Revision WorkBook

English Legal System

H. K. Kanda LLB, MA, Barrister

SECOND EDITION REVISED AND UPDATED BY
Kerry Musgrave LLB, Barrister

HLT Publications

HLT PUBLICATIONS
200 Greyhound Road, London W14 9RY

First Edition 1992
Reprinted 1992
Second Edition 1994

ISBN 0 7510 0448 0

British Library Cataloguing-in-Publication.

A CIP Catalogue record for this book is available from the British Library.

Printed and bound in Great Britain.

CONTENTS

ACKNOWLEDGEMENT

Some questions used are taken or adapted from past University of London LLB (External) and University of Wolverhampton LLB (Honours) by Distance Learning Degree examination papers and our thanks are extended to the universities of London and Wolverhampton for their kind permission to use and publish the questions.

Caveat

The answers given are not approved or sanctioned by the University of London or the University of Wolverhampton and are entirely our responsibility.

They are not intended as 'Model Answers', but rather as Suggested Solutions.

The answers have two fundamental purposes, namely:

a) To provide a detailed example of a suggested solution to an examination question, and

b) To assist students with their research into the subject and to further their understanding and appreciation of the subject of Laws.

INTRODUCTION

This Revision WorkBook has been designed specifically for those students studying English Legal System at undergraduate level. Its coverage is not restricted to any one syllabus but embraces all the core topics which can be found in university and polytechnic examinations.

Each chapter contains an introduction which explains the scope and general contents of the topics covered. This is followed by 'key points' to assist students in studying the essential points of law to properly understand the topic. Recent cases and relevant materials are included where appropriate. Discussion of case law has been kept at a minimum for the sake of simplicity.

Additionally in each chapter there is at least one past examination question, taken in the main from the University of London External examinations. These questions have been selected to cover the most popular issues raised in examinations. The analysis of these questions will help the student to assess the potential range of questions in a topic. Each question is followed by a suggested solution designed to bring the most important issues to the attention of the student and to suggest an appropriate method of answering.

Careful use of the Revision WorkBook will assist the student to develop a good examination technique and also enable him to deal with the wide range of subject matter required for an examination.

In this revised 1994 edition the final chapter contains the complete June 1993 University of London LLB (External) English Legal System question paper, followed by suggested solutions to each question. Thus the student will have the opportunity to review a recent examination paper in its entirety, and can, if desired, use this chapter as a mock examination – referring to the suggested solutions only after first having attempted the questions.

HOW TO STUDY ENGLISH LEGAL SYSTEM

The study of English Legal System will assist a student to understand the mechanics of the system, without which aspects of other subjects will remain puzzling. Many problems, however, are associated with the study of the legal system.

Firstly, the subject consists of a variety of topics, not all connected. Therefore, the volume of information the student must deal with is vast.

However, not all the areas can be easily compartmentalised and many examination questions will require the knowledge of perhaps three or more areas. For example, most questions on criminal procedure will require a knowledge of legal aid, bail and perhaps appeals. In order to manage the quantity of information, students must have a clear picture of the workings of the system. It may be helpful to develop charts indicating, for example, the progress of an accused from arrest through to bail.

Another problem that presents itself is the fact that the rules in many areas are, or have been, under review. This compounds the volume of research required by individuals. Questions on the English Legal System often require an analysis of proposals for reform, the effectiveness of reform and occasionally criticisms of reforms that, although instituted, have perhaps not gone far enough. The only way a student can hope to keep abreast of such developments is by frequent reference to a journal, for example the *New Law Journal*, and by reading a quality newspaper every day.

Relatively speaking, there are perhaps fewer cases to deal with in studying English Legal System than in most other areas of law. However, these cases are used differently. Rather than always referring to a case for its ratio alone, case law is used to illustrate a rule, for example cases that illustrate the approach of the court to statutory interpretation or cases that show how the doctrine of precedent may be avoided. Of course, in order to discover these features, students must read the case itself or parts of it, where time permits. This is a useful exercise and will aid understanding of the area.

REVISION AND EXAMINATION TECHNIQUE

(A) REVISION TECHNIQUE

Planning a revision timetable

In planning your revision timetable make sure you don't finish the syllabus too early. You should avoid leaving revision so late that you have to 'cram' – but constant revision of the same topic leads to stagnation.

Plan ahead, however, and try to make your plans increasingly detailed as you approach the examination date.

Allocate enough time for each topic to be studied. But note that it is better to devise a realistic timetable, to which you have a reasonable chance of keeping, rather than a wildly optimistic schedule which you will probably abandon at the first opportunity!

The syllabus and its topics

One of your first tasks when you began your course was to ensure that you thoroughly understood your **syllabus**. Check now to see if you can write down the **topics** it comprises from memory. You will see that the chapters of this WorkBook are each devoted to a topic. This will help you decide which are the key chapters relative to your revision programme, though you should allow some time for glancing through the other chapters.

The topic and its key points

Again working from memory, analyse what you consider to be the key points of any topic that you have selected for particular revision. Seeing what you can recall, unaided, will help you to understand and firmly memorise the concepts involved.

Using the WorkBook

Relevant questions are provided for each topic in this book. Naturally, as typical examples of examination questions, they do not normally relate to one topic only. But the questions in each chapter *will* relate to the subject matter of the chapter to a degree. You can choose your method of consulting the questions and solutions, but here are some suggestions (strategies 1–3). Each of them presupposes that you have read through the author's notes on key points and question analysis, and any other preliminary matter, at the beginning of the chapter. Once again, you now need to practise working from *memory*, for that is the challenge you are preparing yourself for. As a rule of procedure constantly test yourself once revision starts, both orally and in writing.

Strategy 1

Strategy 1 is planned for the purpose of *quick revision*. First read your chosen question carefully and then jot down in abbreviated notes what you consider to be the main points at issue. Similarly, note the cases and statutes that occur to you as being relevant for citation purposes. Allow yourself sufficient time to cover what you feel to be relevant. Then study the author's *skeleton solution* and skim-read the *suggested solution* to see how they compare with your notes. When comparing consider carefully what the author has included (and concluded) and see whether that agrees with what you have written. Consider the points of variation also. Have you recognised the key issues? How relevant have you been? It is possible, of course, that you have referred to a recent case that *is* relevant, but which had not been reported when the WorkBook was prepared.

Strategy 2

Strategy 2 requires a nucleus of *three hours* in which to practise writing a set of examination answers in a limited time-span.

Select a number of questions (as many as are normally set in your subject in the examination you are studying for), each from a different chapter in the WorkBook, without consulting the solutions. Find a place to write where you will not be disturbed and try to arrange not to be interrupted for three hours. Write your solutions in the time allowed, noting any time needed to make up if you *are* interrupted.

After a rest, compare your answers with the *suggested solutions* in the WorkBook. There will be considerable variation in style, of course, but the bare facts should not be too dissimilar. Evaluate your answer critically. Be 'searching', but develop a positive approach to deciding how you would tackle each question on another occasion.

Strategy 3

You are unlikely to be able to do more than one three hour examination, but occasionally set yourself a single question. Vary the 'time allowed' by imagining it to be one of the questions that you must answer in three hours and allow yourself a limited preparation and writing time. Try one question that you feel to be difficult and an easier question on another occasion, for example.

Mis-use of suggested solutions

Don't try to learn by rote. In particular, don't try to reproduce the *suggested solutions* by heart. Learn to express the basic concepts in your own words.

Keeping up-to-date

Keep up-to-date. While examiners do not require familiarity with changes in the law during the three months prior to the examination, it obviously creates a good impression if you can show you are acquainted with any recent changes. Make a habit of looking through one of the leading journals – *Modern Law Review, Law Quarterly Review* or the *New Law Journal*, for example – and cumulative indices to law reports, such as the *All England Law Reports* or *Weekly Law Reports*, or indeed the daily law reports in *The Times*.

(B) EXAMINATION SKILLS

Examiners are human too!

The process of answering an examination question involves a *communication* between you and the person who set it. If you were speaking face to face with the person, you would choose your verbal points and arguments carefully in your reply. When writing, it is all too easy to forget *the human being who is awaiting the reply* and simply write out what one knows in the area of the subject! Bear in mind it is a person whose question you are responding to, throughout your essay. This will help you to avoid being irrelevant or long-winded.

The essay question

Candidates are sometimes tempted to choose to answer essay questions because they 'seem' easier. But the examiner is looking for thoughtful work and will not give good marks for superficial answers.

The essay-type of question may be either purely factual, in asking you to *explain the meaning* of a certain doctrine or principle, or it may ask you to *discuss* a certain proposition, usually derived from a quotation. In either case, the approach to the answer is the same. A clear programme must be devised to give the examiner the meaning or significance of the doctrine, principle or proposition and its origin in common law, equity or statute, and cases which illustrate its application to the branch of law concerned.

The problem question

The problem-type question requires a different approach. You may well be asked to advise a client or merely discuss the problems raised in the question. In either case, the most important factor is to take great care in reading the question. By its nature, the question will be longer than the essay-type question and you will have a number of facts to digest. Time spent in analysing the question may well save time later, when you are endeavouring to impress on the examiner the considerable extent of your basic legal knowledge. The quantity of knowledge is itself a trap and you must always keep within the boundaries of the question in hand. It is very tempting to show the examiner the extent of your knowledge of your subject, but if this is outside the question, it is time lost and no marks earned. It it inevitable that some areas which you have studied and revised will not be the subject of questions, but under no circumstances attempt to adapt a question to a stronger area of knowledge at the expense of relevance.

When you are satisfied that you have grasped the full significance of the problem-type question, set out the fundamental principles involved. You may well be asked to advise one party, but there is no reason why you should not introduce your answer by:

> 'I would advise A on the following matters ...'

and then continue the answer in a normal impersonal form. This is a much better technique than answering the question as an imaginary conversation.

You will then go on to identify the fundamental problem, or problems posed by the question. This should be followed by a consideration of the law which is relevant to the problem. The source of the law, together with the cases which will be of assistance in solving the problem, must then be considered in detail.

Very good problem questions are quite likely to have alternative answers, and in advising A you should be aware that alternative arguments may be available. Each stage of your answer, in this case, will be based on the argument or arguments considered in the previous stage, forming a conditional sequence.

If, however, you only identify one fundamental problem, do not waste time worrying that you cannot think of an alternative – there may very well be only that one answer.

The examiner will then wish to see how you use your legal knowledge to formulate a case and how you apply that formula to the problem which is the subject of the question. It is this positive approach which can make answering a problem question a high mark earner for the student who has fully understood the question and clearly argued his case on the established law.

Examination checklist

1. Read the instructions at the head of the examination carefully. While last-minute changes are unlikely – such as the introduction of a *compulsory question* or *an increase in the number of questions asked* – it has been known to happen.
2. Read the questions carefully. Analyse problem questions – work out what the examiner wants.
3. Plan your answer *before* you start to write. You can divide your time as follows:
   (a) working out the question (5 per cent of time)
   (b) working out how to answer the question (5 to 10 per cent of time)
   (c) writing your answer

   Do not overlook (a) and (b)
4. Check that you understand the rubric *before* you start to write. Do not 'discuss', for example, if you are specifically asked to 'compare and contrast'.
5. Answer the correct number of questions. If you fail to answer one out of four questions set you lose 25 per cent of your marks!

Style and structure

Try to be clear and concise. Basically this amounts to using paragraphs to denote the sections of your essay, and writing simple, straightforward sentences as much as possible. The sentence you have just read has 22 words – when a sentence reaches 50 words it becomes difficult for a reader to follow.

Do not be inhibited by the word 'structure' (traditionally defined as giving an essay a beginning, a middle and an end). A good structure will be the natural consequence of setting out your arguments and the supporting evidence in a logical order. Set the scene briefly in your opening paragraph. Provide a clear conclusion in your final paragraph.

TABLE OF CASES

TABLE OF STATUTES

1 SOURCES OF LAW

1.1 Introduction

There are a variety of sources of English law. Each source has gained importance in a particular period of history. For example, the advent of law reporting increased the importance of case law. Sources are classified as formal sources, historical sources, legal sources and literary sources.

1.2 Key points

a) *Custom (historical source)*

i) All English law was at one time derived from custom; the law varied from area to area. The development of the Royal Courts, however, allowed the system to develop a 'common law' applicable across the country.

ii) As a source of law, custom has a limited role in modern times because of its restrictive definition: see *The Tanistry Case* (1608) Dav Ir 28. A custom must:

- have been in existence from time immemorial, ie since 1189 or as long as living memory;
- be reasonable: see *Alfred F Beckett* v *Lyons* [1967] 1 All ER 833;
- be certain;
- be obligatory;
- not have been interrupted.

b) *Legislation (legal source)*

i) Legislation is seen as an important source of law as it expresses the will of a democratically elected Parliament and carries out legal and social reforms.

ii) Most legislation is initiated by the Crown. A Bill must go through the relevant procedures in Parliament before it finally becomes law.

iii) The main functions of legislation are as follows:

- reform and revision of the law – the Law Commission and Royal Commissions will generally review the law and make recommendations on reform;
- social impact – legislation has a great impact on social areas of law, such as tax and landlord and tenant law;
- consolidation – statutes are also a valuable means of consolidating various pieces of legislation and common law on a particular subject;
- codification – legislation allows the codification of well developed areas of common law.

iv) There are of course many criticisms of legislation: see 1975 *Renton Committee Report on the Preparation of Legislation.* In the main, the criticisms deal with the fact that statutes are too complex and over-elaborate. This can cause problems in understanding the law and difficulties in its interpretation by the courts.

c) *Subordinate legislation (legal source)*

Parliament itself is unable to legislate on all areas and will often delegate its legislative powers to Ministers and inferior bodies. The legislation so produced has the same force of law as any produced by Parliament itself.

i) The reasons for delegation of legislative powers by Parliament are:

- lack of parliamentary time;
- Parliament's inability to foresee all future contingencies that may require amendments of statutes;
- insufficient expert knowledge for technical legislation;
- to cope with emergencies.

ii) Subordinate legislation is criticised on the basis that Parliament ought not delegate its power to create policy. Furthermore, delegation is made often in broad terms and can lead to abuse.

iii) Subordinate legislation may be controlled in various ways:

- Pre-drafting consultation with advisory and other bodies interested in the proposed legislation.
- The parent statute may require the subordinate legislation to be laid before Parliament. The subordinate legislation may then be subject to a negative or positive resolution.
- Judicial review by the courts where there is a challenge on the basis of procedural or substantive ultra vires.
- Publicity.

d) *Case law (legal source)*

The development of law reporting increased the importance of case law as a source of law. The Incorporated Council of Law Reporting was set up in 1865 and began to produce official Law Reports. Case law is particularly important in the development of the doctrine of precedent.

e) *European law (legal source)*

Section 2(1) of the European Communities Act 1972 incorporates European law into English law.

i) Article 189 of the Treaty of Rome 1957 (the Treaty establishing the EEC) outlines the different types of Community legislation:

- regulations are binding and directly applicable in Member States;
- directives are binding, but must be incorporated into local legislation;
- decisions are binding on those to whom they are addressed;
- recommendations and opinions hold no binding force.

ii) The decisions of the European Court of Justice are applicable in England. The ECJ sees Community law as supreme over national law and this affects the traditional doctrine of supremacy of the UK Parliament, see, eg, *Factortame Ltd* v *Secretary of State for Transport (No 2)* [1991] 1 All ER 70.

f) *International law*

This is a source of the rules accepted by civilised states as determining their conduct towards each other. In order for a rule to be part of international law it must either:

i) be shown to have received express sanction of international agreement; or

ii) have grown to be part of international law by frequent recognition and use.

It is important to note that in order for international law to be binding in the United Kingdom, it must be part of English law.

g) *Equity (legal source)*

The principles of equity are a body of rules which developed in parallel with the common law. Despite their historic roots, they still remain an important source of law today.

i) The historical development of equity:

- Norman conquest of 1066 and the creation of the common law applied by the Royal courts and assizes.
- Special petitions to the Chancellor as the 'Keeper of the King's Conscience'.

- Development of a separate Chancery court applying principles of fairness and the creation of the 'maxims of equity'.
- Conflict between common law and equity.
- 1615 *Earl of Oxford's Case* decided in favour of equity.

ii) Fusion of the two systems:

- Judicature Acts 1873–75.
- One set of courts and procedures applying common law rules and equitable principles.
- Equity always prevails over common law.
- Foundation of modern High Court system.

iii) Creations of equity:

- Rights and remedies.
- Mainly in property law.
- Examples include the trust, mortgages and equitable remedies such as specific performance and injunctions.

iv) Importance of equity today:

- Continuing use of rights and remedies created.
- Maxims of equity still apply in exercise of discretionary remedies.
- Recent developments include promissory estoppel, Mareva injunction, Anton Piller orders and equitable rights for the deserted spouse.

1.3 Analysis of questions

Not every syllabus will include equity as a topic. However, some may consider it important enough to warrant a separate examination question. Questions on the sources of law have been extremely rare in the University of London (External) LLB examinations.

Students attempting this type of question must ensure a thorough knowledge of the different sources. In particular, attention must be paid to the importance of European law as a source.

1.4 Questions

Question 1

What is meant by a source of law? What sources of law have been recognised by the courts? To what extent is international law a source of law?

University of London LLB Examination
(for External Students) English Legal System June 1986 Q6

General comment

A fairly simple question as long as the student does not yield to the temptation of merely writing a list of the different sources of law. Each part of the question must be answered directly and critically.

Skeleton solution

- Identification of sources.
- Explanation of custom.
- Legislation.
- Precedent with case law as illustration.
- European Community law.
- Textbooks.
- International law.

Suggested solution

There are several meanings of the word 'source' as it is used in relation to law. Many writers divide the sources of law into categories; formal, historical, legal and literary sources, and naturally there is a certain amount of overlap between them. A formal source of law is that from which a system of law derives its validity and is a matter of jurisprudence which will not be dealt with here. The historical, legal and literary sources will be examined, especially insofar as they have been recognised by the courts.

Custom

The word custom may be used in several different senses and only in certain limited senses can it be said to have been recognised by the courts. The first use of the word describes the customs of Anglo-Saxon England which varied from village to village and town to town, and had grown up in response to frequently recurring problems. Most local customs governed the more important events in the community such as marriage, succession and how to deal with criminals. Such customs are no longer regarded as a separate source of law since they have either become part of the common law or been incorporated in statute. It is therefore only in this indirect sense that it can be said that Anglo-Saxon custom is recognised by the courts, and few survive today in a recognisable form.

It is possible to establish a local custom by proof of its uninterrupted enjoyment since time immemorial. Local custom is a term used to describe rules of law which apply only in a definite locality. Custom in this sense of the word is a separate source of law and must be settled by judicial decision. The type of local customary rights still existing are such things as rights of way or the right to dry fishing nets (*Mercer* v *Denne* (1905)). If a local custom satisfies certain tests it will be recognised by the courts.

Legislation

Today, legislation is perhaps the most important source of law. It is recognised and followed by the courts and the courts must apply the law as laid down in statutes even if they do not agree with it. Of course one must not overlook the creative role of the judges in construing statutes which are ambiguous or uncertain, but the general rule is that the judges are the declarers of the law and not its makers (jus dicere non jus dare).

Legislation is the principal legal source of law and it has its corresponding literary source in the various publications of statutes, notably the Queen's Printer's Copy. Public general Acts alone account for over 2,000 printed pages each year, supplemented by many thousands more of statutory instruments, Orders in Council and Circulars.

Legislation has not however always been accepted by the courts as absolutely binding. Before the sixteenth century judges enjoyed the same freedom in the application and interpretation of legislative acts as they had in applying and interpreting the common law of their own courts. As J H Baker puts it: 'In applying the spirit of the law, the medieval judges paid scant respect to the letter.' Sir Edward Coke in reporting a case of 1610 wrote: '... it appears in our books that in many cases the common law will control Acts of Parliament and sometimes adjudge them to be utterly void; for when an Act of Parliament is against common right and reason, or repugnant, or impossible to be performed, the common law will control it and adjudge such Act to be void.' There is some doubt, however, as to whether Sir Edward Coke reflected the views of his time. Many scholars feel that he was speaking of long-past ideas without authority. Indeed the Statute of Uses in 1535 gained immediate acceptance by the courts.

There is no doubt that today legislation is unquestioningly accepted by the courts, although the so-called rules of statutory construction do give judges a certain amount of flexibility in deciding what individual sections of statutes really mean.

Precedent

The doctrine of judicial precedent, whereby the decisions of certain courts are binding on other courts, is of comparatively recent origin and is certainly little more than a hundred years old. As early as the time of Edward I (1272-1307) the idea of judicial consistency can be seen in contemporary writings, but this is not the same thing as *binding* precedent. From the sixteenth century onwards cases were cited more frequently, a contributory factor being the development of printing and the improvement in the standard of reporting. In the nineteenth century Baron Parke gave his opinion in the case of *Minehouse* v *Rennell* (1883) that precedents must be regarded in subsequent cases and it was not for the courts 'to reject them and to abandon all analogy to them'. It was not until the reorganisation of the court structure by the Judicature Acts 1873–5 that the task of recognising a hierarchy of the courts became easier. Another major factor in the development of the doctrine of binding precedent was the establishment of the Council of Law Reporting in 1865. This raised the standard of reporting thus making law reports considerably more reliable.

Today precedents are accepted by the courts as being either binding or persuasive, depending partly on whether the legal principle in question was contained in the ratio decidendi or obiter dictum of the case, and partly on the court in which the judgment was given and its place in the hierarchy of the courts.

As a source of law, precedent has lost much ground to legislation in the past century, but still remains one of the primary legal sources of law with its corresponding literary source in the form of law reports.

European Community law

Since the accession of the United Kingdom to the European Communities on 1 January 1973, Regulations, Directives and Decisions of the European Council or Commission are binding in England. Judges in court have to accept the authority of European law. The European legislature has power to make law 'directly applicable' in Member States without the need for the legislatures of the states specifically to enact them into national law. This concept is contained in the European Communities Act 1972, and undoubtedly interferes with the doctrine of the sovereignty of Parliament. The law of the European Communities is a legal source of law and its corresponding literary source are the texts of the Treaties themselves, the Official Journal of the European Communities and the decisions and principles of the European Court of Justice.

Textbooks

Modern textbooks are an indirect literary source of all legal sources. Textbooks and articles in legal journals are used by practitioners for research and a lawyer may adapt the argument of the writer of an article or textbook, but the texts do not carry great authority in court although works such as *Chitty on Contracts* and *Archbold on Criminal Law* are frequently cited. In modern times, with reliable reports and detailed legislation, the scope for textbooks in court has greatly diminished. However, the case of *Woolwich Building Society* v *IRC (No 2)* [1992] 3 All ER 737 (HL) suggests that academic writers may provide a valuable authority when dealing with the scope of common law principles.

When talking of legal textbooks, of course, one had to be careful to distinguish between the ancient textbooks such as Glanvil's treatise *Tractatus de Legibus* written in about 1187, and books by Bracton and Littleton, which are commonly used as original sources of common law and as such are books of authority, and modern textbooks which are not.

International law

International law is the source of the rules accepted by civilised States as determining their conduct towards each other, and towards each other's subjects. In order to prove an alleged rule of international law it must be shown to have received the express sanction of international agreement or it must have grown to be part of international law by the frequent practical recognition of States in their dealings with each other. If international law is to be binding on the courts in this country it must have been adopted and made part of English law.

Question 2

Assess the effects of equitable rights and remedies upon the English legal system. To what extent would you argue that there have been significant developments of equity since the early nineteenth century?

University of Wolverhampton LLB (Hons) by Distance Learning
English Legal System Examination June 1993 Q8

General comment

Questions on equity always require essentially the same material and for that reason can be fairly straightforward. However, this makes it more important for the candidate to deal specifically with the issues the question raises, which here clearly requires something more than a historical discussion.

Skeleton solution

- History and origins.
- Issues of conflict.
- Development of rights and remedies.
- Fusion.
- Development post-1875.
- Evaluation of modern importance, with case law in support.

Suggested solution

Although the foundations of equity can be traced back to the Norman conquest, its impact today remains as strong as ever. Its rights are the basis for many areas of modern law and its remedies are used daily by the legal practitioner of the 1990s. Its role in the English legal system is, therefore, one of both historical creation and modern development and usage.

That historical creation arose from the need to mitigate the harshness of the decisions of the common law developed after 1066. Whilst the Royal Courts and assizes produced the benefits of a widely available legal system applying a consistent set of rules and procedures, they also became rigid and inflexible, ignoring justice in the quest for legal certainty. By the thirteenth century, aggrieved litigants began to petition the Chancellor (at that time a clergyman), as the 'keeper of the King's conscience', in an effort to find a more just solution to their problem. As a consequence of the growth of these petitions, the Court of Chancery developed, where decisions were made on the basis of fairness and reason and so the notion of 'equity' was founded.

Initially, the two court systems operated in parallel, with equity being regarded as a gloss upon the common law. Where the law failed to provide a remedy, equity could operate to 'fill the gap'. However, as both systems became more developed, the situation became one of conflict rather than assistance. Equity began to be criticised by some for its unpredictability and it increasingly found a remedy opposing that offered by the common law. This culminated in the *Earl of Oxford's case* in 1615, in which James I decided in favour of equity as the prevailing rule in the case of conflict.

Equity was now free to develop. It created its own set of rights and remedies which are still in force today. The modern trust, now a core part of the English legal system, was an equitable development, along with many other areas of property law such as the equitable mortgage and the rules of probate.

Remedies were also created to support these rights. The injunction has its foundations in the early development of equity. It served then, as now, as an addition to the common law award of damages.

Alongside these developments, equity also created its own set of rules, the 'maxims of equity', to guide the judge in the use of his discretion in matters of equity. Whilst one of the attractions of equity was that it was based on the judge's discretion and therefore flexible, the maxims led some to criticise equity for becoming as rigid as the common law. Nevertheless, the work of the Chancery courts expanded as equity widened its scope through the late 1700s and early 1800s. By the middle of the nineteenth century it was realised that the two systems could no longer operate as separate bodies and a review of the system was needed.

This reform was achieved by the Judicature Acts of 1873–1875. This legislation provided for procedural fusion of the two systems into one court hierarchy, which is the basis of the modern divisions of today's High Court. The legislation created the King's Bench, Chancery and Probate divisions. Rather than eliminating equity, the Acts, it is submitted, strengthened and confirmed its place in the future. A litigant could now bring his proceedings in one court which would apply both the rules of common law and equity and the Judicature Acts confirmed that in the case of conflict, equity would prevail.

It would be easy to assume that having provided these foundations, the importance of equity as a developing body of law ceased after 1875. However, this is clearly not the case when one examines the many twentieth century developments of equity.

The rights and remedies created before 1873 continue to operate today. Furthermore, they have been refined and added to by modern judges and legal developments. The now established principle of 'promissory estoppel' in contract owes its existence to the judgement of Lord Denning in the *High Trees* case (*Central London Property Trust Ltd* v *High Trees House Ltd* (1947)). The contractual licence, constructive trust and doctrine of part performance are all creations of the judge's equitable discretion in cases such as *Tanner* v *Tanner* (1975), *Binions* v *Evans* (1972) and *Walsh* v *Lonsdale* (1882). The rights of the deserted spouse, an essential part of modern matrimonial property law, are the creations of equity, reinforced by statute.

The development of new and more complex remedies has been as active as that of rights. The order of specific performance is still vital, as was illustrated by the case of *Beswick* v *Beswick* (1968). The injunction is perhaps more widely used than ever before, having a place in many areas of modern law, such as intellectual property rights, as well as its more traditional role. Anton Piller orders and Mareva injunctions have only been created in the last twenty years and they are now an essential part of many legal proceedings (see *Anton Piller KG* v *Manufacturing Processes* (1967) and *Mareva Compania Naviera SA* v *International Bulkcarriers SA* (1975)). The appointment of receivers and orders to account are similarly important parts of modern legal practice which owe their existence to equity.

So the significance of equity in the modern legal system can be clearly illustrated. However, one concept that has perhaps changed is the historic notion of equity as flexible and fair. Whilst the reasoning behind many modern developments is the need to provide a solution which is appropriate to the facts and the changing demands of society, the wealth of guidelines that go with the discretion can be as rigid as any common law rules. For example, to be granted an injunction one must satisfy the complex requirements of the *American Cyanamid* rules (*American Cyanamid* v *Ethicon* (1975)). Anton Piller orders and Mareva injunctions have been criticised by some judges as harsh and draconian and a set of rigid procedures aimed at safeguarding against abuse has developed alongside these two injunctions.

Therefore, equity as a source of law remains as current and as vital a part of the English legal system as ever, although the conscientious Lord Chancellors who first gave life to the idea may wonder at its role today.

2 THE JUDICIARY AND MAGISTRATES

2.1 Introduction

The modern judiciary can be traced back to the twelfth century, although judges were appointed from the ranks of royal clerks. By the fourteenth century a professional judiciary began to emerge. There was until the seventeenth century great political influence over the judiciary. By the eighteenth century, this political influence extended only to appointment and removal.

2.2 Key points

a) *Appointment*

Judges in England are chosen from practising lawyers, mainly barristers, although some circuit judges are solicitors.

i) The Lord Chancellor is a political appointee and member of the Government.

ii) The Lord Chief Justice, the Master of the Rolls, the President of the Family Division, the Vice-Chancellor, the Lords of Appeal in Ordinary and the Lord Justices of Appeal are appointed by the Queen on the advice of the Prime Minister.

iii) Puisne judges of the High Court, circuit judges, and recorders are appointed by the Queen on the advice of the Lord Chancellor.

iv) Justices of the Peace are appointed directly by the Lord Chancellor.

vi) The formal requirements are as follows:

- A Lord of Appeal in Ordinary must have held high judicial office for two years or a Supreme Court qualification (ie, a right of audience there) for not less than 15 years.

- A Lord Justice of Appeal must have a 10 year High Court qualification or be a judge of a High Court: s71(1)(a) Courts and Legal Services Act 1990.
- A puisne judge of the High Court must have a 10 year High Court qualification or have been a circuit judge for at least two years: s71(1)(b).
- Section 71(3)(b) defines High Court qualification as being a right of audience in relation to all High Court proceedings.

vii) The Lord Chancellor has proposed (July 1993) that in future specific vacancies for assistant recorders and circuit judges will be advertised. He is also considering including lay members upon the interviewing panel.

b) *Training*

i) The Judicial Studies Board (JSB) is responsible for training the judiciary. Many have criticised the lack of training and continuing education for judges.

ii) Initial training consists of induction courses for new appointees and time spent sitting with more experienced judges.

iii) Judges are invited to attend periodic refresher courses every three and a half to five years. The JSB also runs annual one day seminars and occasional specialist seminars.

iv) The Runciman Commission (Cm 2263) has proposed the following changes:

- More resources should be allocated to judicial training generally.
- More specialist training should be given on race and gender issues.
- Judges' performance during training should be properly monitored.
- There should be shorter intervals between the refresher courses and attendance should be made compulsory.
- More use should be made of 'mixed' training seminars where all judges attend (whatever their level of appointment) with members of the profession.

c) *Removal*

i) Judges of the High Court and above hold office during good behaviour subject to a power of removal by Her Majesty on an address presented by both Houses of Parliament: Supreme Court Act 1981.

ii) Circuit judges and recorders may be removed from office by the Lord Chancellor on grounds of incapacity or misbehaviour.

iii) Magistrates may be removed by the Lord Chancellor for good cause.

iv) The Royal Commission on Criminal Justice (Cm 2263) has suggested that there should be better monitoring arrangements with a system of performance appraisal by fellow judges and members of the Bar.

d) *Immunity and independence*

i) A judge may not be sued for anything he says or does in the exercise of his judicial office.

- This immunity applies to judges of superior courts even if they act with malice or in bad faith.
- Judges of lower courts are subject to the same immunity so long as they are acting within their jurisdiction.
- Sections 44 and 45 of the Courts and Legal Services Act 1990 governs the position of magistrates' immunity. They may only be made liable if acting outside their jurisdiction and in bad faith.

ii) The judiciary is said to be independent because of its separation from the legislature and executive. Of course, the Lord Chancellor is a political appointee; however, as a matter of convention he keeps his political activities separate from his judicial responsibilities.

e) *Background*

Research has indicated that the judiciary has been dominated by the upper and middle classes (see JAG Griffith, *The Politics of the Judiciary*). This dominance stems from the fact that the Bar has always attracted the Oxbridge educated and the wealthy. The position appears to be changing albeit at a very slow pace. There is now greater participation of women and racial minorities. The Lord Chancellor has recently stated (July 1993) that applications for judicial posts from women and black and Asian lawyers will be encouraged. However, he has rejected measures to ensure a certain proportion of the judiciary are from the ethnic minorities.

f) *The functions of the judge*

i) Supervision of the conduct of the trial.

- The Runciman Commission has proposed that all Crown Court procedures should be supervised by a resident Crown Court judge to speed up the pre-trial process.
- The Commission also suggested that judges should intervene more readily and quickly during the trial to expedite the proceedings.

ii) Arbiter of legal issues.

iii) In most civil cases, the judge is the sole arbiter of fact, law, and quantum of damages.

iv) The interpretation and clarification of the law.

v) In criminal cases, the judge must explain the law and sum up the facts to the jury.

- The Royal Commission on Criminal Justice (Cm 2263) suggests that consideration should be given to the role of the judge in summing up and whether it is always appropriate for him to comment upon the facts.

vi) In criminal cases the judge is also responsible for sentencing the defendant.

g) *Magistrates*

i) Lay justices are appointed by the Lord Chancellor from individuals put forward by local organisations.

- Every attempt is made to appoint a fair mix of sexes, political parties, social classes and races.
- The main requirement is that the magistrate is over 21 and below 60 on appointment.
- A lay justice must normally live or work in the area.
- Lay justices are not required to be legally qualified, but do undergo training.
- The services of a lay magistrate are unpaid except for expenses.

ii) Stipendiary magistrates are full time salaried magistrates.

- In order to be appointed, a magistrate must have a seven year general qualification: s71 Courts and Legal Services Act 1990.
- Stipendiaries are appointed by the Crown or on the recommendation of the Lord Chancellor.
- An advantage of using stipendiaries is that they are said to dispense justice more quickly and fairly.
- The Runciman Commission has suggested that there should be an overhaul of the system of administration of stipendiary magistrates and a more systematic approach to greater deployment of the stipendiaries.

iii) The magistrates' clerk

- The main function of a clerk is to advise magistrates as to law and practice.
- Section 71 Courts and Legal Services Act requires a clerk to have a five year magistrates' court qualification.
- The clerk's role is vital as lay magistrates can only sit if there is a qualified clerk present.
- The clerk is also responsible for court administration and organisation of training of magistrates.

2.3 Recent cases

R v *Mulvihill* [1990] 1 WLR 438

R v *Romsey Justices, ex parte Gale* (1992) The Times 24 January

2.4 Analysis of questions

Questions on the judiciary have only recently appeared in the London (External) LLB English Legal System examinations. They tend to deal primarily with the criticisms of the judiciary. Of course the questions always require some discussion of reforms.

2.5 Questions

Question 1

'The notion of a judge being impartial needs more thought than it is commonly given. Strong views may obviously affect decisions, but general outlook and mental habits can have just as much influence without being so noticeable.'

What criticisms have been made of the general outlook of the English judiciary and its impartiality? What changes to the system of judicial appointment have been recommended in order to overcome these criticisms?

University of London LLB Examination
(for External Students) English Legal System June 1990 Q3

General comment

This is a wide question and requires a general discussion of the background of the judiciary and how this affects their decision-making. It is not a question to be attempted without knowledge of some statistics on composition, etc. Of course, major proposals for reform must be included.

Skeleton solution

- Background of judges.
- Composition of judiciary.
- Independence.
- Influences.
- Reforms.

Suggested solution

What criticisms have been made of the general outlook of the English judiciary and its impartiality? What changes to the system of judicial appointment have been recommended in order to overcome these criticisms?

Berlins portrays the public image of the judge on the one hand as the awesome embodiment of wisdom, independence and impartiality and on the other hand as an elderly, remote, crusty figure who holds views more appropriate to the nineteenth century. Of the Lord Chancellor, Gilbert (of Gilbert and Sullivan) wrote:

'The law is the true embodiment,
Of everything that's excellent.
It has no kind of fault or flaw,
And I, my Lords, embody the law.'

There has been in recent times, however, increasing criticism of the judiciary and many found their disapprobation on the social position of the judge and its inevitable effect on his outlook and, more importantly, the day-to-day decisions he takes in administering justice.

Professor Griffith analysed the social class origins of judges from the period 1820 to 1968. He concluded that over this period the dominance of upper and middle classes is overwhelming.

This is not surprising since our judges are the products of the generation of barristers educated at public schools, Oxbridge, military service and perhaps a brief flirtation with politics. The dignity of their office and the importance of being seen to be impartial and uncontroversial, often demands that they distance themselves from their former habits and haunts and even friends. The result can be an increasing remoteness from the mainstream of society. The longer they serve as judges, the more they may appear to be out of touch with the problems of the ordinary people, with the vicissitudes of most people's daily lives.

It is submitted that the picture is changing slowly – there is an increasing number of women at the Bar and there are appointments from the ranks of the solicitor profession via the position of Registrar. Lord Edmund Davies, a former Law Lord, wrote:

'Judges have friends who get into trouble. Judges have bills to pay, they have arrangements to make. They are not set apart, they are not cushioned. They have to lead pretty normal lives off the bench.'

The English system of justice depends on respect for the judiciary, its independence and its integrity. To some extent that requires the judge to be a slightly awesome figure on a pedestal, and not one of the people. In the words of Berlins he must be:

'Caesar's wife, above suspicion, careful and restrained in what he does and says.'

The independence of the judiciary is a key feature of the system. 'Independence' means that the judges are not controlled by the legislature or the executive – they do not take part in politics and cannot become MPs at the same time. Judges are certainly conservative with a small 'c' and many have loyalties with the Conservative Party. It is to these 'strong views' that the question in hand particularly refers.

In theory, judges must try to put aside not only their own views but also what they know or suspect might be the wider practical consequence of their decisions. Professor John Griffith suggests that the higher judiciary have by their education and training and the pursuit of their profession as barristers:

'acquired a strikingly homogenous collection of attitudes, beliefs and principles, which to them represents the public interest. They do not always express it as such. But it is the lodestar by which they navigate.'

Griffith does not believe that complete neutrality can be achieved in practice. Judges, he argues, by their own inclinations and because of the status of the judiciary as part of the authority within the state, will tend to make conservative decisions which support the existing order as they see it.

Judges vigorously deny that they come to decisions on the basis of political considerations. They argue that it is not in the public interest that judges should be conservative, favour the status quo and be suspicious of new legal theories based on a particular view of social justice. Lord Devlin writes:

'Law is the gatekeeper of the status quo. There is always a host of new ideas galloping the outskirts of a society's thought. All of them seek admission but each must first win its spurs: the law at first resists, but will submit to a conqueror and become his servant.'

If there is a trend to be discerned it is that judges have become more obviously aware of the social, political and administrative circles that form the backdrop to any case before them. They are also much more conscious of public opinion and although they must not formulate their decisions to conform to public opinion, it can have some effect on them.

Similar criticisms are sounded as to magistrates. Statistics show that 84 per cent of magistrates belong to the professional and managerial classes. Many claim that there is too much of a gap between the mainly middle class, white, comfortably off magistrates and the typical defendants who appear before them. The latest figures show that fewer than two per cent of magistrates are black or Asian.

Further, the magistrates' court is still often viewed as a descendant of the old police court. Certainly magistrates are reputed to believe police evidence as a matter of course and as Sir Thomas Skyrme alleges there is at least some evidence that their training does not go far enough to eliminate this prejudice.

Two main proposals for reform of the judiciary have been forwarded: a career judiciary and reform of the selection procedure.

As to selection – at present there is an extremely narrow consultation process – it has been suggested that this be replaced by a committee of wider composition, its membership known to the public.

As to a career judiciary – this would probably be on similar lines to those practised on the Continent. In France, for example, young graduates attend a school for judges where they are familiarised with procedure, sentencing and penology. They serve a probationary period sitting alongside an experienced judge and may take up their 'seat' during their mid-twenties. Young offenders are purposely put before such judges who are, it is deemed, more 'in touch' and more understanding of the needs and problems of the delinquents.

In England, judges attend residential seminars which last for no more than three and a half days. The courses are, it is argued, very valuable but in no way sufficient. A career judiciary would not necessarily improve the situation as the system of precedent depends on having highly experienced judges. The importation of a continental scheme of appointment might well strike at the very heart of the English legal system.

More recently, the Runciman Commission on Criminal Justice, which reported in July 1993 (Cm 2263 Royal Commission on Criminal Justice), has suggested various less radical reforms which may go some way to appeasing critics. The main proposals are directed at improving the training of judges with more frequent refresher courses, better monitoring of performance and special training in gender and race issues. The report also advocates a more active role for judges in Crown Court proceedings and a review of the guidelines on summing up to juries.

With regard to the magistracy, the Commission has suggested that greater use of stipendiary magistrates should be made, ignoring the controversies surrounding the backgrounds of the lay justices.

The Lord Chancellor's department has also put forward some of its own proposals to counteract deficiencies. Vacancies for Justices of the Peace are now widely advertised in the Black and Asian press. In May 1993 it was suggested that vacancies for circuit judges and registrars would also be advertised and lay persons involved in the selection process. And in the autumn of 1993 the Lord Chancellor announced specialist 'race awareness' training for the judiciary.

Clearly, the problems are beginning to be recognised at the highest level. However, it remains to be seen how far these more moderate proposals will be implemented. It is submitted, however, that as long as our judges are mere mortals, they will always be criticised for the frailties of human nature.

Question 2

What are the functions of the professional judiciary and are there any satisfactory methods of 'judging' judges?

University of London LLB Examination
(for External Students) English Legal System 1992 Q1

General comment

A popular but straightforward exam question, which allows you to display knowledge and wider reading. However, to achieve a high mark, it is necessary to have a good structure and relate your material to the question itself.

Skeleton solution

- Role of judiciary and function within the English legal system.
- Selection process.
- General criticisms.
- Methods of censure – official and unofficial – and their effectiveness.

Suggested solution

The members of the professional judiciary are frequently the subject of criticism, but when one considers their influence and role in the English legal system it is easy to see the need for a proper and efficient system of accountability. Before one can assess the methods of 'judging' judges, one must consider their sphere of influence.

A judge's role can range from that of the stipendiary magistrate in the lower courts right through to sitting in the highest appeal court in the land and, indeed, in the case of the Lord Chancellor, being a member of the ruling government. Judges are the 'front line' of the legal system – 'a neutral force between government and the governed' (per Lord Devlin, *The Dockers' Case* (1973)) – the body responsible for the effectiveness of our laws. Within these roles, their task is wide. They must supervise the proceedings before them; they are the sole arbiter of the legal issues, and in the lower courts and in most civil matters, the decider of fact. They must interpret and clarify, give pragmatic effect to the law, as well as being seen to be administering justice. While performing these functions, they must always be seen to be impartial, without apparent bias or intolerance, always with unquestionable authority and undivided attention. Their importance cannot be underestimated. In clarifying and interpreting they may in fact be creating new law and, more fundamentally perhaps, making a far-reaching decision on an individual's future.

So if we ask all this from our professional judiciary, how do we find candidates that can fulfil this role? Clearly, they are all professional lawyers, of varying years' practice depending upon the level of their judicial post. But the actual selection process remains something of a mystery to the outsider. The Lord Chancellor is ultimately responsible for appointing judges, be they a stipendiary magistrate or a Lord Justice of Appeal. His decision is made on the basis of advice from those closest to him and other existing judges. There are no defined criteria or qualifications other than having achieved the required number of years' service, and it is not unusual to find a family practitioner suddenly being made a Chancery judge! While the Lord Chancellor should keep his ministerial role and political views entirely separate from his judicial responsibilities, it is a frequent criticism of the Bench that they are all too much alike and that the Lord Chancellor and his advisers make appointment decisions based too much on personal opinion – the influence of 'the old school tie' is still felt. Certainly by far the majority come from the barristers' side of the profession. There have been calls for a Judicial Appointment Board or even a Minister of Justice. In February 1991, the Law Society actually threatened to take the Lord Chancellor to court to challenge the legality of the 'word of mouth' selection process.

Aside from the faults found in the selection process, other criticisms are frequently heard. Immunity from suit is considered a valuable feature of our judicial system because it is seen to help maintain the independence of the judiciary, but some would say that it merely fosters ignorance and apathy. The judiciary are too old and too elitist, they are out of touch with the realities of life and, in criminal cases especially, with the lives and backgrounds of the parties before them. A common criticism is their social background and attitudes – middle class, middle minded and middle aged.

There would certainly seem to be evidence to support this criticism, at least. Statistics and surveys have frequently shown that both women and the ethnic minorities are drastically under-represented, especially in higher judicial office. Lack of training is another frequent discussion point, as well as the overall role of the Lord Chancellor and his ability to separate his duties from his political post. The widely publicised miscarriages of justice, as well as these criticisms, all suggest that there is a weakness in the system, and it may well lie, as the question suggests, within the system of accountability of judges.

The methods of 'judging' judges come in both official and unofficial forms. Looking first at the official methods, the most obvious is the ability of the Lord Chancellor to dismiss a member of the judiciary. But in reality, this sanction seems to mean little. The Lord Chancellor himself is subject to the whims of political life and will change with the government, and may even change during a Prime Minister's term of office if he or she so chooses. However, the Lord Chancellor is not directly accountable to Parliament and Parliament has no real power to remove him. The Lord Chancellor seems to exercise his disciplinary powers sparingly: not since the Act of Settlement in 1701 has an English judge of the superior court been removed from office (although an Irish judge was dismissed in 1830 for misappropriating court funds). The most severe penalty in recent times seems to be a private admonition of the judge by the Lord Chancellor 'interviewing' him, although sometimes there may be a public rebuke as happened to one senior judge after he referred to the serving Lord Chief Justice as a 'dinosaur'. The closest this form of 'discipline' has got to dismissal is the resignation of Hallett J following his decision in the case of *Jones* v *National Coal Board* (1957), when the Lord Chancellor suggested this would be appropriate. Without the Lord Chancellor's intervention, a judge will remain in office during 'good behaviour' until he retires, which in Lord Denning's case was not until he reached the age of 83 and even then he retired only after the Lord Chancellor had asked him to do so! Not even the Law Lords are actually politically accountable as, although they are members of the upper House of Parliament, they do not take part in the general political debate.

A less direct form of accountability can come through complaints from counsel, solicitors or litigants to the Law Society, Bar Council, Lord Chief Justice or even an MP. However, the matter is then passed to the Lord Chancellor who deals with it in the same way as any matter of discipline – a private interview. The pressure group JUSTICE has suggested that we should have an official complaints committee, but this proposal seems unlikely to succeed.

Perhaps the strongest form of censure can come through the appeal system, although the practicality of this option is questionable. Technically, there is the potential to appeal every case, providing leave is given. Once there, the appellate courts' powers to deal with a case are potentially very wide: the reversal of a judgment, the setting aside of a conviction, a change in sentence or damages awarded. They may also use the opportunity to rebuke judges of the lower courts. Judges have been censured for excessive interruptions, impatience, sighing, falling asleep and even threatening the jury. But how realistic is it to acknowledge this as a method of accountability when it is clearly an admission of failings and error of judgment in the lower courts?

Furthermore, how effective is it when it relies on the resources and willingness of the parties to appeal and does not even guarantee that the judges will be rebuked? Some judges have been frequently admonished by the appellate courts for both their comments and their legal decisions, but it did not remove them from the Bench.

A less direct and unofficial method of censure comes from society itself. The media frequently focuses on a 'newsworthy' decision, because it believes the damages to be excessive, or the verdict unfair, or the sentence too lenient. It is certainly able to create public feeling for its view and may even attract the attention of Parliament. Undoubtedly, allied with pressure groups, the media has played a fundamental role in bringing attention to the recent miscarriages of justice. But since it has no direct control, it serves only as a method of passing comment on judges and can never be a useful form of admonishing them; it can never change a sentence or reinstate a conviction. In addition, its influence is limited by the law itself in the form of sub judice rules and the definition of 'scurrilous abuse' as contempt of court; only press comment which is within the limits of reasonable courtesy and good faith will be tolerated.

Lord Hailsham once diagnosed the judges' disease, the symptoms of which are pomposity, irritability, talkativeness, proneness to obiter dicta and a tendency to take short cuts. Our only real method of dealing with this illusion is by more of the same – having the judges judge themselves. It seems that society, the profession and the judiciary itself acknowledge the flaws in the system but no proposals can ever be agreed to remedy these flaws. Perhaps the real problem lies not so much in how we choose to judge our judges but in the whole selection process and the attitudes our judges bring to the Bench with them.

3 THE DOCTRINE OF PRECEDENT

3.1 Introduction

The doctrine of stare decisis (binding judicial precedent) applies within the hierarchical structure of the courts. The basis of the doctrine is that decisions of higher courts bind those of lower courts. This practice allows the treatment of like cases alike. The modern doctrine emerged in the nineteenth century with the development of a formal system of law reporting. This does not however mean that an unreported case may not be cited as a precedent: see *Roberts Petroleum Ltd* v *Bernard Kenny Ltd* [1983] 1 All ER 564.

3.2 Key points

a) *Reasons for upholding the doctrine*

   i) Fairness

   ii) Predictability

b) *Ingredients of a decision*

   i) Findings of fact.

   ii) Statements of principles of law.

   iii) Judgment based on applying law to facts ie the ratio decidendi.

   iv) Statements made obiter dicta.

c) *The operation of the doctrine*

   i) The European Court of Justice

      - On matters of Community law, the decisions of this court are binding on UK courts.

      - The ECJ is not bound by its own previous decisions, but generally tends to follow them.

ii) The House of Lords

- The decisions of the House of Lords are binding on all other courts.
- Since the 1966 *Practice Statement* ([1966] 1 WLR 1234) the House of Lords is no longer bound by its own previous decisions, but will generally follow them.

iii) The Court of Appeal (Civil Division)

- The decisions of the Court of Appeal are binding on all lower courts.
- The Court of Appeal (Civil Division) is bound by decisions of the House of Lords.
- The Court of Appeal is also bound by its own previous decisions except in very limited circumstances. In *Young* v *Bristol Aeroplane Co* [1946] AC 163, the Court of Appeal made clear the exceptional circumstances in which it would not be bound by its own previous decisions. Firstly, where there are two previous conflicting Court of Appeal decisions. Secondly, where the previous Court of Appeal decision conflicts with a later House of Lords decision, and finally where the previous Court of Appeal decision was made per incuriam. In *Langley* v *North West Water Authority* [1991] 3 All ER 610, the Court of Appeal said that departure from a previous Court of Appeal decision should only be considered if the earlier one was manifestly wrong.

iv) The Court of Appeal (Criminal Division)

- The decisions of this court are binding on all lower courts.
- The Court of Appeal (Criminal Division) is bound by the decisions of the House of Lords.
- The Criminal Division of the Court of Appeal is not required to follow its own previous decisions, where to do so would cause injustice to the appellant: *R* v *Gould* [1968] 1 All ER 849.

v) The High Court

- All divisions of the High Court are bound by the decisions of superior courts.
- Where the court sits as a court of first instance, it is not bound by its own decisions, but will tend to follow them: *Colchester Estates* v *Carlton Industries* [1984] 3 WLR 693.

vi) Other courts

- Are bound by the decisions of the superior courts.
- Are not bound by their own previous decisions.

d) *Persuasive authorities*

i) Privy Council decisions are highly persuasive

ii) Ratio of Scottish courts

iii) Ratio of Commonwealth courts

iv) Ratio of foreign courts

v) Obiter dicta statements. *Donoghue* v *Stevenson* [1932] AC 562 and *Hedley Byrne & Co* v *Heller & Partners* [1964] AC 465 are both examples of cases with influential obiter dicta.

e) *Avoiding awkward precedents*

At times a court may feel that it does not wish to adhere strictly to the doctrine of precedent and may therefore seek to avoid the application of a precedent. It may do to in a number of ways.

i) Distinguishing

Cases ought only to be distinguished where it is 'reasonable' to do so, generally upon dissimilar facts.

ii) Overruling

This is allowable within the hierarchical structure of courts. It is an important means by which a degree of flexibility is maintained within an inherently rigid doctrine. Consider also the concept of prospective overruling.

iii) Statements made 'per incuriam' (literally 'through want of care'), eg without the court having considered relevant cases.

3.3 Recent cases

Secretary of State for Trade and Industry v *Desai* (1991) The Times 5 December

Langley v *North West Water Authority* [1991] 3 All ER 610

3.4 Analysis of questions

In questions on precedent, students are generally required to critically analyse the use of the doctrine. In some questions specific areas of precedent may require examination. Students ought to be able to give examples of case law to explain the operation of the doctrine.

3.5 Questions

Question 1

A government committee is considering proposals to abolish the doctrine of precedent. Draft a memorandum for the committee considering (a) the desirability or otherwise of doing so and (b) whether there are particular areas of law where exceptions or special provisions may be necessary.

University of London LLB Examination
(for External Students) English Legal System June 1987 Q9

General comment

This type of question, which asks the candidate to adopt a hypothetical position as the writer of a memorandum or report, invites, perhaps, a more imaginative approach than a straightforward essay question. Whilst the examiner may welcome the attempts of a candidate who enters quite fully into this charade, in that it provides a welcome relief from the usual run of answers, it is easy to appear 'clever' and a little silly if one adopts the role too thoroughly and attempts to be humorous.

Skeleton solution

- Explain precedent and how it operates.
- Advantages of the doctrine: certainty; predictability.
- *Practice Statement* 1966.
- Conflict between House of Lords and Court of Appeal.
- Avoidance of the doctrine.

Suggested solution

This memorandum will first consider the desirability of abolishing the doctrine of precedent and then go on to deal with those areas where there might be a need for exceptions or special provisions if the doctrine were to be abolished.

a) The current system of stare decisis which obtains in common law jurisdictions depends fundamentally upon two principles. First, that like cases should be treated alike and this is, in turn, based upon the not unreasonable assumption that the law should deal with litigants in a similar fashion where their situations are similar as it is apparently fair so to do. Secondly, the judgment of a higher court should bind the decisions of a lower. The crucial word here is 'bind', for other systems of law such as those found on the Continent have a system of precedent but there the judges are not 'bound' to follow the decisions of superior tribunals even if they almost always do so.

   Among the advantages of the English system are said to be certainty and predictability. As judges must follow the decisions of superior courts there is less scope for an individual judge to interpret the law idiosyncratically and perhaps therefore unfairly. This means that lawyers can be more sure of the likely outcome of a case under the system of stare decisis and thus save their clients (as well as the other party) from unnecessary trouble and expense.

   There can be not doubt that certainty is a highly desirable characteristic of the law for it would otherwise appear to be a lottery or ever-changing, like the old jibe about equity being like the Chancellor's foot. Certainty may, however, have disadvantages in that it may provide a system of such rigidity that individual injustices occur when particular cases cannot be fitted into the general scheme forged by the law. It can be countered on behalf of the common law that the development of law according to decided cases provides a reasonable degree of flexibility, in that it relates to the change and modification of principles according to the needs of the times.

It may now be observed that the law no longer needs to be developed through precedent in the same way as it was in earlier times. The role of common law has diminished in relation to the more pervasive influence of statute law. And yet the concept of precedent is still in some respects paramount, for once an Act has been passed by Parliament it remains for the judiciary to interpret it. As the interpretations of the judges are part of the system of precedent these specific decisions become part of the Act, rather like barnacles sticking to the hull of a ship. This can be especially problematic where a judicial decision appears to go against the spirit of an Act, such as happened in the House of Lords' decision in *Anderton* v *Ryan* (1985) on the Criminal Attempts Act 1981.

Since the *Practice Statement* of 1966, the House of Lords has reserved the right to vary its own previous decisions when it is just to do so. Thus the House's error in *Anderton* could be corrected in *R* v *Shivpuri* (1986). It might have been easier if the earlier decision were regarded simply as a wild extravagance which did not need to wait for a subsequent case for it to be discarded. A similar situation arose with the House of Lords decision in *Junior Books* v *Veitchi* (1982), although there the judgment was substantially contracted in its effect by the Court of Appeal.

It may seem strange that this could happen, as the Court of Appeal is bound to follow the decision of the House of Lords and, indeed,was peremptorily reminded of this by the House when Lord Denning presumed to give 'gratuitous advice' to subordinate judges as to the wisdom of following the law in *Rookes* v *Barnard* (1964). This raises two matters; first, that not every case ends in the House of Lords and therefore an error may be perpetuated in the lower courts simply because the losing litigant did not have the means or the interest to pursue the case just to clarify the matter for others.

Secondly, an inferior court may be able to avoid the binding effect of a superior decision by 'distinguishing' it. This is a perfectly respectable process where there are good grounds on which to do this – the ratio of a decision has, after all, been described by Professor Goodhart as the material facts of the case plus the decision thereon. The material facts of a case are by no means easy to determine in many situations. There is always a possibility that a judge may distinguish a case on the basis of a false assessment of what constitutes material facts and some judges may indulge in a form of logic-chopping in order to obtain the desired result where a case does not easily fit within the existing precedent.

The proliferation of cases, especially now that lawyers have recourse to sophisticated information retrieval systems such as the computer-based LEXIS, suggests that the system of precedent is already breaking under the strain of its own weight. The House of Lords have already indicated that they are not prepared to accept other than properly reported cases and judges have complained about cases being cited to them unnecessarily. It can appear that a similar fact-situation rather than a principle of law is what barristers now seek to urge upon the judges. Amongst this richness of specific instances there is a grave danger of losing the thread of principle.

The current situation is worse than it was when the number of cases was merely confusing to the layman. It now confuses the lawyer as well, making research tiresome and expensive. The time has surely now come when the common law had done its task of developing guidelines for the courts. Much common law has been reduced to statutory form anyway. It may seem ridiculous that judges can pile on their own words as essential elements of the Acts which they are interpreting.

As we progress towards European integration and with the increasing importance of European Community Law, it may seem preferable to discard the system of rigid common law principles, as they have largely served their purpose and could fall into desuetude along with those other sources of English law, textbooks and custom.

b) In the 1966 *Practice Statement* the then Lord Chancellor stated that, whilst the use of precedent was an indispensable foundation for deciding cases in that it provided a degree of certainty upon which individuals could rely and legal rules could be developed in an orderly fashion, too rigid adherence could lead to individual injustice and restrict that development. Thus, although previous decisions of the House were to be treated as normally binding, the House could depart from precedent where it appeared right to do so.

The House was especially aware of the danger of disturbing retrospectively the basis of contracts, property settlements and fiscal arrangements as well as the need for certainty in the criminal law. These are evidently the areas in which special care needs to be taken if the doctrine of precedent were to be abandoned. Nonetheless it may be seen that there has been a change of attitude in the courts in respect of tax cases so that the liberal principles with regard to the arrangements of one's affairs in *Inland Revenue Commissioners* v *Duke of Westminster* (1936) have been supplanted by *Ramsay (WT)* v *Inland Revenue Commissioners* (1981) and *Furniss* v *Dawson* (1984).

Whilst the abandonment of the harsh view of the rights of child trespassers in *Addie* v *Dumbreck* (1929) allowed *British Railways Board* v *Herrington* (1972) to provide a more humane attitude, there is no doubt that there are matters where a judicial decision can throw existing situations into considerable disarray. This is not so objectionable when it is a question of a change in the law by Parliament but a decision such as *Street* v *Mountford* (1985) can cause chaos in the drafting of landlord and tenant documents.

There is always the possibility of appeal in these cases but there is a final point that may be made about the likely consequences of change in the use of precedent. It might bring us closer to the European system and this might be an argument for a European style of appointing judges. Few of those now appointed might be willing to serve substantially as functionaries and the quality of the judiciary might suffer.

Question 2

Is the doctrine of precedent a means of discovering what the law is, or a means of justifying a decision?

University of London LLB Examination
(for External Students) English Legal System June 1988 Q5

General comment

A straightforward discussion question which needs no introduction. Try and justify your answer with references to authorities. Many approaches are possible in a question such as this.

Skeleton solution

- Definition.
- Use of precedent.
- Role of interpretation.
- Illustrative case law.

Suggested solution

The doctrine of judicial precedent, the principal way in which the law develops in Common law jurisdictions, relies on the concept of stare decisis. This means that where a decision exists on a particular point a later court confronted with those facts, or similar facts, ought to follow the earlier decision unless clear reasons are advanced for not following it. While this crude enunciation of the principle will apply to courts of the same or inferior level it does not of course apply to courts of higher appellate standing. Until 1965 it was said that the House of Lords could not depart from its own previous decisions, while today it is thought that they can depart from their own decisions. None of this is terribly important in practice because the courts are still bigger law makers than Parliament and 'new' law is being created judicially every day of the legal term.

Let us examine the present system to see whether judges are judicial law makers who use precedent as a means of justifying their decision once made, or whether the doctrine of precedent is genuinely a way of discovering what the law is. Few lawyers can believe that the common law is latent and can be discovered by revealing it bit by bit in the authorities. A larger number of lawyers believe that precedent is a way of justifying a decision once made. But by far the greatest number of lawyers believe, I suspect, that judges are carrying out both functions; they are exposing the core of principles behind the decisions in an area and they are aiming to arrive at the just and logically sound decision in a particular case and are seeking to justify this conclusion with reference to authorities and fit their own case within those authorities.

I feel sure that under our system of precedent judges feel compelled to follow earlier decisions to an almost unnecessary extent, and that while there is scope for law making the general nature of decisions is evolutionary rather than revolutionary. In other words judges will seek the principle underlying the precedents in a particular area and will try to fit the facts of the case within that principle. If they are unable to do this they will look for another line of authorities within which to fit the case. It is only when there are no decisions on an area that they will have to create new law. Then it may be a matter of statutory interpretation, namely what was Parliament's intention? Otherwise it may be appurtenant to other areas in which case they will be able to draw on earlier authorities. Thus in the law of landlord and tenant where the Rent Act 1977 applies the courts on many occasions have had to decide the meaning of a 'sham' transaction, ie one for the sole purpose of evading the Act which in some way pretends to be of a different nature than the substance of the agreement entered into. In deciding the meaning of a sham transaction the courts were able to have some recourse to tax cases in which the same question had been considered in relation to tax avoidance. Thus cases like *Furniss* v *Dawson* (1984) were considered in a Rent Act context.

I would like to illustrate the above point with reference to the authorities. The very reason why Lord Denning was considered such a controversial judge was because he departed from the established, but implicit, nature of precedent in this country. The courts developed in the 1950s and 1960s a concept known as the 'deserted wife's equity' – based on matrimonial rights to occupy property rather than contractual. Authorities to state that the concept was incorrect in property law were ignored. It was held that when a wife to a marriage was deserted she had an irrevocable licence enforceable in equity against third parties to occupy the matrimonial home. This was in the nature of a mere equity and thus flew in the face of precedent which required an equitable interest before it could be binding on a third party purchaser.

The line of authority was started by Lord Denning in 1952 (*Bendall* v *McWhirter*) and was reversed and heavily criticised by the House of Lords in the case of *National Provincial Bank* v *Ainsworth* (1965). It was held that you look at who the property was vested in and whether the wife has any proprietary interest in the house and do not grant her an interest in land merely by virtue of her occupation as wife. The case illustrates the way the courts are bound by precedent even though justice would be better served by departing from it. The point is illustrated by a multitude of other Lord Denning cases which grant a wife proprietary rights by virtue of being a mistress and therefore contributing to the work on the common home, eg *Gissing* v *Gissing* (1971). These cases owe a lot more to the tenacity of a particular judge and much less to precedent and have been the subject of much criticism. But, they have succeeded in starting a new line of authorities and have carried out a social policy by giving a wife or mistress a protection she would not otherwise have. The Denning line of cases is now sufficiently advanced to render it impossible for the courts to ignore them and thus they can tighten up the law only: *Burns* v *Burns* (1984), not overturn the earlier decisions.

I seek to illustrate with the above discussion that the courts are basically conservative in approach and will generally be at pains to make a particular case gel with authority.

This will particularly be the case in areas such as property where conveyancers need to be able to convey property with the minimum of pitfalls. The argument, as in the mistress cases, is between fairness to the parties and administrative convenience to the general public. In most cases the courts will of necessity give higher priority to producing a logical workable precedent which practitioners can work with than with doing justice inter partes in the particular case. Lord Denning was an exceptional judge because he departed from this concept. In conclusion, therefore, I would say our doctrine of precedent is employed to justify decisions once made. In truth however I believe that neither statement represents an accurate reflection of the behaviour of the courts.

Question 3

Could the Court of Appeal issue a practice statement having a similar effect to that issued by the House of Lords in 1966? Would there be any point in its doing so?

University of London LLB Examination
(for External Students) English Legal System June 1991 Q1

General comment

A very common type of question. Analysis of the role of precedent is required as well as thoughts about the structure of the appeals process. The overlap with the powers of the legislature should be discussed. Plenty of good material from Denning and others but a statement of their views without your own critique will not be enough. Of course the main thrust of the question is in the second sentence; but try to decide what *sorts* of point there could be.

Skeleton solution

- Purpose of appeals. Law's impact on society. Certainty v flexibility.
- What was the 1966 *Practice Statement*?
- What is the CA system at the moment and why?
- What flaws are there? Why do they need changing?
- What alternatives to a practice statement by CA exist? Think of some.
- Conclusion.

Suggested solution

The correct balance between certainty and flexibility in an appeals system is much debated. Some consider justice to be best served by the former concept, allowing all relations to be conducted in a sure knowledge of the consequences. Others contest that life can never be perfectly forecast and situations will arise that require changes in the legal rules governing relations between people and with the state. In the 1966 *Practice Statement* the House of Lords adjusted the balance in favour of greater flexibility in certain circumstances.

The House of Lords' statement is a conservative one; it speaks in favour of certainty so that the individual can conduct his affairs and for the orderly development of the law. The accompanying press notice indicated that the power would be sparingly used and indeed the court has tended to reverse the Court of Appeal's decision without over-ruling the House of Lords' precedent. Clearly the Lords feel disinclined to say that their previous decisions were wrong and either distinguish between the facts of cases (often on tenuous grounds) or imply that each case is to be decided on its own merits, resulting in two apparently contradictory authorities. Considerable sacrifices in certainty flow therefore even from this reserved increase in flexibility. The Practice Statement justifies such changes in the law where the precedent would lead to individual injustices or restrict the proper development of the law, but reserves such power to the House of Lords only.

In contrast to the House of Lords the Court of Appeal is bound by its previous decisions unless one of the exceptions to *Young* v *Bristol Aeroplane Co Ltd* (1944) can be made out. There has been considerable debate as to whether these exceptions should be widely or narrowly applied, extended or restricted. It is also accepted that stare decisis should in criminal appeals be subject to the more important consideration of the liberty of the subject. Nonetheless, the fundamental position is that the Court of Appeal is subject to its own previous decisions. Lord Denning MR tried without success for this convention to be altered; he argued in *Davis* v *Johnson* (1979) that as a matter of principle the Court of Appeal should be able to depart from its previous decisions if convinced they were wrong. The principle is that justice should be done in each individual case and this is supported by the practical view that in many cases the Court of Appeal is the last resort for the penurious litigant. However in Denning's words he received a 'crushing rebuff' from the House of Lords. Sympathetically, Lord Salmon agreed with the inherent right of a court to regulate its own activity but argued that total agreement of all the Lord Justices was necessary in order to change such a practice. It seems unlikely that such unanimity would ever be reached among the members of the Court of Appeal and, in the absence of the more liberal Lords of the late 1970s, unlikely that the House of Lords would countenance such a step.

Of all the arguments in favour of greater flexibility in the Court of Appeal the fact that it is financially impossible in many cases to appeal to the House of Lords makes such a change very desirable. The Lord Justices are experienced lawyers accustomed to setting precedents that are well reasoned and long lived. However Lord Salmon pointed out that simply the number of Lord Justices would introduce too much uncertainty into the appeals process. It is felt that this second tier of judges serves as a quality control on the judgments of the lower courts, assuring litigants of a high quality of justice at moderate cost. The Court of Appeal should play the strict constitutional role of applying the law as it exists and leave the quasi-legislative development of the law to the Lords. Many would argue that this is arrant nonsense since in reality the careful distinguishing of authorities and the malleability of legal principles allow the Court of Appeal to make law in all but name. If this view is accepted then giving the Court of Appeal the right to depart from its previous decisions avoids deception and increases clarity in the law.

However, there are alternative ways in which to avoid this irreconcilable debate. If the House of Lords is to be the developer of the law as of right then access to such judgment must be improved. Lord Salmon has suggested that power be given to the Court of Appeal to refer cases to the House where they disagree with the decision they were bound to make by precedent. Such appeals would be paid for from public funds; however this system still envisaged argued submissions before the Lords, preparation and research and all the procedure of a proper appeal. A more efficient method could be devised whereby the Lords review the arguments and evidence adduced in the lower courts and give their judgment in writing when they are satisfied. This could even be done as 'pro bono' work by their Lordships, giving them an active role in initiating the reviews as guardians of the growth of the law. Such an approach would clarify the three tier appeals system that we have without inhibiting the Court of Appeal or making the House of Lords redundant.

It is hard to estimate exactly how many cases of injustice go unchanged because the litigants cannot challenge precedent in the Court of Appeal and cannot afford the House of Lords. The Practice Statement gives the Lords considerable discretion in departing from its previous decisions when it is 'right to do so'. Extending this wide a power to the Court of Appeal, no matter how conservatively used and limited to special circumstances, would overbalance the system towards uncertainty and injustice. However since the legislature cannot have time for legal modifications the access to the House of Lords in their role as law makers should be improved.

4 STATUTORY INTERPRETATION

4.1 Introduction

The approach of the judiciary to interpretation of statutes is indicated by reference to the rules discussed below. The choice of approach depends on both the problem with the statute and the judge's conception of his own function.

4.2 Key points

a) *Main problems with statutes*

i) Unexpressed words

ii) Broad terms

iii) Ambiguous words

iv) Unforeseeable developments.

b) *The rules of interpretation*

i) The mischief rule: *Heydon's Case* (1584) 3 Co Rep 7a

Regard must be had to the four-stage analysis:

- what was the common law before the making of the Act?;
- what was the mischief or defect for which the common law did not provide?;
- what remedy did Parliament provide?; and
- the true reason for the remedy.

In the light of the above, the judge's task is to suppress the mischief and advance the remedy. This rule is used primarily where words are ambiguous.

ii) The literal rule

Words must be given their ordinary meaning: *Sussex Peerage Case* (1844) 11 Cl & F 85. This encourages precision drafting.

iii) The golden rule

This approach allows the court to depart from the ordinary meaning of words where their application leads to an absurd result: *Grey* v *Pearson* (1857) 6 HL Cas 61; *River Wear Commissioners* v *Adamson* (1877) 2 App Cas 743.

iv) Contextual approach

A four stage progressive analysis which introduces a combination of elements of the established approaches: see Sir Rupert Cross: *Statutory Interpretation* (1976); *Maunsell* v *Olins* [1974] 3 WLR 835; *Federal Steam Navigation Co Ltd* v *Department of Trade and Industry* [1974] 1 WLR 505.

c) *Aids to interpretation*

i) Internal aids

- Other enacting words
- Long and short title
- Preamble
- Headings: see *DPP* v *Schildkamp* [1971] AC 1
- Side notes and punctuation – generally not to be used.

ii) External aids

- Historical setting
- Dictionaries
- Textbooks
- Statutes in pari materia
- Statutory instruments
- Government publications – to discover the mischief
- Parliamentary materials – since the important case of *Pepper* v *Hart* [1992] 3 WLR 1032, the House of Lords may now refer to Hansard subject to the guidelines given in the decision.
- Rules of language
- Presumptions.

4.3 Recent cases

R v *R (a husband)* [1991] 4 All ER 481 (HL)

R v *Highbury Corner Magistrates' Court, ex parte Di Matteo* [1992] 1 All ER 102

Pepper v *Hart* [1992] 3 WLR 1033

4.4 Analysis of questions

Statutory interpretation is a favourite examination topic, both for the examiner and the student. The most common error made by students is to write general accounts of the rules. The questions are either in essay form or in the form of a problem that requires the application of the rules of interpretation. Students ought to ensure they are able to illustrate the principles with case law.

4.5 Questions

Question 1

Section 2 of the Disclosure of Information Act 1988 provides as follows:

'1) If any person having in his possession or control any document, or information which has been entrusted in confidence to him by any person holding office under Her Majesty or which he has obtained owing to his position as a person who holds or has held office under Her Majesty, communicates the document, or information to any person, other than a person to whom he is authorised to communicate it, that person shall be guilty of an offence.

2) If any person receives any document, or information, knowing, or having reasonable ground to believe that the document, or information, is communicated to him in contravention of this Act, he shall be guilty of an offence, unless he proves that the communication to him of the document or information was contrary to his desire.'

a) Alec, a civil servant, had microfiches containing personal details of members of the public taken from answers to a census. Fearing that his department was (unlawfully) going to supply the microfiches to the police, he placed them in a safe at his bank, telling Bill, the bank manager, to take great care of them because they were 'red hot'.

b) Charles, a trade union official, received complaints about the food and recreational facilities at a secret research establishment. He reported these complaints to the civil servant in charge of the establishment.

c) Dave, a journalist, overheard a conversation between two Treasury officials about the forthcoming Budget. He wrote an article 'leaking' details of the Budget.

Alec, Bill, Charles and Dave have been charged under s2. Advise them.

University of London LLB Examination
(for External Students) English Legal System June 1988 Q6

General comment

This question covers quite a wide area and only those who know a little about official secrets legislation should attempt it. Be careful to answer the problems facing the three individuals and do not become too bogged down in the rights and wrongs of this legislation, which is of course very similar to the real life Official Secrets Act 1911, s2, an historic piece of legislation if ever there was one. This question also requires a reasonable eye for statutory interpretation.

Skeleton solution

a)
- Alec's liability within s2(1).
- Bill's knowledge of A's position.
- Bill's liability under s2.

b)
- Charles' liability under s2(1).
- Application of literal rule.
- Liability of the recipient of information.

c)
- David's liability.
- Literal meaning of words.

Suggested solution

The wording of the fictitious s2 of the Disclosure of Information Act 1988 follows closely the wording of the all too real s2 of the Official Secrets Act 1911. That section was designed to catch the important category of persons who are not spying for a foreign government but who without legal control would 'leak' information of a nature that is harmful to the national interest. Section 1 of the Act dealt with spies and s2 dealt with people other than spies. Thus the problem with s2 from the start was that it was too broad in scope and caught innocent recipients as well as those who deliberately set out to harm the national interest. The section covers Crown servants as well as independent contractors and any knowing recipients of information.

Applying the Disclosure of Information Act 1988 to the facts in the three examples, it would appear that Alec is guilty of an offence under subs(1). This subsection bites on Crown servants who '*communicate* documents, or information to any person, other than the person to whom he is authorised to communicate it'. Here Alec clearly communicates the information that has been entrusted to him in confidence and the mens rea element of the offence is present because of this communication.

The question now to answer is whether Bill, the bank manager, is liable as a knowing recipient of the microfiches under subs(2) of the Act. The 'knowing' (ie the mens rea) element is made up of being aware that Alec is a civil servant and is therefore entrusted with a duty of confidence. It would not be necessary for the prosecution to show at Bill's trial that Bill knew the precise contents of the microfiches, only that he knew or had reasonable cause to believe that the information was conveyed in contravention of the Act. This requirement is surely satisfied here by the surrounding circumstances of Bill's receipt of the information. He is told that the microfiches were 'red hot' and he should know that Alec is a civil servant. These two facts ought to have enabled him to identify the nature of the information. In both Alec's and Bill's case it will not matter that the nature of the information is harmless to national security or the state interest.

Part (b) of this question illustrates how absurd the working of s2 of the Disclosure of Information Act may be, because here it seems Charles may be liable. Subs(1) of that section provides that a person may be liable where he has obtained information by virtue of his office, as a civil servant, and has communicated that information to any person other than a person to whom he is authorised to communicate it. Nothing is said in the section about communication to another Crown servant and the section clearly was not intended to apply to situations such as these. However, technically he has communicated information, ie complaints about food, that he has not been authorised to communicate and therefore he is technically guilty of an offence.

According to subs(2) of the section the civil servant who Charles communicates with is also technically guilty of an offence because he is the unauthorised recipient of information, unless he is able to show that he is an unwilling recipient in that the communication was contrary to his desire.

Of course in practice Charles would not be prosecuted on these facts but the absurd result that he could technically be liable stems from the catch-all wording of the section. Furthermore, there is no defence of communicating information in the public interest within s2 of the Disclosure of Information Act and this is yet another glaring deficiency in the 1911 Act, the wording of which this section closely follows.

This last comment leads up to an answer to the liability of Dave (c). Clearly the two civil servants are not guilty of an offence because they have not 'communicated' the information (the actus reus of the offence) and do not have any mens rea (knowing communication). What though of the liability of Dave? Dave has not received the information on the budget 'contrary to his desire'. On the contrary it is very much to his advantage that he is able to obtain information in this way and publish it as a 'leak', it is a pre-budget scoop for the newspaper concerned.

I think the question of Dave's liability must come down firstly to the meaning of the words 'received' and 'information', for learning of information is not necessarily the same as 'receiving' information. Also the prosecution must show that the 'information is communicated to him in contravention of the Act', and that Dave knew or had reasonable grounds to believe that the information was so communicated.

I do not believe that these facts can amount to a 'communication', nor do I think that Dave's acts are enough to amount to receipt of the information and therefore I am very doubtful as to Dave's liability for the offence. This again illustrates how silly this Act is because the one person who has done an act harmful to the public interest, Dave, is the least likely to be criminally liable.

Question 2

Assume that on 1 February 1989, a Public Indecency Act became law and that the Act provides:

'An Act to maintain decency in all public places.

Section 1. A person who commits any act of indecency, or who displays any indecent painting, drawing or other material in any theatre, gallery, exhibition or other public place shall commit an offence.'

How would this statute operate in the following circumstances?

a) Guy runs a members' club which is well known as a meeting place for homosexual businessmen. To make a last protest against the Act, he showed a film, depicting homosexual acts, on the evening of 31 January 1989. Someone, however, had tampered with the clocks at the club, and the film ended at 12.15 am on 1 February.

b) On 1 July the new farce 'No Trousers, Please, We're Scottish' is to open in the West End of London. One of the moments of 'humour' in the play occurs when Bill, an actor, must lose his kilt to reveal – with his back to the audience – that he has nothing under his shirt-tail.

The police have charged Guy under s1; a member of the League for Clean Theatre managed to get into the dress rehearsal of the new play and as a result the League has begun a private prosecution against Bill.

University of London LLB Examination
(for External Students) English Legal System June 1989 Q5

General comment

This question requires a good understanding of the rules of statutory interpretation. You must not, in this type of question, merely list the available approaches. Instead, an attempt must be made to display how the courts are likely to interpret the statute and what approach is best suited to its interpretation.

Skeleton solution

a)
- Is the statute in force?
- Guy's liability – strict?
- Application of ejusdem genesis rule.
- Application of mischief rule.
- Use of extrinsic materials.

b)
- Bill's liability – literal interpretation?
- Mischief rule.

Suggested solution

a) The first issue is to consider whether the Act was in force at the time of the alleged offence. From the facts, it appears that the Act received the royal assent on 1 February, and would be deemed to be in force at one instant past midnight on that date. Thus for nearly 15 minutes the film was being screened in possible contravention of the Act.

However, Guy did not realise that the film would run over into 1 February and it might be argued that he lacked any intention to commit the offence, and merely wanted to protest before the Act was law. However, the wording of the section may be interpreted to make the offence one of strict liability.

Obviously Guy is not committing an act of indecency; his liability if any, would come under the 'display' part of the section. Using the literal rule, the showing of a film is a display, but is a film within the category created ejusdem generis by the words 'painting, drawing or other material'? It could be argued that 'painting, drawing' creates a class of visual material, or alternatively that they are static and since the film is moving, it is not within the Act.

Since there is this variety in meaning, the mischief rule may be used. The long title refers to the need to maintain decency in all public places, and it would seem that this would encompass a film.

The next issue is whether the members' club is ejusdem generis with 'theatre, gallery, exhibition or other public place.' Arguably, since the public do not have automatic access to the club, it would not be within the section. The club requires some kind of membership formality to be complied with, whereas theatre, gallery etc do not. Also 'theatre, gallery, etc' are all places where the public would go to see some kind of display, whereas the club is for social purposes.

The mischief rule would again be resorted to, in order to ascertain Parliament's intention. Hansard may now be used in limited circumstances following the House of Lords decision in *Pepper* v *Hart* (1992). Law Commission reports could legitimately be looked at to determine Parliament's intention: the *Black Clawson* case (1975).

Lastly it would be necessary to establish that the film was in fact indecent. Many films hint at homosexuality without in fact being indecent. Much would depend upon the way in which this particular film dealt with the subject.

b) The Act would clearly be in force when Bill performs this action in the play, but we are not told when the dress rehearsal takes place. Whether the League can maintain a private prosecution depends upon the Act; normally sensitive prosecutions require the consent of the Director of Public Prosecutions or the Attorney-General.

Bill's liability, if any, would be for committing an act of indecency. The Act refers to 'any act of indecency' and is therefore literally very wide in scope. Whether the incident amounts to indecency is again a question of fact, and the circumstances in which the activity takes place are important. The fact that this is a farce, where traditionally this kind of joke is commonplace may mean the activity is not indecent, whereas were Bill to do the same thing at a railway station it might be!

Secondly the act must take place in a 'theatre, gallery or other public place.' Although this occurs in the theatre, it does not occur whilst the theatre is a public place. There would however be the possibility of a prosecution based on the activity at a performance.

As discussed earlier, if there is ambiguity the mischief rule could be employed to resolve the issue as to whether Parliament intended this sort of activity to be covered.

Question 3

May a judge, faced with a statutory provision which seems to produce an absurd or unjust result, simply say that Parliament has made a mistake?

University of London LLB Examination
(for External Students) English Legal System June 1990 Q2

General comment

This question requires an analysis of the judge's role in interpreting statutes. It also requires discussion of the means available to a judge to avoid the literal interpretation of words.

Skeleton solution

- Functions of a judge.
- Use of the golden rule to avoid literal interpretation.
- Discovering Parliament's intention.

Suggested solution

It is the function of judges in relation to legislation to apply it. If, however, the wording of the legislation is ambiguous, or its extent uncertain, its meaning or scope will need to be interpreted or construed first.

F A R Benion, a former parliamentary draftsman, in statute law identified a number of doubt factors. First, ellipsis: this is where the draftsman omits words necessarily implied. Secondly, broad terms: words or phrases of wide meaning, eg 'mechanically propelled vehicle' as in *Smart* v *Allan* (1963). Thirdly, political uncertainty: provision may be politically contentious or the Bill may have lacked clear objectives. Fourthly, unforseeable developments – eg the ingenious schemes of tax avoidance exploiting loopholes in the existing law. Fifthly, the fallible draftsman: inadequate wording, printing or drafting errors and conflict within or between statutes.

A judge confronted with a statutory provision which apparently produces an absurd or unjust result cannot simply say that Parliament got it wrong. Acknowledgement of such a 'mistake' is the unique competence of Parliament and this operates through the medium of repeal and new enactments. Rather, a judge interprets and applies the current law as embodied in the statute in question – theoretically he has no creative role to play therein. In his task of statutory interpretation he is assisted by certain rules and presumptions and in addition there are available some intrinsic and extrinsic aids to construction. J Willis in *Statute Interpretation in a Nutshell* (1938) said:

'A court invokes whichever of the rules produces a result that satisfies its sense of justice in the case before it ... the courts treat all three as valid and refer to them as occasion demands, but naturally enough do not assign any reasons for choosing one rather than another.'

The question calls for discussion in particular of the so-called golden rule since this is employed in two ways: firstly: it is used in a narrow way to modify the literal rule in order to avoid an absurdity. In its second broader application, it is sometimes used in preference to the literal rule where the words used can have only one literal meaning. This is especially so where considerations of public policy intervene to discourage the adoption of an obnoxious interpretation.

The reader should note at the outset that a pre-condition to use of the golden rule is the *rejection* of the literal rule. By the literal rule, the words used in a statute must be given their plain, ordinary, or literal meaning. The objective of the court is to discover the intention of Parliament as expressed in the words used (*Stock* v *Frank Jones (Tipton) Limited* (1978). If the words used are quite clear they must be applied even though the result is absurd, or even though the interpretation may inflict hardship on those affected by the legislation, eg *Leedale* v *Lewis* (1982). Thus, unless it can be shown that the statutory framework or the legal context in which the words are used require a different meaning, the words of the statute should be assigned their natural and ordinary meaning (as per Lord Scarman in *Shah* v *Barnet London Borough Council* (1983).

Lord Denning writing extra-judicially in *Discipline of Law* (1979) and also *The Closing Chapter* (1983) argues that the actual words used in the statute are merely the starting point and not the finishing point. Furthermore, he aired his view from the bench in *Nothman* v *Barnet London Borough Council* (1978):

'The literal method is now completely out of date ... it is no longer necessary for the judges to wring their hands and say "There is nothing we can do about it." Whenever the strict interpretation of a statute gives rise to an absurd and unjust situation, the judges can and should use their good sense to remedy it.'

Literal interpretation which promotes hardship/absurdity is thus mitigated by use of the golden rule. The golden rule lays down that if the words used are ambiguous the court should adopt an interpretation which avoids an absurd result. *Adler* v *George* (1964) concerned a prosecution under the Official Secrets Act 1920 which made it an offence to obstruct H M Forces 'in the vicinity of' a prohibited place. The defendants had obstructed H M Forces '*in*' a prohibited place and the Divisional Court held they were guilty of the offence.

It must be stressed that the golden rule can only be used where there is a sensible alternative interpretation. If there is only one interpretation, or the second interpretation is as absurd as the first, the literal rule must be applied even though the result might be ridiculous, unless that is, the result would be so undesirable that the court can be persuaded to adopt the golden rule in its broader sense (outlined above).

The present question asks whether or not the judge is entitled to say that Parliament has made a mistake. The present writer argues that the judge is not so entitled but that with the assistance of extrinsic aids the judge may discover the more general intention of Parliament and perhaps conclude that, after more detailed research, Parliament has not erred after all.

Use of extrinsic material, including travaux preparatoires, as an aid to statutory interpretation is restricted. In recent years the strict rules have been relaxed. Thus reports of the Law Commission, Royal Commissions, the Law Reform Committee and other official committees have been considered by judges, eg *Black-Clawson International Limited* v *Papierwerke, etc* (1975). Moreover, in *Anderton* v *Ryan* (1985) the House of Lords virtually ignored the report of the Law Commission which preceded the Criminal Attempts Act 1981. This error led to a bad decision which was overruled in *R* v *Shivpuri* (1986).

Previously, Hansard remained a closed book, although Lord Denning had powerfully disagreed with this view. In *Davis* v *Johnson* (1979) Lord Scarman cited two main reasons for not referring to the Parliamentary debates. First, he claimed that such material constitutes an unreliable guide to the meaning of what is enacted; second, counsel were not permitted to refer to Hansard in argument.

However, the recent decision of the House of Lords in *Pepper* v *Hart* (1992) reverses this approach and allows the court to refer to Hansard, provided it is clear what the intention of Parliament was. There was a notable dissent by Lord McKay, the Lord Chancellor, who feared it might lead to excessive citations by counsel.

There are few today who deny that the interpreter of legislation exercises some creative role. To describe the extent of judicial creativity in statutory interpretation, Reed Dickerson in *The Interpretation and Application of Statutes* (1975) uses the simile of the restorer of an ancient vase:

'Here he is guided by the adjacent contours, and if he is skilful the result blends well enough to attract little or no attention. His job is harder if the vase has been decorated, but the difficulty is small if the decoration follows a discernible pattern.'

In this activity there is certainly some creativity but it is of the lowest order. It still falls within the general heading of 'ascertainment of meaning' in the sense of discovering something that is in a real sense latent in the material and certainly does not amount to saying that Parliament got it wrong.

5 ARREST, SEARCH AND SEIZURE

5.1 Introduction

The Police and Criminal Evidence Act 1984 (PACE) was passed as a result of recommendations from the Phillips Commission. The provisions of PACE deal principally with police powers. PACE empowered the Home Secretary to issue Codes of Practice for the exercise of police powers within PACE. These are seen as a guide to the conduct of criminal investigations by the police. This chapter will consider the provisions of PACE and the relevant codes of practice connected with these powers.

Students should check whether police powers forms part of the English Legal System or Constitutional Law syllabus for their examining board.

A STOP AND SEARCH POWERS

5.2 Key points

a) *Police powers to stop and search*

Section 1 makes provision for the general power of the police to search a person or vehicle. This power can only be exercised if certain conditions are satisfied.

i) Section 1(3) – allows the power to be exercised if the police constable has reasonable grounds for suspecting that he will find stolen or prohibited articles.

ii) Section 1(1) – this type of stop and search may only be carried out if the person or vehicle is in a public place.

iii) Section 1(4) and (5) – with regard to persons or vehicles that are on land adjacent to dwellings, these may only be searched if the constable has reasonable grounds for believing that:

- the person does not reside in that dwelling; or
- the person or the vehicle is not there with the permission of the owners of that dwelling.

b) *The purpose of the search*

The police may only stop and search if they have reasonable grounds to suspect that stolen or prohibited articles will be discovered.

i) Stolen goods

Stolen goods are those goods acquired contrary to ss1–7 Theft Act 1968 and also s15, goods obtained by criminal deception, and handling within s22.

ii) Prohibited articles – s1(7) and s1(8)

Section 1(7) stipulates that prohibited articles include the following:

- Offensive weapons – s1(7)(a)
  - any article made or adapted to cause injury or
  - intended for such use by him.
- Prohibited articles – s1(7)(b)
  - articles made or adapted for use in the course of an offence (see s1(8) for the relevant offences)
  - intended by the person for such use by him
  - the offences concerned here are burglary, theft, and offences under ss12 and 15 Theft Act 1968.

iii) If the search results in the discovery of stolen or prohibited articles, s1(6) allows them to be seized.

c) *Reasonable grounds for suspicion*

The Codes of Practice give guidance as to the meaning of reasonable grounds for suspicion. Some factors to be considered are:

i) nature of the article;

ii) the time and place the person is seen;

iii) behaviour of the person.

Reasonable suspicion cannot be based on personal factors – age, colour, etc.

d) *Conduct of searches*

Once s1 conditions are satisfied and the police have reasonable grounds, the search can continue within the procedure laid out in s2. The police constable must give:

i) his name and the name of the station to which he is attached;

ii) the object of the search;

iii) the grounds for conducting the search.

e) *Duration of detention*

To avoid delay persons or vehicles to be searched may only be detained for a reasonable time. What is reasonable is a question of fact.

B POWERS OF ENTRY, SEARCH AND SEIZURE ON PREMISES

5.3 Key points

a) *Exercise of power with warrant issued by a magistrate*

The warrant is generally issued where there are reasonable grounds for believing that:

i) a serious arrestable offence has been committed (s116; Schedule 5); and

ii) the material in the premises is likely to be of substantial value to investigations; and

iii) the material is likely to be relevant evidence.

In addition one of the conditions within s8(3) must be satisfied:

i) it is not practicable to communicate with any person entitled to grant entry to the premises or access to the evidence; or

iii) entry to the premises will not be granted without a warrant; or

iii) the purpose of the search could be frustrated unless a constable can secure immediate entry to the premises.

The procedure for the application and execution of warrants is governed by ss15 and 16. A warrant remains valid only for one month, after which time it lapses and must be returned to the court. The search must take place at a reasonable hour and if anything is found, it may be seized.

b) *Exercise of power without warrant*

Section 17 allows a constable to enter and search premises if he has reasonable ground for believing the person he is seeking is on the premises and for one of the following purposes:

i) to execute a warrant of arrest;

ii) to arrest a person for an arrestable offence;

iii) to recapture a person who is unlawfully at large; or

iv) to save life, limb or serious damage to property.

c) *Powers of seizure*

Section 19 confers a general power of seizure of property where the police are lawfully on any premises. A police officer may seize anything he has reasonable grounds for believing:

i) is obtained in consequence of the commission of an offence; and

ii) is evidence in relation to an offence under investigation or any other offence; and

iii) it is necessary to seize to avoid concealment, loss or alteration.

Once seized these articles may be retained so long as is necessary in all the circumstances.

C POWERS OF ARREST

5.4 Key points

a) *Arrest without warrant: s24*

The power of arrest here lies with both private citizens and the police. The power exists for offences where sentence is fixed by law and for offences for which there is a minimum five year sentence. The danger for a private citizen in making such an arrest is the possibility of an action in false imprisonment for a wrongful arrest.

b) *Arrest for non-arrestable offences*

Only the police have this power and it can be exercised if it appears that a service of summons is inappropriate and any of the general arrest conditions in s25(3) is satisfied, ie:

- the name of the suspect is unknown or cannot be discovered; or
- there are reasonable grounds for doubting that the name the suspect gives is his real name; or
- the address the suspect gives is improper; or
- the constable has reasonable grounds for believing arrest is necessary to prevent the suspect from:
  - causing physical injury to himself or some other person; or
  - suffering physical injury; or
  - causing loss or damage to property; or
  - committing a public decency offence; or
  - causing unlawful obstruction of the highway.

c) *The procedure following arrest*

Once arrested the suspect must be taken to a police station as soon as is practicable: s30. Once at the station the suspect is under the supervision of the custody officer.

i) If there is sufficient evidence the suspect must be charged. Once charged he ought to be released with or without bail unless:

- his name or address cannot be ascertained or are suspected to be false; or
- he would abscond or interfere with the investigation; or
- there are reasonable grounds for believing that he ought to be detained for protection of himself or any other person or damage to property.

ii) There is provision within s40(1) for a suspect's continued detention if the above provisions apply. However reviews of the situation must take place to determine if continued detention is justified.

iii) Once arrested, if the suspect is not charged, s41 allows him to be held for 24 hours. After this time he must be released unless his detention is authorised by a police officer of at least the rank of superintendent or by the authority of a magistrate's warrant.

iv) After charge and detention the suspect must be brought before a magistrates' court as soon as practicable.

d) *Interrogation and the right to legal advice*

i) Section 56 allows an arrested person to have a friend or relative informed of his arrest. Delay is only permitted if the suspect is being detained for a serious arrestable offence and there is authority for the delay from a superintendent. This authorisation will generally be given where there is a possibility that allowing contact will lead to interference with evidence or personal injury to others or will alert other suspected persons or hinder the recovery of property.

ii) The right to consult a solicitor – suspects are often at a disadvantage because of a lack of knowledge of their rights or the powers of the police. The cautioning of suspects of their right of silence is not sufficient protection. Section 58(1) of PACE redresses the balance and allows a person arrested to consult a solicitor at any time. Delays may be authorised for the reasons given in (d)(i) above: *R* v *Samuel* [1988] 2 All ER 135. An added protection for the detainee is that he can request a copy of the Codes of Practice.

The Royal Commission on Criminal Justice (Cm 2263) has proposed a tightening of the rules and procedures in this area. These are aimed at ensuring a suspect is fully aware of his right to legal advice and that he is sure that he is waiving it.

e) *Confessions*

i) Section 76(2) provides for a confession to be excluded from evidence if it is obtained:

- by oppression; or
- in consequence of anything said or done which was likely in the circumstances to render any confession unreliable;

unless

- the prosecution can prove beyond reasonable doubt that it was not so obtained.

ii) Oppression is defined by s76(8) as being torture, inhuman treatment, and degrading treatment, and includes the use or threat of violence.

iii) The court has a discretionary power to exclude a confession if it would have an adverse effect on proceedings: s78; *R* v *Sang* [1980] AC 402.

5.5 Analysis of questions

This area is frequently examined. Students must ensure they are familiar with the Police and Criminal Evidence Act 1984 and the Codes of Practice. Questions are usually based on the rules of arrest, search and seizure. The area of confessions should also be revised carefully.

5.6 Questions

Question 1

Jonathan and Trevor Bailey (two black youths aged 14 and 17) are jogging down a street with Orville Locks, a black youth association worker and keen athlete, dressed in a tracksuit. A police car pulls up and two police officers, PC Spotter and PC Quick Draw, stop them and demand to search the pack which Orville is carrying. Finding a length of lead piping and four wallets, PC Quick Draw exclaims 'Got you! No more steaming for you lot!' (Steaming is a version of mugging carried out by groups of young people dressed in training/jogging gear who run past individuals and grab their bags. Recent research known to the police had shown that 90% of the individuals arrested for mugging in the past two years were black.)

Orville is taken away in a police van while Jonathan and Trevor are taken to a local police station.

After being cautioned, Jonathan and Trevor are questioned in separate rooms, with tape recorders operating. Trevor asks for a solicitor, but his request is refused. He is questioned for two hours and released. Jonathan is kept for two days and questioned extensively. Jonathan said he did not need a solicitor as that meant one more person would be present to ask him questions! On the second day the police discover that Jonathan is only 14 and bring a police typist into the room to act as an appropriate adult. Jonathan, who is crying and obviously distressed, now claims that Orville is 'always saying that he knows how to make quick money', and that 'sometimes we run into people on the street and Orville grabs their bags while we make lots of noise'.

Assess the effect of the procedures followed and whether Jonathan's statements amount to a valid confession.

University of London LLB Examination
(for External Students) English Legal System June 1992 Q8

General comment

This is a very detailed and lengthy question which required a thorough knowledge of the Police and Criminal Evidence Act 1984 and the connected case law. A question of this type should always be read thoroughly and a careful plan made so that a well structured answer can be given.

Skeleton solution

- Legality of police stopping the three parties.
- Legality of arrest.

Each detainee should then be dealt with individually. The following matters should be discussed where applicable:

- Legality of search;
- Conditions of questioning and detention;
- Admissibility of evidence.

If issues have been discussed in relation to one person, it is not necessary to repeat your points; simply refer the examiner to the relevant issues and your previous discussions.

Suggested solution

The introduction of the Police and Criminal Evidence Act (PACE) and the accompanying Codes of Practice in 1984 was designed to safeguard the rights of detainees by clarifying the exact extent of police powers on a statutory basis. It is the details of that legislation that must be discussed here in relation to each of the parties.

Turning first to the action of the police in stopping Jonathan, Trevor and Orville, ss1–3 of PACE give the police a power to stop and search anyone they have reasonable grounds to believe is carrying stolen or prohibited articles. These include articles intended or made for use in connection with theft. The police must have reasonable grounds for suspecting they will find these articles. This must be something more than a hunch, something concrete. While PACE and the Codes do not say exactly what would constitute a 'concrete' reason, it is clear that the suspect's personal factors or stereotyping by the police are not sufficient. They should be looking at the behaviour and location of that person, and at the time of day. From the information given there would appear to be no grounds for suspicion at all other than the fact that they are black, which is clearly insufficient. Therefore, this initial action by the police would appear to be in breach of PACE.

Orville is then searched and, following the discovery of the lead piping and wallets, the three are apparently arrested. The legality or otherwise of the search is dealt with below. The power of arrest is established by, inter alia, s24 of PACE which provides that a constable may arrest anyone he has reasonable grounds for suspecting has committed, is committing or is about to commit an arrestable offence. Arrestable offences are also defined by s24 and include theft related matters. The basis of the reasonable grounds of suspicion is presumably the articles found in Orville's pack. If the grounds are the arrestee's race, this would not be sufficient, as discussed above. When exercising the power of arrest, the police must make it clear that they are arresting that particular person and on what grounds. No technical language need be used, but, if the arrest is to be lawful, it must be clear to the arrestee (*Christie* v *Leachinsky* (1947)). It is debatable whether the words used here are sufficient to fulfil that need for clarity, but this would be a matter for the magistrate or jury to decide at any subsequent trial.

It is now proposed to deal with the treatment of the parties individually.

Orville

The actions of stopping and arresting Orville (O) have been dealt with above. This still leaves the question of the legality of the search. Sections 1–3 of PACE also provide the grounds for detaining a person in order to search them, providing the grounds already discussed are fulfilled. Furthermore, the Codes of Practice emphasise the need to gain the detainee's permission to search whenever possible, to always state a reason for the search and to make a record of the search and reasons as soon as is practicable. On the facts given, it would appear that a 'demand' was made of O rather than a request. No details are given on the issues of grounds being given or records being made, but the case law is clear that failure to give a valid reason for the search will lead to it being unlawful (*R* v *Fennelly* (1989)). There is, therefore, a strong case to suggest that the search of O's pack is unlawful.

However, this does not necessarily make the evidence obtained inadmissible. Under s1 of PACE the police are within their powers to seize anything obtained as a result of the search. Here, s78 of PACE is important in providing for the exclusion of unfairly obtained evidence. This preserves the common law discretion of the court to exclude evidence which it considers unfair, having regard to the circumstances in which it was obtained. In dealing with this area, the judges have varied in their approach. Often a breach of PACE is looked for (clearly an issue here), but in *R* v *Keenan* (1990) the court suggested that a breach did not automatically lead to exclusion, and in *R* v *Mason* (1988) the Court of Appeal pointed out that the courts were not the place to discipline the police. However, Lord Lane LCJ in *R* v *Alladice* (1988) said that where the police have acted in bad faith the courts will have little difficulty in ruling any confession inadmissible under s78 (if not s76, discussed below). If this evidence against O is to be excluded, he must hope that the court follows Lord Lane's approach to s78.

The only other matters in relation to O are his departure in the police van, which of itself does not suggest any problem, and the statement of Jonathan, which is discussed below.

Trevor

One of the first things we are told about Trevor (T) is his age. However, at 17 he is technically an adult for the purposes of PACE (a juvenile being someone under 17) and so there are no special rules regarding his treatment.

The legality of his arrest has already been discussed, and so the main issue is the lawfulness of his detention. On the facts given it is assumed that the custody officer complied with all the requirements of PACE on T's arrival at the police station, including the right to have someone informed (s56). The key fact is the refusal of access to legal advice. We are told that T clearly asked for and was refused access to a solicitor. Section 58 of PACE established the right to legal advice for all detainees if they so choose (and clearly T has done so). Only in exceptional circumstances can this access be delayed. These are detailed in s58 and apply where the police are dealing with a serious arrestable offence and have reasonable grounds for believing that access to a solicitor would lead to evidence or witnesses being affected, or accomplices being alerted. Serious arrestable offences are specified in s116 and do not include the facts in question. Furthermore, the courts have shown the seriousness with which they regard this right, especially in the case of *R* v *Samuel* (1988) where it was emphasised that delay would only be justified in exceptional circumstances. It would appear, therefore, that there has been a blatant breach of s58 in relation to T.

There is no information given regarding any evidence being obtained from T so admissibility is not in issue here. We are told that he was released after two hours of questioning; this is just within the guidelines of the Codes which specify a break every two hours.

Jonathan

By far the most important issues in this case surround the treatment of Jonathan (J). At only 14 he is clearly to be regarded as a juvenile and, while this does not require any special treatment with regard to the powers of stop and search and arrest, there are very important requirements regarding detention.

Again, it is assumed that the custody officer has complied with the initial requirements, including s56. However, in addition to s56 there is an extra requirement which places the onus on the police to make sure an appropriate adult is informed of the juvenile's arrest and detention. For the purposes of the Act, an appropriate adult is a parent, guardian or a social worker, or any other appropriate person unconnected with the police. Furthermore, that adult should be present throughout any questioning and has the right to intervene on the part of the juvenile or to ask for legal advice on his behalf.

It is apparent from the facts that initially the police did not know J's age. However, the Codes of Practice suggest that whenever a detainee *appears* to be a juvenile, he should be treated as such until he is *proved* to be older. This makes the duty on the police more onerous and undermines any defence by the police that they did not realise J was a juvenile, especially since he was some years under 17. As soon as the police apparently realised J's age they attempted to find someone. This would perhaps absolve them from initial fault. Nevertheless, when they confirmed J's age, they still failed to fulfil requirements by bringing in the police typist who clearly is not an appropriate adult as defined above. They are, therefore, again in breach of PACE on this matter, even if only towards the end of J's detention.

Another issue which the facts raise is J's refusal of a solicitor. This is prima facie not a problem provided he clearly understood his right to legal advice and the nature of that right (*R* v *Vernon* (1988) and *R* v *Hughes* (1988)). His attitude suggests he may not have done, although there are insufficient facts to corroborate or refute this point.

We are also told that it was during the 'second day' that the police discovered J's age. This immediately raises issues regarding the length of detention. Section 41 of PACE allows an initial period of 24 hours. After that, further detention must be authorised in accordance with ss42 or 43 and is only permissible where dealing with a serious arrestable offence. It may be that J is still within the 24-hour limit depending on the time of arrest, but this is not clear from the facts, and the fact that he is being detained for a second day clearly suggests a considerable time in detention.

We are also told that J is questioned extensively. Again, although no specific facts are given, the length and conditions of questioning may be a problem. The Codes suggest a break every two hours with regular meals and proper sleep.

By the time J makes his statement he is clearly distressed. At the very least, there has been one breach of PACE with the failure to have an appropriate adult present (note that his brother has long been released by this stage). The main issue is the admissibility of that evidence. Here, ss76 and 78 of PACE may both be applicable. Section 76 specifically provides that the court must exclude confessions obtained by oppression (s76(2)(a)) or which are unreliable (s76(2)(b)). It is submitted that the most appropriate point here is the issue of unreliability. The Codes of Practice themselves suggest that juveniles by their very age may be prone to giving unreliable evidence (hence the need for an appropriate adult). However, the cases in this area have established that the unreliability must be as a result of something said or done by someone rather than the state of the detainee himself (*R* v *Goldenberg* (1988), where the defendant was a heroin addict). In the present case we must look at the actions of the police and the breaches of PACE that have taken place in relation to J. Furthermore, the circumstances to be considered are those prevailing at the time (ie J's youth and distress) and not what the police perceived them to be. There would seem to be a strong case for arguing for exclusion under s76(2)(b), but this would be the decision of the court.

Section 78 is also applicable in this matter. Although it deals with all evidence, it clearly includes confessions. As discussed in relation to Orville, the case law in this area is not conclusive. However, in the case of *R* v *Delaney* (1989) the failure to provide an appropriate adult was considered a sufficient ground for exclusion. Again, the approach of Lord Lane in Samuel offers the most assistance to the defence here.

While both sections may be pleaded together, and both would probably use a voir dire to decide the issue (though this is not compulsory with regard to s78), s76 has an advantage for the defence as the burden is placed on the prosecution to prove that the statement is not unreliable rather than on the defence as is the case under s78.

In conclusion, the police actions throughout suggest breaches of PACE of varying severity and would appear to provide potentially strong arguments for the exclusion of evidence. Apart from this, Jonathan, Trevor and Orville may well wish to consider a civil action against the police or a complaint to the Police Complaints Authority based on their treatment.

Question 2

Angelo is a student of very scruffy appearance. In his spare time he is renovating an old car and yesterday bought some tools and cans of spray paint for this purpose. He was returning to his lodgings when he was stopped by Police Constable Hurd, who asked what was in his carrier bag. Despite Angelo's explanation PC Hurd took the bag and on examining its contents told Angelo that he was under arrest on suspicion of being 'connected' with a raid on Angelo's college by 'Animal Liberation' protesters who had caused considerable damage to laboratories and sprayed slogans on the buildings. PC Hurd then searched Angelo's bedroom, and found another student's lecture notes which Angelo had stolen. When he proposed to search the room of Angelo's friend Bertie the latter pushed him away, using highly offensive language, before locking the door and refusing him entry.

Angelo has now been charged with theft of the lecture notes and Bertie with obstructing the police.

Advise Angelo and Bertie.

University of London LLB Examination
(for External Students) English Legal System June 1989 Q4

General comment

The question requires a good knowledge of Part I of the Police and Criminal Evidence Act 1984 (PACE).

Skeleton solution

- Powers of the police to stop and search – s1 PACE.
- Effect of the Codes of Practice on 'reasonable suspicion'.
- Grounds for arrest without warrant.
- Legality of the search – s32 PACE.

Suggested solution

Section 1(2) of PACE gives a general power to constables to search a person, provided the constable 'has reasonable grounds for suspecting that he will find stolen or prohibited articles' as a result of the search (s1(3)). Ultimately the existence of such 'reasonable grounds' must be a question of fact, although Annex B of the Code of Practice for the Exercise by Police Officers of Statutory Powers of Stop and Search issued under s66 of the Act, and of general application in its interpretation, gives guidance. The constable need not be certain that an unlawful article is being carried, nor does he have to be satisfied of this beyond reasonable doubt. But there must be some concrete basis for the constable's suspicion, related to the individual concerned, which can be considered and evaluated by an objective third person. Reasonable suspicion may arise from the nature of the property observed or being carried or suspected of being carried, coupled with other factors including the time, place and suspicious behaviour of the person concerned or those with him.

It would appear that there is nothing in Angelo's behaviour to mark him out as a suspect. Hurd's explanation for his searching him would appear to be due to the fact that he is a student, of somewhat scruffy appearance. But the Code provides that reasonable suspicion cannot be supported on the basis simply of a higher than average chance that the person has committed or is about to commit an offence, merely because he belongs to a group within which offenders of a certain kind are relatively common, eg scruffily dressed people. Thus it is likely that there was no basis for the stop and search. Nor do the requirements of s2 and s3 appear to have been complied with.

Where a constable has reasonable grounds for suspecting that an arrestable offence has been committed, he may arrest without a warrant anyone whom he has reasonable grounds for suspecting to be guilty of an offence either: (a) for which the sentence is fixed by law; or (b) for which a person of 21 years of age or over (not previously convicted) may be sentenced to imprisonment for a term of five years. The situation is one that would have been intended by the legislature to fall within its provisions: someone is suspected of committing an act of criminal damage. Hurd rightly tells Angelo that he is under arrest, and the ground for the arrest as required by s28. He does not say that Angelo was guilty of the offence of damaging laboratories and spraying the buildings with slogans (criminal damage), merely that he was 'connected' with it. This is rather flimsy, and may lead one to suppose that Hurd had inadequate grounds for making the arrest.

Once a suspect has been arrested he must be taken to a police station as soon as practicable after his arrest: s30(1). Hurd is probably within his rights in searching Angelo's room while he is in the area. An officer is entitled to search premises in which the suspect was arrested, or in which he was present immediately before his arrest, in order to discover evidence relating to the offence for which the arrest was made, if the arresting constable has reasonable grounds for believing that such evidence exists: s32(2) and (6), but Angelo was not in his lodgings. Therefore such a search must be justified under s18. This enables premises in Angelo's control to be searched for evidence relating to the offence or other similar or connected offence. Arguably the lecture notes do not come within this category, and their service would not be justified.

Therefore it may be that the lecture notes could be excluded under s78, since in all the circumstances of the case, to admit them as evidence would have an adverse effect on the fairness of proceedings.

With respect to Hurd's attempted search of B's rooms, s17 only empowers him to arrest a person for an arrestable offence or for one of a number of specified offences. Again Hurd may have criminal damage in mind as an arrestable offence. In addition, under subs17(1)(e) powers of entry and search are only exercisable if the constable has reasonable grounds for believing that the person whom he is seeking is on the premises. But in cases where premises consist of two or more separate dwellings (eg two rooms in a house or hostel) the powers are limited to any parts of the premises which the occupiers of any dwelling comprised in the premises use in common with the occupiers of any other such dwelling. Bertie is thus fully within his rights to obstruct Hurd.

Question 3

Detective Constables Freebie and Bean were searching for a car used in a robbery and spotted it apparently abandoned in the residents' car park outside a block of flats. Simple, who lived there, reached into the car and removed a small package. He ran off when challenged by Freebie but was caught by Bean and bundled into the DCs' car and taken to the police station. On the way, he confessed that he had intended to keep the contents of the package if they proved valuable. No note was made of this confession. When the package was opened at the police station it was found to contain jewellery from the robbery. Simple was questioned for two hours about the robbery, no mention being made that any advice might be available to him. He once again admitted that he had intended to steal the package from the car and asked to see a lawyer. This was refused. After a further three hours' questioning he agreed that he had taken part in the robbery and was thereupon charged with that offence.

After seeing a solicitor Simple withdrew his confession to the robbery saying that he had been frightened and confused when he made it. You are now asked to advise whether:

a) the procedures followed by the police were lawful, and;

b) Simple's confession to taking part in the robbery is likely to be admissible.

University of London LLB Examination
(for External Students) English Legal System June 1990 Q8

General comment

A typical question on police powers. The question requires discussion on the powers available to the police to arrest and search suspects. Discussion on the Codes of Practice and the subsequent admissibility of the confessions is essential.

Skeleton solution

a)
- Arrest without warrant.
- Grounds for reasonable suspicion.
- The right to legal advice.

b) • Does S's confession fall within s76 PACE? Identify the breaches of the Code of Practice.

Suggested solution

a) The procedures

The powers of the police to arrest, search, seize and interrogate are now largely to be found in PACE. All subsequent references are to this Act unless otherwise stated.

The powers of arrest are covered under s24 of the Act and clearly F and B act within their rights under s24(6):

'When a constable has reasonable grounds for suspecting that an arrestable offence has been committed, he may arrest without a warrant anyone whom he has reasonable grounds for suspecting to be guilty of the offence.'

We can presume that F and B did not have a warrant – possession of a warrant would, however, have provided a fortiori a defence to any action for false imprisonment. F and B's suspicions are undoubtedly reasonable – Appendix B of the Code of Practice related to statutory powers of stop and search says:

'Reasonable suspicion, in contrast to mere suspicion, must be founded on fact. There must be some concrete basis for the officer's suspicion, related to the individual concerned, which can be considered and evaluated by an objective third person.'

F and B witnessed S's appropriation of the package, they thus acted within their powers, having more than mere suspicion, founded on facts.

S was detained in the residents' car park outside the flats of which he was a tenant. By s1 a constable may search and detain any person or vehicle in a public place if he has reasonable grounds for suspecting that he will find stolen or prohibited articles.

F and B had such reasonable grounds – the car had been used in the robbery which they were investigating. 'Public place' is defined in s1(1) as a place 'to which people have ready access ... but which is not a dwelling'. S's detention therein seems to be lawful.

By virtue of s28 of the Act an arrest is unlawful unless and until D is informed that he is under arrest and of the reason for the arrest as soon as is practicable. The Code of Practice further states that a caution should be given on arrest and its meaning explained. We are not told whether or not such procedures were complied with – if not, the arrest can be said to be prime facie unlawful.

S is 'bundled' into the car. Section 117 provides that in the execution of powers conferred by the Act a constable may use reasonable force, if necessary.

According to s30(1) an arrested person should be taken to the police station 'as soon as practicable' after his arrest – this presents no problem in the given situation.

Section 58(1) entitles a person in police detention to consult a solicitor, if he so requests, privately at any time. There is power under s58(8) for an officer to authorise delay in certain circumstances, in which case the arrested person must be told of the reason for the refusal. It does not seem that this presumptive right should have been denied to S since on the facts his case does not fall within the exceptions. Moreover, paragraph 6 of the Code of Practice on Detention, Treatment and Questioning also deals with the right to legal advice and stresses that an arrestee who asks for legal advice may not be interviewed or an interview continued unless he has received it. There seems to be a blatant breach of the rules here.

In addition to the right to legal advice there is also a right to have a friend, relative or other person informed of the arrest. S does not appear to have been made aware of this right.

As regards the interrogation and detention: S was held and questioned for five hours and then charged. The five hours' detention is lawful since by s41 a suspect can be detained for up to 24 hours without charge. As to the interrogation itself – this should have been broken with periods of respite every two hours – there is no mention of such breaks in the facts and this could perhaps amount to oppression within the ambit of s76 (see post).

b) The confessions

Three separate confessions were made by S.

i) Confession in the police car re theft of the package.

ii) Confession at the police station as to the theft of the package.

iii) Confession at the police station as to the robbery.

The first two confessions are of no concern in the present question since S admits making them. The third confession S now wants to withdraw.

It should be noted at the outset that the admissibility of evidence obtained by breaches of the criminal law on the part of the police involves the balancing of two opposing law interests: *Lawrie* v *Muir* (1950) per Lord Cooper:

Firstly, the interest of the citizen to be protected from illegal or irregular invasions of his liberties by the authorities; and

Secondly, the interest of the state to secure that evidence bearing upon the commission of a crime and necessary to enable justice to be done shall not be withheld from courts of law on any mere formal or technical ground.

The confession may be given in evidence and has not been excluded by the court in pursuance of s76 of the Act. S's confession would be excluded if it falls within the scope of s76(2). By this section a confession will be excluded if it has been obtained by oppression or in consequence of anything said or done which was likely in the circumstances existing at the time to render unreliable any confession made by him.

'Oppression' is defined in s76(8) as including 'torture inhuman or degrading treatment and the use or threat of use of violence'.

S will complain in the mainstay of the following breaches of the Code of Practice; refusal of legal advice and insufficient breaks in questioning. In *R* v *Fulling* (1987) Lord Lane CJ said that:

'... "oppression" in s76(2)(c) should be given its ordinary dictionary meaning'.

The word is thus defined in the Oxford English Dictionary:

'Exercise of authority or power in a burdensome, harsh or wrongful manner: unjust or cruel treatment of subjects, inferiors etc, the imposition of unreasonable or unjust burdens.'

Certainly, the power has been exercised in a burdensome manner. Further, in *R* v *Samuel* (1988) Hodgson J said that the decision to withhold legal advice, as sprovided for in s58, could rarely be justified on the basis that the solicitor himself might deliberately or inadvertently alert others involved in the offence (of the grounds specified in s58 permitting the denial of such advice). However, the decision in *R* v *Samuel* should not be taken to mean that any breach of the requirements will invalidate any confession which is obtained as a consequence thereof. In *R* v *Alladice* (1988) Lord Lane CJ dismissed an appeal where access to a solicitor had been refused. He concluded that the interviews had been conducted correctly and that the only difference the presence of a solicitor would have made would have been to provide additional advice as to the appellant's right to say nothing. In the light of this decision S's confession may remain admissible under s76.

Section 78 PACE deals with the exclusion of unfair evidence. In *R* v *Mason* (1988) the Court of Appeal held that 'evidence' included a confession, although this was expressly dealt with by s76.

Thus a confession can be excluded on the grounds of its unfairness as well as on the s76 grounds of oppression and unreliability.

By s78 the judge has a general discretion to exclude evidence which:

'Having regard to all the circumstances in which the evidence was obtained, the admission of the evidence would have such an adverse effect on the fairness of the proceedings that the court ought not to admit it.'

Thus, the judge may in his absolute discretion exclude the confession as to the robbery as being unfairly obtained evidence.

6 PROSECUTION AND BAIL

6.1 Introduction

In October 1986, the system and responsibilities of prosecution underwent major change with the introduction of the Crown Prosecution Service. However, the police still play a major role in criminal prosecutions. This chapter will summarise the various prosecutors and their functions.

A PROSECUTION

6.2 Key points

a) *The police*

The police initiate most prosecutions, principally because they are in the best position to investigate crimes and as they have wide powers of arrest. Once the accused is charged, the Crown Prosecution Service (CPS) will take over the prosecution. The police will however continue to assist the CPS in the collecting and giving of evidence.

b) *The Crown Prosecution Service*

i) The CPS was created by s1 of the Prosecution of Offences Act 1985. The Director of Public Prosecutions (DPP) is its head and is required to take over all criminal proceedings initiated by the police. He may also take over any other prosecution initiated by a private individual or other body. The DPP acts under the supervision of the Attorney-General.

ii) The principal importance of the CPS is its independence from the police and it is the CPS that takes the responsibility of deciding whether a particular prosecution should continue. The CPS is also in a position to discontinue proceedings in magistrates' courts: see s23 of the 1985 Act.

The Runciman Commission on Criminal Justice has proposed that the CPS should be given power to discontinue proceedings up to the beginning of trial in the Crown Court.

c) *Government bodies*

Most non-police prosecutions are initiated by other government bodies, for example the Health and Safety Executive, the Inland Revenue and the Serious Fraud Office.

d) *Private individuals*

Private individuals are in a position to prosecute other individuals, a right retained by s6 Prosecution of Offences Act 1985. They will generally do so where the police display insufficient interest in bringing prosecution: see eg *Whitehouse* v *Gay News Ltd and Lemon* (1978) 68 Cr App R 381.

e) *The decision to prosecute*

Not every criminal offence is prosecuted. The decision to prosecute is at the discretion of the prosecutor. It will largely be based upon the extent and quality of evidence available and the seriousness of the offence.

There is, generally, no prosecution for technical infringements of the law. Often the police will issue instead a caution. This is principally used in relation to juvenile offenders and works by way of warning, so that although no prosecution takes place, the likelihood of prosecution is greater for subsequent offences.

It is extremely rare for the court to interfere in the exercise of action in making the decision to prosecute, see: *R* v *Commissioner of Police of the Metropolis, ex parte Blackburn* [1968] 2 WLR 893.

f) *Commencing a prosecution*

There are two methods available for commencing any prosecution.

i) Laying an information

An information is a statement of the suspected offence – it may be either written or oral. This method is generally used for less serious offences. The appearance of the defendant may be secured by either an issue of summons or a warrant for arrest.

- Where a summons is required the information may be dealt with by the magistrates' clerk. Once a summons is obtained, it is issued to the accused and he is informed about when he is to appear before the magistrates to answer the allegations made against him.
- Where a warrant is required, the information must be in writing and on oath and it is the magistrate who must deal with the matter.

ii) Charging

This procedure is used for more serious offences and generally by the police. The charge is written down on the charge sheet and read over to the accused.

He is then either detained or bailed. The charge sheet is then sent to the magistrates' court.

B BAIL

6.3 Key points

Bail is defined simply as the release of a person subject to a duty to surrender to custody at a particular time and place. It can be applied for both at the police station and at court.

a) *A right to bail*

i) Section 4 Bail Act 1976 gives the accused a right to bail. However, this does not mean that the accused may not be refused bail. The section does not apply to all stages of the proceedings. The importance of this right is that it is for the prosecution to show why bail ought to be withheld.

ii) Section 4 applies to give a right to bail in cases that do not fall within Schedule 1 of the Bail Act. In these cases there is no statutory presumption in favour of bail and the defence would have to plead for bail.

iii) Cases in which there is no right to bail:

- when the custody officer is considering bail for an arrestee from the police station, after charge; or
- when the magistrates' court has summarily convicted the accused and commits him for sentence to the Crown Court; or
- where the accused has been convicted or sentenced by the magistrates or Crown Court and is appealing against conviction or sentence.

b) *Factors to be taken into account*

Paragraph 9 of Schedule 1, Part I gives the court some guidance on approaching the issue of bail. The following ought to be considered in determining whether bail should be granted:

i) the nature and seriousness of the offence;

ii) character, antecedents, associations and community ties ie, job, home, wife, children;

iii) past record for answering bail;

iv) strength of the prosecution's case.

c) *Grounds for refusing bail – imprisonable offence*

Schedule 1 lists the circumstances in which bail may be refused. This applies where the defendant is accused or convicted of at least one imprisonable offence.

The defendant need not be granted bail where

i) the court is satisfied that there are substantial grounds for believing that if he is released he will:

- fail to surrender to custody; or
- commit an offence; or
- interfere with witnesses or obstruct the course of justice *or*

ii) the court is satisfied he should be kept in custody for:

- his own protection; or
- if a juvenile, for his own welfare; or
- where he is already serving a custodial sentence; or
- he has already been bailed, absconded and been arrested.

d) *Grounds for refusing bail – non-imprisonable offence*

Schedule 1, Part II allows the court to refuse bail if:

i) on a previous occasion the defendant failed to surrender to custody; or

ii) the court is satisfied that the defendant ought to be kept in custody for his own protection/welfare; or

iii) the defendant is already serving a custodial sentence; or

iv) he has already been bailed, absconded and been arrested.

e) *Conditions on bail*

The court may grant unconditional bail under s3 Bail Act 1976, in which case the only obligation is to surrender to custody at the time and place required.

However, the court is permitted to attach whatever conditions it deems fit. The most common conditions are:

i) to ensure the defendant surrenders to custody, the court may require a surety to undertake to pay a sum of money to the court if the defendant fails to surrender;

ii) the defendant may be required to report to a particular place at particular intervals;

iii) the defendant may be required to live at a particular address;

iv) the court may impose a curfew on the defendant.

f) *Appealing against refusal to grant bail*

Where bail is refused, a record is made of the decision and the reasons for it. The defendant may if he wishes obtain a copy.

Appeal against a magistrates' decision may be made to the High Court. Section 22 of the Criminal Justice Act 1967 governs the jurisdiction of the High Court in this respect and provides for the High Court to grant bail or vary any conditions to bail imposed by the magistrates.

Appeal to the Crown Court is also possible. The Crown Court may grant bail, if it is refused by magistrates, in the following cases:

i) where the magistrates remanded the defendant in custody after hearing a full bail application; or

ii) where the magistrates have committed the defendant to the Crown Court for trial or sentence; or

iii) where the defendant was convicted by the magistrates and refused bail pending appeal to the Crown Court.

g) *Failure to surrender*

A person released on bail is guilty of an offence if he fails to surrender to custody: see s6(1) of the Bail Act 1976.

6.4 Analysis of questions

Prosecution and bail is rarely examined on its own. It may however be included as part of another question. Students ought to familiarise themselves with the workings of the Crown Prosecution Service and its problems.

6.5 Questions

Question 1

Answer *both* parts:

a) Describe in outline the organisation of the Crown Prosecution Service in England and Wales; and

b) 'It has never been the rule in this country – I hope it never will be – that suspected criminal offences must automatically be the subject of prosecution' (Lord Shawcross). Discuss.

University of London LLB Examination
(for External Students) English Legal System June 1987 Q4

General comment

This is a difficult question in both parts. Both parts of the question are sufficiently general to be capable of being handled in so many ways that it is hard to penetrate the mind of the examiner to see what he may have been seeking for when the question was set. This is not to say that questions have a particular answer that the examiner expects, it is just that one can usually recognise some of the points that are likely to be found in an answer.

Skeleton solution

a)
- Historical perspective on the Crown Prosecution Service (CPS).
- Role of the Director of Public Prosecutions.
- Role of CPS lawyers.

b)
- Reasons for close scrutiny of cases.
- Public benefit for undertaking prosecution.
- Consideration of available evidence.

Suggested solution

a) The Crown Prosecution Service was set up in October of 1986 as a result of the Phillips Report on Criminal Procedure. This seminal report gave rise to the Police and Criminal Evidence Act 1984 and the Prosecution of Offences Act 1985. The intention was to redefine police powers with regard to search, seizure, arrest and interrogation and to put the prosecution of offences into the hands of a completely new body. The two Acts may be seen as complementary in this respect. Until then prosecutions had been undertaken by the police themselves who had fulfilled two functions. First, to decide in what situations to prosecute. This is essentially an executive decision quite divorced from investigative or fact-finding tasks of the police or their functions in detecting or preventing crime. It is not unreasonable to assume that the decision to prosecute should be left to another body.

The second function undertaken by the police before Crown Prosecution Service was initiated was the actual conduct of the prosecution. This relates to the marshalling of the appropriate evidence and the presentation of the case of the court. It is not surprising that in view of the specialised forensic nature of the process that many police authorities had already recruited their own Prosecuting Solicitors' Departments. This formed the basis of the Crown Prosecution Service. The prosecuting solicitors could conduct a case in the magistrates' court and would brief barristers when a case was to be dealt with in the Crown Court. There were 36 prosecuting solicitors' offices and there are 13 Crown Prosecution Area offices today.

Before the establishment of the Crown Prosecution Service the more serious crimes were dealt with by the Director of Public Prosecutions, and police forces were obliged to report these offences to the Director and sometimes could not prosecute without his authority. The Director of Public Prosecutions was the natural head of the new service. It was hoped that the Crown Prosecution Service would provide for greater national consistency in the prosecution of offences for, although it remains a regionally based service, it is nationally organised.

It might be churlish to say that it would be easier to write about the *dis*organisation of the Crown Prosecution Service. There have been many accounts of lost papers and poor preparation and advocacy. Many agents – barristers and solicitors in private practice – have had to be employed at higher rates than full-time members of the service because of the shortage of staff and this is generally attributed to the relatively poor pay offered to full-time Crown Prosecutors. Staff shortages have been linked to a somewhat hasty timetable of reorganisation and morale is undoubtedly low. Nonetheless, the concept of a Crown Prosecution Service remains a good one and, even if the current difficulties are more than teething troubles, it must be made to succeed.

b) A major criterion in deciding whether to prosecute an offender must be the likelihood of success. Failure is both expensive and embarrassing in that the defendant has been put to unnecessary trouble and exposure to risk while the prosecutor may appear to be incompetent or the law and the prosecution a species of harassment. Of course, not every suspected criminal offence can be the subject of prosecution. First, it is necessary to see whether an actual offence has occurred, second, whether a perpetrator can be identified and apprehended. Nulla poena sine lege remains a good maxim. It seems unwise in general to prosecute an offence without a proper consideration of whether there is a criminal offence disclosed in the particulars of indictment.

To prosecute for a suspected criminal offence where none turns out to have been committed seems an equally strange way of proceeding. Coroners' juries are no longer able to name the person they believe guilty of a murder because it tends to force the hands of the police and, in any event, it may be ill-considered allegation. With all due respect to the case of *R* v *Fuschillo* (1940), it would seem odd to prosecute a person who appears to have committed what is suspected to be an offence. If fresh evidence were to be discovered subsequently to an unsuccessful prosecution it could not be used, for the defendant, once acquitted, is not subject to double jeopardy, and could plead 'autrefois acquit'. The automatic prosecution of suspected offences might involve too much premature shooting of the police's bolt.

Another major criterion is the consideration of the public benefit to be derived from a prosecution. Although there is not a time limit for the prosecution of indictable offences, summary offences must be prosecuted with six months. An offence committed many years before might not be worth prosecuting at a later date. It might be considered oppressive to do so.

For that matter the prosecuting authorities have a discretion as to whether to prosecute at all. The police cannot attempt to prosecute every actual offence and there must be some reasonable discretion at this stage. Thus the dropping of litter is unlikely to be prosecuted and most police officers would not even warn a person in those circumstances. Even first offences of the possession of small amounts of the less harmful controlled drugs are unlikely to be the subject of prosecution. In these circumstances the police are more likely to issue a caution, either formally or informally. There are regular provisions for the administering of a formal caution by a uniformed police officer and this is often used in the case of juveniles or minor shoplifting cases. The prosecution of the television personality Lady Isobel Barnet for shoplifting a few years ago led to her suicide.

There are many cases where prosecution will not be merited in the circumstances of a case but there are at least two problems that flow from this. One is the assumption which may easily be made that a person brought before the courts has been previously cautioned and that this therefore is effectively a second offence. Secondly, there is a visible danger in allowing anyone other than an open court of law to decide on the appropriate course of action once a person has been accused of having committed an offence. There are occasional allegations that people of influence have been able to avoid prosecution, although this normally refers to minor offences. It is both impossible and undesirable that every suspected person or offence should be subject to formal prosecution. Commonsense must be allowed to enable some discretion to be used in these situations.

Question 2

Critically assess the advantages of TWO of the following:

a) tape recordings of confessions of accused persons in the police stations;

b) the general right to bail created by the Bail Act 1976;

c) the discount on sentence allowed to an accused person who pleads guilty.

University of London LLB Examination
(for External Students) English Legal System June 1988 Q2

General comment

The key word here is 'critically'; your judgment is asked for on three topical areas of criminal justice. 'Critically assess' means look at the advantages and disadvantages of both the theory and practice of the three areas and perhaps come to a conclusion as to what the Government should now do to remedy any defects. It should not be forgotten that those who do best in exams are generally those who have original ideas on an area.

Skeleton solution

a)
- Section 60 of the Police and Criminal Evidence Act 1984 (PACE), introduction of tape recordings.
- Challenges on evidence obtained without recordings.
- Disadvantages of tape recordings.

b)
- Consideration of s4 Bail Act 1976.
- Exceptions to the general right to bail.
- Options available to a defendant on refusal of bail.

c)
- Individualised sentencing.
- How can guilty pleas be seen as a mitigating factor?

Suggested solution

a) Section 60 of PACE lays a duty on the Home Secretary to, by statutory instrument, introduce the tape recording of interviews of criminal suspects throughout England and Wales. Since the passing of the Act the new system has been widely introduced and many forces have moved completely to the new system. Before looking at the merits and demerits of tape recording let us examine briefly the advantages and disadvantages of the new and old systems (still employed by some forces, especially those in rural areas).

The old system involved a police officer, usually together with a fellow officer, when interviewing the suspect in either taking down verbatim in question and answer format what is said. Alternatively, he could keep a note in his 'pocket book' or the fellow officer could keep a note in his pocket book. The trouble was that this pocket book note was often in summary form because the officer wanted to save time by not noting down every word. When the matter came to court there were frequent challenges to statements obtained by either of the above methods because it was said other things were said by the police or the accused which were not recorded in the note book. These challenges wasted a lot of time at the trial. Also the police officers wasted a lot of time writing up interviews, either verbatim or later on where pocket book notes were transferred to sheet paper.

The trouble with the new system is that it is expensive and slow. It is expensive because the equipment is more costly and sometimes several tapes are needed for one interview and because the interviews are slower and therefore wasteful of police manpower. Tape recorded interviews are slower because every word of the interview is recorded start to finish, even requests for a cup of tea. Much irrelevant material is recorded which has no bearing on the case and sometimes the jury have to listen to this at the trial. The advantages are a dramatic reduction in the number of challenges at the trial and at other stages. There can be no doubt about what was said. Eventually therefore, the new system should speed up the trial and make the criminal justice system a little more efficient.

b) Bail is a right not a privilege as the Bail Act 1976 makes plain: s4. However, this 'right' is not in practice a right because there are a wide range of circumstances where bail will not be granted. There is much concern also that magistrates do not grant bail in all the cases that they should do and there are often cases where, against the strict letter of the law, magistrates refuse bail and it is necessary for the accused to go to a higher court before being granted bail (often to the consternation of the judge). Bail may also be granted by the police prior to the accused's first appearance before court.

Section 4 provides that the accused 'shall be granted bail except as provided in Schedule 1'. This right to bail continues from the date of the first appearance up to the date on which he is acquitted or convicted. Therefore the right continues during the trial and the judge must give reasons for overnight (and sometimes over-lunch) detention. The exceptions to this general right provided in Schedule 1 are that, in the case of an imprisonable offence:

a) The accused would:

   i) fail to surrender to custody;

ii) commit an offence while on bail;

iii) interfere with witnesses or otherwise obstruct the course of justice. Or

b) The accused needs to be kept in custody for his own protection. Or

c) Because of lack of time since commencement of proceedings the court is unable to say one way or the other because it does not have the information required to answer (a) or (b) above.

If the magistrates refuse bail at one appearance the defendant can only make a renewed application to the bench if there has been a 'change of circumstances'. In practice it is very difficult to show this; for example, a grant of legal aid is not considered a change of circumstances. Therefore most defendants who are refused bail either go (most commonly) to the Crown Court or to the High Court to a judge in chambers, to argue that the magistrates at the lower court exercised their discretion in the wrong way. Often they do; a high percentage of appeals against refusal of bail are successful. It has recently been suggested that the change of circumstances restriction on reconsidering applications for bail in the lower court should be removed, as appeal to the higher court is wasteful of time and money and unjust to the accused.

Criticism of the present system centres around the high percentage of cases in which bail is refused rather than over-liberality. Research has shown that in cases where bail is granted pending trial only a very small number of defendants commit offences while on bail, less than one per cent. Also on moral grounds it must be right to try and incarcerate as small a number of people as possible pending trial or conviction. These people are after all innocent until proven otherwise – why should they be treated like criminals?

Therefore it has been said that the law needs to be drafted in a clearer way so that magistrates are in no doubt of the accused's right to bail. Also perhaps magistrates need better training in such matters. Such things as the change of circumstances restriction need to be removed. At a time of prison overcrowding it is now imperative that something is done, both for practical and for moral reasons.

c) Depending on the potential effect and strength of mitigation personal to the defendant on the trial judge, it may lead the sentencer to pass an individualised sentence whose aim is not to punish the defendant but to help rehabilitate him, or, if a tariff sentence is imposed, to a penalty somewhat less severe than that warranted by the offence viewed in isolation.

A common mitigating factor pleaded on behalf of defendants is that the defendant pleaded guilty. A judge must not increase the sentence he passes because the accused pleaded not guilty, even if he believes that the accused has committed perjury: *R* v *Quinn* (1932); or because the defendant's defence involved grave allegations against the police: *R* v *Skone* (1967); or because by pleading not guilty the defendant has forced the prosecution to call witnesses who found giving evidence distressing or harmful, eg child witnesses to sexual offences.

However, it is well established that a guilty plea attracts a lighter sentence than a conviction following a not guilty plea: *R* v *Cain* (1976).

Pragmatism is probably the major reason for treating a guilty plea as mitigation. If every defendant pleaded not guilty, the legal system could not cope with the extra work involved. If there was no advantage to pleading guilty, why should any defendant give up the chance of an acquittal, however remote? Therefore, in order to save public time and money, defendants should be encouraged to plead guilty. It is in the public interest to give a discount on sentence even if a guilty plea was not motivated by the defendant's contrition for the past and his determination to reform for the future. There is no precise percentage by which the sentence should be reduced on account of a guilty plea. The Court of Appeal Criminal Division cases have suggested that between one-quarter and one-third off the tariff custodial sentence would be proper, though this percentage may be reduced the stronger the case is against the defendant, ie had he pleaded not guilty he would have stood little chance of an acquittal.

7 CLASSIFICATION OF OFFENCES AND COMMITTAL PROCEEDINGS

7.1 Introduction

The classification of offences is vital to determine the mode by which they are to be tried. For this purpose offences are divided into three main categories, namely, offences triable only on indictment, offences triable summarily and offences said to be triable either way.

7.2 Key points

a) *Classification of offences*

   i) Indictable offences are generally the more serious offences such as murder, manslaughter, robbery, rape. These offences are triable only on indictment, ie triable by both judge and jury in the Crown Court.

   ii) Summary offences are the least grave offences, many of which do not carry a sentence of imprisonment. The offences are triable summarily in the magistrates' court.

   iii) Triable either way offences are offences of medium gravity. These offences vary in seriousness and include offences such as theft and handling stolen goods. As such they are triable in either the magistrates' or the Crown Court.

b) *Determining the mode of trial*

   Where an offence is summary or indictable, it must be tried accordingly. A choice only presents itself in relation to offences triable either way. Procedure:

   i) The charge is first read to the defendant. The magistrate will hear submissions from both the prosecution and defence regarding the suitability of a mode of trial.

      - Should the magistrate decide that trial on indictment is appropriate, the defendant is informed and that decision is final.

- Where the magistrate considers that summary trial is more suitable the defendant is informed that if he consents, he may be tried by magistrates. The defendant then is put to his election and may choose where he is to be tried. He is also informed of the magistrates' court's power to commit him to the Crown Court after conviction if the court feels that its powers of punishment are insufficient.
- Once the magistrate decides on trial on indictment or the defendant chooses this mode, committal proceedings will follow before trial.
- The Runciman Commission has proposed major changes in this area. Essentially, these involve the prosecution and defence agreeing which court the case should be tried in. Only if the two sides fail to agree will the magistrates decide.

c) *Committal proceedings*

At this stage of the proceedings the court is not concerned with guilt or innocence, but merely with whether there is a prima facie case against the defendant. This may be determined in either of two forms of committal proceedings.

i) Long form committal: s6(1) Magistrates' Court Act 1980

In this mode of committal the prosecution brings its evidence before the court, including its witnesses. The witnesses can be cross-examined by the defence. The defence is entitled to make a submission of no case to answer where:

- there is no evidence shown to prove an essential element of the offence; or
- the evidence of the prosecution was discredited by cross-examination or the evidence is so unreliable that it would be unsafe to convict.

ii) Short form committal: s6(2) Magistrates' Court Act 1980

In this form of committal all the evidence comes before the court in the form of written statements. The form of these written statements is governed by s102 of the Magistrates' Court Act 1980. The following conditions must be satisfied:

- the statement must be signed by its maker; and
- the statement must contain a declaration of truth; and
- there must be no objection by either party to its production in evidence.

In this form of committal the defendant must be legally represented but the defence may not make a submission of no case to answer. The advantage of this method of committal is that it saves time and expense.

iii) Royal Commission on Criminal Justice proposals:

- The present system of committals should be completely abolished.

- Instead, the defendant would be able to make a submission of no case to answer and this would be considered on the papers with oral arguments from both sides if necessary.
- The submission would be based on legal argument and so, where dealing with an indictable offence, it should be considered by the Crown Court, and by the stipendiary magistrates for either way offences.

Once a defendant has been committed the examining justices will consider the following issues as appropriate.

i) Alibi warnings – should be made where the defendant wishes to rely upon an alibi. Section 11 of the Criminal Justice Act 1967 prohibits, save with the leave of the trial judge, the defendant from adducing evidence of an alibi, unless he gives notice of the particulars of the alibi to the prosecution either in the magistrates' court or within seven days of the committal proceedings.

ii) Bail applications can also be made at this stage.

iii) Legal aid applications are also considered.

7.3 Analysis of questions

If examined, it is likely that this subject area will arise in a question also raising other issues. For example see Question 1 in Chapter 9 which deals with classification of an offence, entitlement to legal aid and bail applications.

Students must be familiar with the classification of offences in order to consider whether a choice of trial exists. An understanding of the procedure and advantages of each type of committal is also useful.

7.4 Question

See Question 1 in Chapter 9.

8 SUMMARY TRIAL

8.1 Introduction

Summary trial generally takes place before three lay magistrates or a single stipendiary magistrate. The procedure of summary trials is governed by the Magistrates' Courts Act 1980. The only limitation on the criminal jurisdiction of the magistrates' court is subject to geographical limitations.

8.2 Key points

a) *Attendance and representation*

In some cases the defendant is not required to be present at summary trial: s12 Magistrates' Court Act 1980. A defendant is permitted to plead guilty by post where the maximum penalty for the offence is no more than three months.

b) *Information and plea*

The first stage in a summary trial is the clerk 'putting the information' to the defendant and asking for a plea. Should the defendant plead guilty, sentencing is the next stage. Where the plea is not guilty, the trial will follow.

c) *Summary trial procedure*

i) The prosecution will begin the proceedings with a short speech that gives some background information on the prosecution's evidence and will include a brief description of the facts of the case.

ii) The prosecution must then bring evidence to show beyond reasonable doubt that the defendant is guilty. Usually, witness evidence is called. It is particularly advantageous to have oral evidence, as it allows the magistrate to evaluate a witness's credibility and gives the defence an opportunity to cross-examine.

iii) Written statements of evidence may, however, be used in certain circumstances:

- s9 of the Criminal Justice Act 1967 allows the admissibility of written evidence in cases where the evidence is undisputed and certain formalities are complied with.
- s105 of the Magistrates' Courts Act 1980 permits written evidence taken from a witness who is ill and unlikely to recover or is dead. This is permissible so long as notice is sent to the other side.
- s42 Children and Young Persons Act 1933 permits certain types of evidence from children to be in written statements.

iv) There are three stages in witness evidence: firstly the examination in chief; secondly, cross-examination by the defence, during which time the defence has an opportunity to ask questions and attempt to discredit the witness; and finally re-examination, which allows the prosecution to deal with any unfavourable answers given in cross-examination.

v) At the end of the prosecution case, the defence may make a submission of no case to answer, and if the magistrates agree with this, they may acquit the defendant.

vi) The defence need not adduce any evidence as it is for the prosecution to prove the case.

vii) The magistrates will then make their decision, taking advice from their clerk as necessary.

8.3 Analysis of questions

This area is simple and rarely examined. However, if they are to attempt a question in this area, students must ensure an understanding of the procedure and importance of summary trial in the criminal process.

8.4 Question

See Question 1 in Chapter 9.

9 TRIAL ON INDICTMENT

9.1 Introduction

Indictable offences are tried in the Crown Court by both judge and jury. This mode of trial is also used for triable either way offences, either where the defendant elects it or the magistrate decides it is the suitable mode.

9.2 Key points

a) *Arraignment*

This is the process by which each count is 'put' to the defendant for his plea. There are several different pleas available in the Crown Court.

i) Guilty – this plea must be entered by the defendant and not by his counsel. Once the plea is entered, sentencing follows.

ii) Not guilty – the defendant denies the charge and trial will follow.

iii) Guilty to a lesser offence – this plea must be accepted by both the prosecution and the judge. If not, the defendant must change his plea to either of the above: see s6(1)(b) Criminal Law Act 1967.

iv) Autrefois acquit and autrefois convict – these pleas apply where the defendant has already been acquitted or convicted on a previous occasion.

b) *Pleas*

i) Ambiguous pleas – where a plea is ambiguous, the judge will explain to the defendant the necessity for a clear plea and a second arraignment should follow. Should the plea remain ambiguous, a plea of not guilty will be entered for the defendant.

ii) Voluntary pleas – an appeal court may quash a conviction and order a retrial should it be proved that the plea was not made voluntarily. A plea is involuntary if the defendant is placed under pressure by the defendant's counsel or the judge.

iii) Inability to plead – where the defendant does not give a plea, a jury is empanelled to decide if the defendant is either:

- 'mute by malice', in which case his acts are deliberate and a plea of not guilty will be entered on his behalf and the trial will continue (see s6(1)(c) Criminal Law Act 1967); or
- 'mute by visitation of God', in which case the proceedings will be adjourned to find a method of communication. Where there is doubt, a jury is empanelled to decide whether the accused is fit to be tried: see s5 Criminal Procedure (Insanity) Act 1964 as substituted by ss2 and 3 of the Criminal Procedure (Insanity and Unfitness to Plead) Act 1991.

iv) Change of plea – the defendant may change his plea at any stage of the trial before sentence is passed. Any change is subject to the judge's consent.

v) Plea bargaining – not all methods of plea bargaining are acceptable.

c) *Trial procedure*

i) Empanelling a jury – a jury panel of between 20–25 people is summoned, out of which 12 will be retained as jurors and sworn in.

ii) The prosecution's case – the prosecution will in its opening speech explain the process of the trial to the jury and also inform them of their role. The prosecution will then give the background of its case against the defendant. After this the prosecution will call its witnesses and the defence will have opportunity to cross-examine them.

The Royal Commission on Criminal Justice has suggested that the defence should have the choice of being able to make an opening speech immediately after the prosecution's.

iii) Submission of no case to answer – this submission is made in the absence of a jury and it is for the judge to decide. Should he decide there is no case to answer, the jury is called back and will be directed to acquit; if not the trial will continue.

iv) The defence will then put its case, and call its witnesses.

v) Closing speeches will be made by both the prosecution and defence.

vi) Summing up – the judge will summarise the case to the jury. There are several issues he must bring to their attention:

- the respective roles of judge and jury;
- the burden and standard of proof;
- explanations of the law;
- evidential rules;
- reminder of all material evidence;

- direction as to the appointment of a foreman;
- the need for a unanimous decision.

vii) The verdict – after the summing up, the jury will retire to the jury room for their deliberations. The three possible verdicts they could return are guilty, not guilty or guilty of a lesser offence.

Majority verdicts are only allowable under the judge's direction where the jury have deliberated for at least two hours and 10 minutes.

viii) The Runciman Commission has suggested various measures aimed at speeding up the whole process.

9.3 Analysis of questions

Questions on this area tend to be problem questions that require advice to a client who has been arrested and charged with an offence (generally theft). The questions require detailed knowledge of determining the mode of trial and committal proceedings. Less emphasis has been placed on the procedure of the trial itself. These questions are often combined with legal aid, bail and, on occasion, with appeals.

9.4 Recent cases

R v *Harper-Taylor and Bakker* (1988) 138 NLJ 80

R v *Pitman* [1991] 1 All ER 468

9.5 Questions

Question 1

Your client Pierre (37), a hotel porter, has been arrested and charged with the theft of a ring worth £5,000 from a hotel guest. He tells you he is not guilty. Advise him:

a) in which court he will be tried and how this will be determined;

b) whether he will be entitled to legal aid to prepare and conduct his defence; and

c) on the merits of an application for bail. Pierre worked in England for 10 years; he lives at the hotel and is unmarried with no relatives in this country. He had no police record. He fears he will now lose his job.

University of London LLB Examination
(for External Students) English Legal System June 1987 Q6

General comment

This is not a difficult question for those who have worked hard to understand the basics of procedure in the criminal trial. It is made harder to answer in that it also requires the candidate to have revised legal aid and the matter of bail. These are, however, all quite easy to deal with if the candidate has done the work because this question needs only the minimum of thinking or planning, although it is vital to be fast because of the amount of material to handle and thus it is important to be clear and precise.

Skeleton solution

a)
- Classification of the offence.
- Determination of mode of trial.
- Pierre's election and advice on the effect of his choice.
- Committal proceedings for trial on indictment.

b)
- Application to Crown Court.
- The means and merits test and how it is applied.

c)
- Possible reasons for the police to object to bail.
- Likelihood of refusal.

Suggested solution

a) Theft is an offence triable either way, ie the offence may be dealt with either by the magistrates or by the Crown Court. The procedure is that Pierre will be brought before the magistrates at the earliest possible opportunity and then the prosecution and the defence will make representations as to the appropriate mode of trial. In view of the sum of money concerned and the circumstances of the theft (which involve a breach of trust) it is likely that the magistrates would decline to try the case themselves. In any event, as Pierre may well prefer trial by jury, this is not a problem. Even if the magistrates are willing to try Pierre summarily he must be asked if he consents to this mode of trial. My advice in these circumstances would be to seek trial by jury because this is rather too serious for magistrates to deal with and there is a better prospect of acquittal before the jury than before the magistrates. The temptation of trial before the magistrates, even if it were to be offered, would be that the case would be decided more quickly, but this is not of paramount concern. Pierre should realise that if he is found guilty, he is quite likely to be sentenced to a custodial term. A jury trial in this instance is more advisable.

The magistrates would not proceed to immediate trial in any event as Pierre is going to plead not guilty and this would involve an adjournment in order for the prosecution to prepare its case. However, we must now consider what will happen if the magistrates commit Pierre for trial to the Crown Court. There are two forms of committal, the 'old style' under s6(1) of the Magistrates' Court Act 1980 or the 'new style' under s6(2). The first is a committal where the magistrates proceed as examining justices to hear the evidence in full, including the testimony of witnesses which is then taken down into the form of depositions. The new style committal, which is a much briefer matter, is permitted where the defendant is legally represented and it is agreed that there is a case to answer. This is the only purpose of the committal proceedings: to ensure that Pierre has a case to answer. He is not obliged to reveal the nature to his defence at this time, unless it is an alibi defence.

Pierre, whom I take to be of French origin, may wish to be reassured that the committal for trial to the Crown Court does not mean that he is likely to be found guilty, as may be the case in France. The committal proceedings in this country are, in some respects, a formality and the English examining magistrates do not undertake their job with the thoroughness of the French.

Summary trial is conducted in most instances by a bench of three part-time, unpaid non-lawyers who are advised by a legally qualified clerk. They deal with the finding of facts and, if they find the defendant guilty, they proceed to sentence within the powers given to them. In the Crown Court Pierre's guilt must be determined by a jury of 12 ordinary citizens, after a summing up speech by a judge who is legally qualified and experienced. The judge acts as an umpire in the proceedings as these are conducted in an adversarial fashion with the prosecution calling witnesses who then give evidence orally before being cross examined by the defence. The judge is responsible for passing sentence if Pierre is found guilty by the jury.

b) Pierre should apply to the Crown Court for legal aid and he stands a good chance of obtaining this. There are two tests, one a means test, the other a merits test. A court may, but is not obliged to do so, grant legal aid where it is desirable in the interests of justice. Under the Widgery criteria established in 1966 the defendant should be granted aid where the charge is a serious one so that the accused is in jeopardy of losing his liberty, job or reputation. This is a real possibility here. It does not appear that the second criterion is applicable, ie that a serious question of law is raised, but a reasonable third point is that legal aid may be justified where the defendant does not speak English very well and thus requires representation as he cannot state his own case.

c) There is an entitlement to bail but the police may object although there is no special reason to think that they are likely to do so here. The reasons most relevant here for objecting to bail may be summarised as follows:

   i) The defendant is likely to abscond. This obviously relates to the seriousness of the charge and the roots that the defendant has in the community. Certainly, Pierre has something of a problem here but there are always possible conditions that can be attached to bail, such as the need to surrender a passport, or a requirement that the accused should reside in a certain place. Equally, the defendant may be required to report to the police station daily and Pierre could always make an offer to be bound by some condition or offer a surety, although it may not be necessary.

   ii) The defendant is likely to re-offend whilst on bail. There is no suggestion of this and it would seem highly unlikely. It would be important to see what the reaction of the hotel would be in these circumstances as Pierre might well be suspended from work and this would have a negative effect on the chances of obtaining bail. A helpful reference from his employers would go a long way here.

   iii) The defendant is likely to interfere with witnesses or obstruct the course of justice. This seems unlikely in the present case.

It therefore seems likely that Pierre would obtain bail.

Question 2

Advise your client who has just been charged with theft of the detailed court procedures that will follow.

Written by Editor

General comment

Here the candidate is asked to outline the main court procedures for the client who has just been charged with theft – beginning with his appearance before the magistrates' court. Note that theft is an offence 'triable either way' and, depending on the mode of trial selected, may be tried either on indictment or summarily, by magistrates. The emphasis of the question appears to be mainly on the initial procedures before trial – though some mention of the trial procedures should be made.

Skeleton solution

- Theft is triable either way, therefore determine mode of trial.
- If summary trial is chosen, trial procedure.
- If trial on indictment is chosen, committal proceedings.
- Trial procedure in the Crown Court.
- Participation of the jury.

Suggested solution

All criminal offences are classified according to the manner in which they may be tried; indictable (most serious, trial by jury), summary (least serious, magistrates only) and offences 'triable either way' (either method may be selected, depending on the individual case). Theft is an offence 'triable either way' – see s17 and Schedule 1 Magistrates' Courts Act 1980 (MCA). Once the accused has been arrested, and charged, he should be brought before the magistrates, who sit first as 'examining justices', without undue delay.

Since theft is triable either way, the first procedure before either committal proceedings or summary trial can take place is to determine the mode of trial; ss18–21, 23 of MCA. The charge is read to the accused and both prosecution and defence may make representations as to which mode of trial would be most suitable. Except where the prosecution is conducted by one of the Law Officers, the prosecution cannot require trial by jury. The magistrates must consider, having regard to all the circumstances, which mode they consider appropriate bearing in mind the gravity of the offence and whether their powers of punishment are likely to be adequate (see: *Practice Note* (1990)). If the theft is serious, either because it involves a relatively large amount or because of some other reason (eg breach of trust) the usual course is committal for trial by jury: *R* v *King's Lynn Justices, ex parte Carter* (1969). The basic rule is that the accused has a right to elect trial by jury, though if he prefers summary trial the magistrates are able to insist themselves that trial be by jury. It is only if both the magistrates and the accused prefer summary trial that this is selected.

Once the manner of trial is determined, the court may proceed immediately with trial or committal proceedings – though adjournments are available if preparations are not complete.

If summary trial is chosen:

Summary trial is trial by magistrates alone viz, either a panel of lay justices (JPs), between two and five in number, or by a stipendiary magistrate (a professional, salaried, lawyer of at least seven years' standing). If the bench consists of lay justices, then they will receive advice on points of law and procedure from the clerk – a professional lawyer, though he takes no part in reaching the formal decision of the bench.

The charge is read by the clerk and the accused is asked how he pleads – guilty, or not guilty. If he pleads 'not guilty' then trial takes place. The prosecution (usually CPS) then examines the informant (ie the police officer, or other person who laid the information stating the offence alleged to have been committed) and other witnesses who may help to prove the guilt of the accused. The accused is then entitled to cross-examine those witnesses, ie try to test their testimony by further questions in order to raise doubts about his guilt or their testimony, and may also give evidence on his own behalf – though if he does, then he is subject to cross-examination by the prosecution. In certain cases written depositions (statements) may be used as evidence, in order to save time in calling witnesses. In theft, the burden of proof will rest as normal on the prosecution who must prove his guilt 'beyond reasonable doubt'. If the defendant has called evidence, then he makes a final speech to the court (he is entitled to two if he calls evidence – one before and one after the evidence), followed by the prosecution. The court then retires to consider its decision. If the court find the accused guilty, they will then proceed to sentence him. If the accused has pleaded guilty in the first place, then the court will proceed directly to sentence.

Sentence is preceded by a consideration of the accused's record (if any) and circumstances, and there is usually a 'plea in mitigation' by the defendant (or his representative) to attempt to convince the court that the accused deserves a lesser sentence than they might impose. There may be an adjournment before sentence, in order that the accused's record be investigated or to decide the most appropriate sentence.

Though the magistrates consider the character of the accused at the stage of deciding whether trial should be summary or not (which is relevant to their view of whether their sentencing powers are adequate), they may discover subsequent matters relevant to sentencing, eg that the offence involved some serious matter such as an abuse of position (see *R* v *Woodley* (1979)) or that his character and 'antecedents' (background circumstances) make their powers inadequate – six months' imprisonment or £5,000 fine in the case of offences triable either way. If this is the case, they may then commit the accused to the Crown Court for sentence (s38 MCA) – usually heard by a circuit judge or recorder sitting with two magistrates. The Crown Court may pass any sentence on the accused which it could have done had the trial been on indictment.

If trial by jury is chosen:

Before trial takes place the examining justices must hold a preliminary inquiry, called 'committal proceedings' to determine whether there is sufficient evidence for the case to proceed to trial. The question is whether the evidence placed before the court raises a *prima facie case*, viz that there is evidence upon which a reasonable jury could convict. It is irrelevant that the court would not itself convict, unless (of course) it is because the evidence is so weak that no reasonable tribunal of fact could convict. The function of such a procedure is clear – to 'filter out' cases which are so weak that they would waste the time of the court.

There are now two types of committal proceedings (s6 MCA) – with and without consideration of the evidence. Most are now without consideration of the evidence (often confusingly called 's1 committals') since this saves much time. However, such committals (s6(2) MCA) may only take place on the agreement of the accused if all the evidence is in the form of written statements (s102 MCA), the accused has a solicitor acting for him in the case (s61 CJA 1982) and there is no submission of 'no case to answer' viz the defence submits that the evidence presented reveals no offence (eg because one element of the offence is not proved or even considered). The main types of case where a committal without consideration would be inappropriate include those where no case is revealed on the evidence, or identification is in issue, or the makers of the written statements could be discredited in cross-examination.

On a committal *with* consideration of the evidence (s6(1) MCA), the prosecution presents evidence to the court (both written and oral), which the defence may cross examine, and notes are taken of the statements of witnesses and certified by the magistrates (depositions).

The defence then has a choice whether to examine the makers of statements etc, viz test their accuracy (otherwise it is conceding that the statements are correct) and to challenge them if possible – though the standard of proof in committal proceedings is low (ie prima facie case). The defence may then present its own case, which is not usually done since it reveals the defence case in advance (losing the advantage of surprise at trial) and is unlikely in most cases to make much difference once the prosecution evidence is accepted – again because of the low standard of proof. It is also open to the defence to submit 'no case to answer' (see above), though this will only succeed if the evidence demonstrates no offence – since the magistrates are not restricted to committal on the charges presented, but may commit on any offence revealed by the evidence (providing it is suitable for trial by jury).

Before committing, the bench has the charges read to the accused on which it finds there is a case to answer and gives the usual 'alibi warning' (viz that notice must be given to the prosecution if an alibi defence is to be relied upon), along with any other orders which it considers necessary, eg restrictions on publicity, bail and legal aid. It must be decided whether the accused should be granted bail (conditionally or unconditionally) and legal aid for trial. If the magistrates consider bail inappropriate (eg because the accused is likely to abscond – see Schedule 1 of the Bail Act 1976), they will commit the accused in custody.

The usual rule is that a bill of indictment should be preferred within 28 days of committal, though this rule is not mandatory. The indictment will contain the list of charges against the accused, each detailed in a separate paragraph ('count') which gives the essential details of the offence ('particulars'): see the Indictment Rules 1971. (Other methods are available to commence proceedings in the Crown Court, though rarely used, eg voluntary bill of indictment.) Trial should usually take place between two and eight weeks after committal, but this rule is not mandatory.

Trial on indictment is held in the Crown Court and is by judge and jury. There are a number of different types of judges who may sit in the Crown Court, their rank depending on the seriousness of the offence(s) charged, eg murder is usually tried by High Court judges – others are circuit judges, recorders, deputy circuit judges and assistant recorders.

Triable either way offences are Class 4 and are usually tried by circuit judges or recorder.

Trial on indictment begins with the 'arraignment', viz the counts are put to the accused who must plead to them. If the accused fails to plead clearly, or remains mute, a plea of 'not guilty' is entered on his behalf. It is also possible for the accused in certain cases to 'plead guilty to a lesser offence', which is possible in certain cases where the offence charged involves a lesser offence (eg if murder is not proved, it is still possible to convict for manslaughter) – though this depends on the co-operation of the prosecution and judge in accepting a plea of guilty for one offence in return for not proceeding with the charge preferred. This would not be possible in a theft case as the offence does not contain a lesser offence.

If the accused pleads 'not guilty' then trial proceeds, the jury is then selected and sworn in and the trial begins with the opening speech by counsel for the prosecution and the course of trial proceeds largely as in a summary case, with examination of witnesses by each side, and cross-examination (and occasionally re-examination if necessary). At the end of the prosecution case, the defence may make a submission of 'no case to answer', which if successful will lead to the judge directing the jury to acquit.

Save in the most exceptional cases, the burden of proof is on the prosecution to establish the guilt of the accused – though counsel should not press for conviction in any circumstances, but should proceed impartially to ensure that justice is done. Moreover, there are restrictions on the evidence which can be presented to the jury; evidence of the accused's character, disposition or previous convictions is not usually admissible since it would be too prejudicial to the accused. Hearsay evidence is excluded on grounds of unreliability.

At the end of the defence case, defence counsel makes a speech summarising the case from the accused's point of view. The judge (if the prosecution does not wish to call evidence in rebuttal of the defence case (*R* v *Flynn* (1957)) then 'sums up' the case to the jury, paying particular attention to the elements of the offence which the prosecution must prove, the burden of proof and any other points which are of importance (eg directions on the strength of identification evidence).

The jury then retires, and deliberates in secret (s8 Contempt of Court Act 1981). When they have reached a conclusion, they return into court and the foreman gives the verdict. If the accused is found guilty, or has pleaded guilty in the first place, the judge then proceeds to give sentence. The procedure here is the same as on summary trial – antecedents are read out, a plea in mitigation is made, etc. The powers of the Crown Court are, of course, much greater than a magistrates' court and vary from unconditional discharges and fines, to life imprisonment. Imprisonment is not possible for any person under the age of 21, though Young Offender Institutions (once called 'borstals') are available for the under 21s. If this is a first offence, then it is unlikely to carry imprisonment (unless very serious indeed).

Appeal lies to the Court of Appeal (Criminal Division) on matters of conviction and/or sentence from the Crown Court. From the magistrates' court appeal can lie to the Crown Court, or a case may be 'stated' on a point of law to the Queen's Bench Divisional court.

10 SENTENCING

10.1 Introduction

Where the accused has pleaded guilty or been convicted, he must then be sentenced. Certain factors must be considered before the court decides on a sentence for the defendant. This chapter will consider the pre-sentencing procedures and will then list all the sentencing options available to the court.

10.2 Key points

a) *Procedure before sentencing*

i) Where the defendant pleads guilty to an offence, before sentence is passed it is the duty of the prosecution to recount the facts to the judge.

ii) The defendant's antecedents must be made known to the judge. Usually a police officer dealing with the case is responsible for this and will give his evidence on oath. The procedure for this is laid down in a *Practice Direction* [1966] 1 WLR 1184, and it will generally include details of the following:

- age;
- education;
- employment;
- domestic and marital status;
- income;
- date of his last release from prison;
- previous convictions.

The defence may cross-examine or challenge the truth of allegations.

iii) Reports on the defendant are an important part of this procedure. Under s3 of the Criminal Justice Act 1991 proceedings must be adjourned in certain circumstances to allow for the preparation of reports, eg where the court is considering a custodial sentence. The major types of reports are:

- Pre-sentence reports, formerly called social inquiry reports, prepared by probation officers. These reports will deal with the defendant's social background and will make recommendations as to how he ought to be dealt with.
- Community service reports must be prepared if the court wishes to make a community service order. They are required to consider the defendant's suitability for such a sentence.
- Medical and psychiatric reports must be considered, where a judge wishes to detain a defendant in a mental hospital.
- Reports of juveniles will be required to be prepared by social workers involved.

iv) The defence may also make an attempt to persuade the judge to pass a more lenient sentence by entering a plea in mitigation. The defence will ensure that the following issues are considered:

- any factor that makes the offence look less serious;
- any explanation for the commission of the offence;
- any developments in the defendant's future to indicate that he is unlikely to offend again.

b) *Sentencing options for offenders over 21 years of age*

i) The Criminal Justice Act 1991 attempted to create a hierarchy of sentencing bands based on the idea of 'proportionality':

Discharge (conditional or absolute)	Most lenient – no specific criteria required.
Fine	No specific criteria required.
Community orders	Only appropriate where the offence is too serious for a financial penalty.
Custodial sentences	If the seriousness of the offence demands or there is a need for public protection. Court may attach various ancillary financial or property orders.

ii) Imprisonment

Where the offence has a term of imprisonment attached, that sentence may be imposed. However, if the defendant has not been imprisoned before, the court cannot sentence him to imprisonment without considering the requirements of s1(2) of the Criminal Justice Act 1991. These are:

- the offence (or offences together) is so serious only a custodial sentence is justified; or
- the offence is a violent or sexual offence and only a custodial sentence would be adequate to protect the public from harm from the offender.

Sentences of imprisonment may run concurrently or consecutively. The defendant is usually entitled to a remission of one third of his sentence for good behaviour. There is also the opportunity to apply for parole after six months.

iii) Suspended sentences

Where a court passes a sentence of not more than two years, it may order that it is suspended for a period of not less than one and not more than two years: see ss22–27 Powers of Criminal Courts Act 1973. The Criminal Justice Act 1991 has amended s22 so that a court may not pass a suspended sentence unless 'it can be justified by the exceptional circumstances of the case' (s22(2)(b)).

A suspended sentence may be combined with a financial order but not with a probation order.

Should the defendant commit an offence during the period of suspension, the sentence may (and probably will) be brought into effect.

iv) Fines

The magistrates' court may at present impose a maximum fine of £5,000. The Crown Court is only limited by the amount specified by statute for that offence. Section 18 of the Criminal Justice Act 1991 introduced the controversial concept of unit fines in the magistrates' court where the seriousness of the offence and the defendant's ability to pay are translated into units which decide the level of fine. The 1993 Criminal Justice Bill has proposed the abolition of 'unit fines' as they have proved unworkable.

v) Hospital orders

Sections 37–43 of the Mental Health Act 1983 provide for such orders to be made, to have the defendant detained to receive treatment for a mental disorder. These orders are only made if it is the only way to deal with the offender.

vi) Community service orders

Section 14 of the Powers of Criminal Courts Act 1973 requires certain conditions to be satisfied before such an order can be made:

- the defendant must be over 16;
- the offence must be imprisonable;
- the defendant's consent is required;

- in the light of reports prepared, the defendant is suitable for community service;
- there must be an available vacancy within the area in which the defendant lives;
- a community service order must be for a maximum of 240 hours and a minimum of 40 hours.

vii) Probation

Sections 2–6 of the Powers of Criminal Courts Act 1973 provides the conditions under which a probation order may be made:

- the defendant must be over 17;
- defendant must consent to the probation order;
- the period of supervision under the order must be between six months and three years;
- failure to comply with the conditions of probation will result in a fine of up to £200 or a different sentence for the original offence.

Generally, the main requirement of such orders is that the defendant makes fixed visits at set times to his probation officer. Other requirements may also be included:

- residence (s2(5) Powers of Criminal Courts Act 1973);
- treatment (s3 Powers of Criminal Courts Act 1973);
- activity (s4A Powers of Criminal Courts Act 1973);
- prohibition on certain activities.

For 'community orders' from October 1992, see ss6 and 10 of the Criminal Justice Act 1991. See also ss8, 9 (probation orders), 11 (combination orders) and 12, 13 (curfew orders) of the 1991 Act.

viii) Conditional and absolute discharge

The court is empowered by s7 of the 1973 Act to discharge a defendant who is found guilty. An absolute discharge has the effect of completely absolving the defendant. A conditional discharge however operates in the following way:

- there is no punishment on the condition that no offence is committed during a specified period;
- the specified period should not exceed three years;
- if a further offence is committed, the defendant will also be sentenced for the original offence.

c) *Additional sentencing options for offenders under the age of 21 years*

(These options are also applicable to 'adult offenders')

Detention and imprisonment

i) Detention in young offender institutions

Duration of order:

Range is from three weeks to number of years. Length of sentence is governed by age:

- Defendant aged between 15 and 17 years old inclusive: two months to 12 months.
- Defendant aged between 18 and 20 years old inclusive: 21 days to the maximum for the offence.
- Sentences for more than one offence may be served concurrently or consecutively, but an offender aged under 18 should not be detained for more than one year.
- Sentences cannot be suspended where the offender is under 21.

ii) Detention at Her Majesty's pleasure

Section 53 of the Children and Young Persons Act 1933 allows a young offender aged 18 or under to be detained:

- where convicted of murder or manslaughter; or
- where the offender is older than 14 and has been convicted of an offence for which the maximum sentence is 14 years or more; or
- a defendant aged 16 or over has committed an offence which involves indecent assault on a woman; and
- no other method of sentencing is suitable.

iii) Custody for life

If the defendant is aged between 18 and 20 years old and has been convicted of an offence which carries life imprisonment.

Other types of sentence

The Criminal Justice Act 1991 introduced widespread changes:

iv) Community sentences

Section 6(1) Criminal Justice Act 1991.

This consists of one or more community orders:

a) probation;

b) community service;

c) combination order;

d) curfew;

e) supervision;

f) attendance centre orders.

The basis for the type of order is governed by age of the offender and seriousness of the offence:

Orders a) – d) can only be given to offenders older than 16 years.

Order e) for defendants aged between 10 and 17.

Order f) for defendants aged between 10 and 20 years.

The consent of the offender may be required for some orders.

a) Probation orders

The offender must be aged 16 years or over and the duration of the order will be between six months and three years.

The order involves supervision by a probation officer and is aimed at rehabilitating the defendant for protecting the public and/or preventing the defendant from committing further offences. It may be combined with requirements of residence or treatment at a probation centre or a particular activity.

b) Community service

Can only be used for offenders of 16 years or older for an imprisonable offence.

c) Combination orders

Introduced by the Criminal Justice Act 1991.

Involves probation and community service. The defendant must be at least 16 years old and have been convicted of an imprisonable offence.

The probation order may range from 12 months to three years and the community service from 40 to 120 hours. This type of order would only be used where a pre-sentence report has been given.

d) Curfew orders

Section 12 of the Criminal Justice Act 1991.

Requires the consent of the offender.

Duration is up to a maximum of six months.

Experiments involving electronic monitoring or 'tagging' have been tried but were not regarded as very successful.

e) Supervision

Section 7 Children and Young Persons Act 1969.

Duration can be up to three years and the supervisor is usually the local authority.

Order may include specific requirements such as residing in a certain place or treatment for a mental condition.

No offender consent is required to the general order.

f) Attendance centre orders

This order requires defendants to attend a centre run by police officers in order to encourage the use of spare time in a constructive manner: see ss16–19 Criminal Justice Act 1982. See also s67 of the Criminal Justice Act 1991.

v) Binding over of parents

Where dealing with an offender the court may order his parents or guardian to undertake to take proper care and control of him: s58 Criminal Justice Act 1991.

Where the offender is under 16, the court must generally do this. If the parents fail to comply they forfeit a sum of up to £1,000.

vi) In addition to those mentioned, some of the sentencing options applicable to offenders over 21 years of age are also applicable here:

Fines

Conditional and absolute discharges

Binding over (to keep the peace)

Deportation (for non-British citizens over 17 years of age)

Hospital order (to receive treatment)

d) *Sentence discounts and 'plea bargaining'*

'Plea bargaining' and sentence concessions in general are very controversial.

The only way the system operates in England is as follows:

- A guilty plea to the sentence charged will attract a discount of $^1/_4$ to $^1/_3$ off the sentence.
- A system of 'plea arrangement' whereby the defendant pleads guilty to a lesser offence in exchange for the more serious being dropped.

There are careful guidelines as to how the system should operate in order to avoid the judge appearing biased or the defendant being pressurised: *Practice Direction* [1976] Crim LR 561.

The Royal Commission on criminal justice has proposed:

- that the present system should be made much clearer;
- the earlier in proceedings that the guilty plea is, the higher the discount should be;
- judges should be allowed to indicate maximum sentence on the facts;
- policy should be kept under constant review.

10.3 Analysis of questions

Sentencing is rarely examined on its own. It tends to be combined with questions on criminal procedure. However, as there have been some changes to sentencing made by the Criminal Justice Act 1991 and the Children Act 1989, more emphasis may be given to this area in the examination. London University has asked questions specifically on sentence discounts (see below).

10.4 Questions

Question 1

See Question 2(c) in Chapter 6.

Question 2

Plea-bargaining is prohibited because it is said to place unfair pressure upon the accused and to militate against a fair trial. Could a similar criticism be made about the practice of awarding sentence concessions to those who plead guilty?

University of London LLB Examination
(for External Students) English Legal System June 1992 Q3

General comment

This question requires a great deal of careful thought. Although the information that must be dealt with is not particularly complex, to tackle the question effectively necessitates careful planning and consideration of structure.

Skeleton solution

- Clarify the actual status of sentence concessions, etc, in this jurisdiction.
- Results in unfair pressure?
- Results in unfair trial?
- Conclusion, including attitudes of the profession and future status.

Suggested solution

Plea bargaining and sentence concessions are among the most controversial areas of the criminal legal system and, with the recent proposals from the Bar Council's working party, they are again topical.

The exact status of sentence concessions for guilty pleas in the English legal system is not without confusion. In practice, the technical guidelines and the realities are often different. So far as any form of plea bargaining exists, it takes two forms. Firstly, that of offering a guilty plea to the sentence charged. Secondly, pleading guilty to a lesser offence on the indictment in return for no evidence being offered for a more serious offence – 'the plea arrangement'. One needs to examine the use of these before considerations of fairness and pressure can be looked at.

The offering of a guilty plea is a well-known practice. While no promises are, or can be, given by the judge, it is established practice that a plea of guilty will count as a mitigating factor as it allows the defendant to show his contrition and remorse. Unofficially, it has been suggested that it may serve to reduce the sentence by a quarter or one-third. According to the case of *R* v *Davis* (1979) it is 'common knowledge' that a sentence concession will be given for a guilty plea. The plea arrangement is also widely used and is, in reality, a form of plea bargaining. However, the frequency with which these situations arise has in no way served to eradicate the problems that seem to come with them.

The use of the guilty plea is relied upon by the adversarial system. Without criminal cases being 'settled' in this way, the courts simply could not cope with the volume of work. Over 70 per cent of crown court cases are dealt with by a guilty plea. This clearly is an advantage in that it may allow more 'important' cases to be heard fully and sooner. Similarly, it relieves some of the pressures of lack of funding and saves witnesses the ordeal of giving evidence. If one could be sure it was only used by the guilty, the use of the plea could be advantageous. For the defendant it guarantees a sentence of less severity than a conviction of guilty. For the prosecution it alleviates the problems of a heavy case load and the time and expense of conducting the trial, as well as being a guaranteed 'win'. However, Baldwin and McConville (among others) believe they have clearly identified a problem of the innocent pleading guilty. This may start in the police station with an innocent detainee making a confession in order to obtain bail. However, the case of *R* v *Richards* (1967) made it clear that even the slightest suggestion by the police that a plea of guilty would lead to a mitigation of sentence would make any resulting confession inadmissible and this approach would seem to be confirmed by the relevant sections of the Police and Criminal Evidence Act 1984. But it has already been suggested that it is common knowledge and may not require an overt suggestion from the police for the detainee to feel under pressure to plead guilty in order to go home, believing he can prove his innocence at a later date. Criticism has also been made of undue pressure from counsel and a lack of fight on the part of legal representatives. An abnormally high rate of guilty pleas on the North Eastern circuit was explained by one judge as being due to northern common sense!

The plea arrangement is also not without criticism. There are allegations of overcharging, where the prosecution will overload the indictment with more offences than they could realistically prove in order to obtain a guilty plea to the offence they are most concerned with. Similarly, it may mean the prosecution obtains a successful outcome for a case that may have proved very weak at trial. It obviously could act as pressure on the innocent defendant who may feel the 'system' is against him and decide not to risk being convicted of a more serious offence.

Clearly, the potential for undue pressure is there. This would undoubtedly mitigate against a fair trial as the defendant who pleads guilty never has the opportunity to put his case and force the prosecution to fulfil its legal and evidential burdens. But it should also be noted that there are attempts to alleviate the problem. Unlike some other jurisdictions, the English prosecution cannot exert any influence or make any suggestions on the length or type of sentence. It can only 'bargain' about the charges that will be offered. The role of judge and counsel in this area is confused, but attempts have been made to clarify this by case law and rules of professional conduct. With regard to plea arrangements, the judge cannot interfere and so it is up to the prosecution counsel what charges should be pursued and which should be left on file. But the judge does not have to agree with the plea arrangement, the most notorious example of this being in the trial of the 'Yorkshire Ripper' where the judge refused to accept a plea of guilty to manslaughter on the grounds of diminished responsibility, regarding it as in the public interest that a full trial for murder should take place (and the defendant was subsequently convicted). The case of *R* v *Turner* (1970) and the subsequent July 1976 *Practice Direction* (1976) sought to make the role of counsel and judge in plea 'bargaining' crystal clear. While it is perfectly permissible for the counsel to advise his client that a plea of guilty may lead to a lighter sentence, it should always be emphasised to the defendant that he must only plead guilty if he is! The accused must have and feel that he has complete freedom of choice. There should be complete freedom of access between *both* counsel and the judge, but no indication of length of sentence must ever be given, nor implied to the client in conference. The judge must never be seen without both sides being present and the practice has become that approaches to the judge in chambers should only be made if absolutely necessary and may be turned down. Counsel is under a duty to relay to his client what exactly happened in the judge's chambers so no false assumptions can be made or inferences drawn: *R* v *Cain* (1976). While these might appear to be ample safeguards, subsequent case law has shown that abuses of the system remain. Private communications between counsel and judge were condemned in *R* v *Harper-Taylor and Bakker* (1988) and as recently as last year, 15 years since *Turner* and the *Practice Direction*, a conviction had to be quashed due to improper behaviour regarding sentence concessions: *R* v *Pitman* (1991).

The evidence would seem to suggest that the risk of undue pressure is great, although not perhaps so great as in some other jurisdictions where the prosecution plays a more active and direct role in the sentencing decision. The future status of the practice is uncertain. Recent case law suggests the rules of conduct are unclear or ignored. This situation looks unlikely to change if the proposals of the Bar's working party are to be followed in which the working party suggested that plea bargaining is an option to be recommended to obtain the efficient disposal of business in the crown court, and that guidance on sentence lengths would help the guilty defendant come to a decision sooner and stop wasting court time. More recently, the Runciman Commission on Criminal Justice (1993) has recommended that the whole system should be clarified and kept under review. It is also recommended that the size of discount for a guilty plea should be proportionate to how soon in the proceedings it is given and that the judge should be able to indicate the maximum sentence he is inclined to give in the case. It remains to be seen whether these proposals will be adopted though they would appear to do little to address the problems of unfair pressure on the accused. But perhaps in a system of justice that is said to be the envy of the world we should be more interested in the quality of decision making rather than in the efficiency of administration, whatever the financial cost.

11 THE JURY SYSTEM

11.1 Introduction

Although of much earlier origin, by the beginning of the nineteenth century the concept of jury trial was safely entrenched into the English legal system and considered to be an important safeguard for the individual. Lord Denning MR in *Ward* v *James* [1966] 1 QB 273 regarded the jury as the 'bulwark of our liberties'. The participation of lay persons in criminal trials may also be seen as giving credibility to the criminal justice system. However, trial by jury is now increasingly limited to serious criminal cases, as a majority of criminal cases are tried by magistrates' courts.

11.2 Key points

a) *Jury trial in civil cases*

The vast majority of civil cases are tried by a judge alone. There are, however, some civil cases in which there may be trial by jury.

i) Section 6 of the Administration of Justice (Miscellaneous Provisions) Act 1933 (see now s69(1) of the Supreme Court Act 1981) allows a right to jury trial in cases of fraud, defamation, malicious prosecution and false imprisonment. Even in these cases there is a possibility of refusal especially where there are long and complex documents to be considered: see *Rothermere* v *Times Newspapers* [1973] 1 WLR 448 and 'Repeal the Contempt of Court Act 1981 s8' [1990] NLJ 1257 .

ii) In all other civil cases, the decision to allow a jury trial rests with the court's discretion: see s69(3) of the 1981 Act, and, eg, *Ward* v *James* [1966] 1 QB 273. The reasons for refusing trial by jury are bound up with the need to:

- assess fair compensation;
- maintain uniformity in awards;
- encourage predictability, allowing for settlement out of court.

b) *Jury trials in criminal cases*

The only criminal cases in which trial by jury is now used are those triable on indictment in the Crown Court. As most cases are tried summarily, trial by jury is only used for more serious offences.

c) *Qualifications*

i) Any person between the ages of 18 and 70 may serve on a jury provided that person:

- is registered on the electoral roll (the Runciman Commission has proposed that better efforts should be made to ensure that the electoral role is as comprehensive as possible);
- has been ordinarily resident in the UK for at least five years; and
- is not ineligible or disqualified for jury service.

ii) A person is disqualified if he:

- has been sentenced to imprisonment for life or to a term of five years or more, custody for life or youth custody for a term of five years or more; or
- has had passed on him a sentence of imprisonment of any duration during the last ten years or any order of community service during the last ten years; or
- has been placed on probation during the last five years.

iii) A person is ineligible for jury service if he falls within one of the categories identified by Schedule 1, Part I to the Juries Act 1974:

- judges;
- magistrates;
- police officers;
- lawyers;
- the clergy (the Royal Commission suggests they should in fact be eligible);
- the mentally ill.

iv) Excusal: ss8–9 Juries Act 1974

The following persons may claim to be excused from jury service as of right:

- doctors;
- nurses;
- Members of Parliament;
- members of the armed forces.

v) Deferral: s120 Criminal Justice Act 1988

The court may defer jury service if the person summoned shows a good reason. This power is entirely within the discretion of the court.

The Runciman Commission has proposed a scheme whereby alternative dates should be offered to people unable to attend.

d) *Checking and challenging of jurors*

i) The defence may challenge the presence of particular jurors. Jurors may be challenged for cause on three grounds: see s12(4) Juries Act 1974:

- the juror is in fact not qualified; or
- the juror is for some reason biased; or
- the juror may reasonably be suspected of bias against the defendant.

ii) The prosecution may also challenge jurors. They do so by means of a stand by. The *Practice Note* [1988] 3 All ER 1086 provides the circumstances in which the prosecution may exercise its stand by rights:

- where information justifying this right is discovered by a jury check and the Attorney-General authorises the stand by; or
- where a particular juror is manifestly unsuitable and the defence agree.

The effect of a stand by is that the particular juror is not selected, but must wait until the end of the jury selection process and then only if there are no other jurors left on the panel will he become a member of the jury.

iii) Jury checks by the police are permitted in exceptional cases (see *R* v *Mason* [1980] 3 All ER 777):

- if it appears that a juror may be disqualified;
- if it is believed that a juror was involved in a previous aborted trial where there had been an attempt to interfere with jurors; or
- where the police consider it particularly important that no disqualified person serve on the jury.
- The Royal Commission proposes to separate this role from the police by allowing records to be checked by the court using the new national criminal record system currently being implemented.

iv) Jury vetting is the investigation of jurors' backgrounds to ensure that there are no unsuitable jurors. There is much controversy on whether jury vetting should continue as it undermines the idea of random selection. The *Practice Note* issued by the Attorney-General in 1988 ([1988] 3 All ER 1086) now allows the check of a juror's background:

- if it is a case of national security;

- where it is a case involving terrorists, the police can check the criminal records of a juror to ensure that he is not disqualified.

e) *Empanelling the jury*

Once 12 jurors have been chosen from the panel summoned, they are sworn in.

f) *Secrecy of the jury room*

The jury conducts its deliberations in secret and its verdict is not accompanied by reasons. Jurors may not be questioned on their deliberations, opinions or arguments: see s8 Contempt of Court Act 1981.

g) *Retention of the present system*

Some of the arguments for retention of the present system can be briefly summarised as follows:

i) the independence of the jury from the judiciary and executive provides a safeguard for the defendant;

ii) the lay participation in the form of the jury contributes to the public's confidence in the criminal justice system;

iii) the combined judgment of 12 jurors is particularly useful in the evaluation of evidence and in judging the credibility of witnesses.

Conversely, the following are examples of the arguments against the retention of juries in the criminal justice system:

i) there is doubt on the ability of randomly selected jurors to carry out satisfactorily their task of fact-finding in complex criminal cases (this is especially so where there are many defendants);

ii) the jury may be too easily swayed by counsel's arguments or by strong minded individuals within their number.

The Runciman Commission has called for amendment of s8 of the Contempt of Court Act 1981 to allow proper research into how juries reach verdicts.

h) *Alternatives to the present system*

i) Trial by judge alone.

ii) Trial by a judge and two lay assessors.

iii) Trial by judge with a lay magistrate.

iv) The Runciman Commission on Criminal Justice has proposed various amendments to the present system:

- That for either way offences the defendant should no longer have a right to insist on trial by jury (see Chapter 7).

- Changes could be made in all areas to improve the quality of jury decisions, eg selection; checking; ethnic representation; training and instruction.

11.3 Recent cases and articles

R v *Ford* [1989] 3 All ER 445

Guinness plc v *Saunders* [1990] 1 All ER 652

Beta Construction Ltd v *Channel 4 TV Ltd* [1990] 1 WLR 1042

H v *Ministry of Defence* [1991] 2 All ER 834

Kingshott v *Associated Kent Newspapers Ltd* [1991] 2 All ER 99

R v *Bean* (1991) The Times 1 May

R v *Green* (1991) The Times 31 December

'Repeal the Contempt of Court Act 1981 s8' [1990] NLJ 1257

Mike McConville 'Shadowing the Jury' [1991] NLJ 1588

11.4 Analysis of questions

Questions on the jury system are nearly always based on arguments for and against its retention. Another issue which may come up is reform of the jury system. Students must be prepared to illustrate their arguments with case law.

11.5 Questions

Question 1

Critically evaluate the statement that 'juries are expensive and slow: for these reasons, jury trial should be abolished.'

University of London LLB Examination
(for External Students) English Legal System June 1989 Q6

General comment

A question which requires imagination and the ability to marshal both sides of an argument.

Skeleton solution

- Reasons for trial by jury.
- Role of the jury in the Crown Court.
- Selection process.
- Arguments against retention.

Suggested solution

Trial by jury is still felt by many to be the inalienable right of a free-born Englishman. But many disquieting cases recently have cast doubt on whether this institution should be held to be so sacrosanct.

Firstly, it should be noted that 98 per cent of all criminal trials take place summarily in the magistrates' court, so very few defendants are tried by a jury.

Because juries are only used for the more serious criminal offences, it may be thought that the gravity of the offence justifies the expense and the slowness which attend the institution of the jury. The possible deprivation of liberty for a serious offence may be considered to outweigh any considerations of expense and slowness. Nevertheless public funds are limited, and money spent on juries means money denied to some other worthy cause. So it is right that the jury should periodically come up for scrutiny.

The jury is likely to be approved of by a 'defence-minded' person, as a jury tends to be far less 'prosecution-minded' than magistrates or a judge sitting alone. But it may well be that juries nowadays are too 'defence-minded', and thus justice fails to be done. The defendant used to be able to challenge up to three jurors without disclosing any cause (peremptory challenge); this however, was abolished by the Criminal Justice Act 1988. He may then challenge as many jurors as he likes on the ground that they are not qualified to serve; that they are biased; or that they are reasonably suspected of bias.

Jury vetting is the process by which the prosecution are given information on potential jurors and can then use that to ask the juror to stand by for the Crown. This has been attacked as unconstitutional and has been subject to new guidelines following the outcry over the Criminal Justice Act 1988.

The province of the jury is to sum up facts, not law. Fact-finding should be a matter of commonsense, and the presence of 12 jury persons should serve to eliminate bias in a way that cannot be achieved by a judge alone. Nevertheless the complexities of modern life mean that the factual situations of some cases will be way above the heads of the average jury person; some fraud cases may require the finest brains to comprehend them. Some jurors may be exceedingly poor judges of character; magistrates or a judge sitting alone are likely to be far more sophisticated and accurate in their assessments. Nevertheless some judges may be exceedingly out of touch with life in modern Britain: in the seventies there was the notorious case of a judge who had not heard of the lunchtime radio programme 'The World at One'!

Many criminal cases must be seen in their social context: the jury, since it is randomly selected from a wide selection of the population, is best able to reflect the views of society. Juries can be a barometer of public feeling on the state of the law. A notable example of this is the case of Clive Ponting, who was charged with offences under the Official Secrets Act with respect to his divulging information to an MP about an alleged Government cover-up. He was acquitted, perhaps largely because of the public outcry against a sentence of imprisonment passed on a secretary, Sarah Tisdall, in similar circumstances. However, one may wonder whether a judge or magistrates would not have been similarly swayed by public feeling.

There are many powerful arguments against the jury. The present law of evidence, which many might consider to be excessively favourable to the accused, is much distorted by the need to accommodate the biases and inexperience of the jury and to keep from them matters which would unduly prejudice them against the accused.

Unlike a judge or magistrates who have been trained to assess evidence rationally, the average person is no model of rationality. Juries often bring in perverse verdicts. Although Lord Hailsham has said that the perverse verdict is the justification for the jury, one may well wonder whether justice is being done in such a case. As unsophisticated people, jurors may be too easily swayed by good oratory from counsel, or dominated by two or three strong-minded individuals from among their number.

There have, in the past, been allegations that juries are being tampered with. In some cases it has been suspected that defendants have been acquitted because jurors were afraid of what might happen to them if they convicted. In a society which is becoming more violent, and criminals more ruthless, this concern can only increase.

Sir Robert Mark, a former Commissioner of the Metropolitan Police, has stated that 'confidence in the jury system is essentially a matter of faith and is based on no evidence whatsoever'. The jury system is ripe for overhaul.

Question 2

'The whole question of trial by jury is one that raises strong emotions, and views about the value of the jury are unlikely to be much affected one way or the other by the evidence of empirical research.'

Why does discussion of the jury raise strong emotions? What have researchers discovered about jury decisions in criminal trials and do their findings support the view that jury trial should be abolished?

University of London LLB Examination
(for External Students) English Legal System June 1990 Q7

General comment

Students should NOT be tempted to give a rendition of the pros and cons of trial by jury – this will not secure a pass mark.

Timing may be a problem since the essay is wide ranging and all three points must be covered.

Skeleton solution

- The development and role of the jury system.
- Findings of researchers in relation to the composition of juries.
- The reasons for doubtful jury decisions.
- Recommendations on reform.

Suggested solution

Trial by jury is an ancient and democratic institution. It provides an opportunity for the layman to participate in the administration of the legal system, to reassure the rest of us that justice is being done in individual cases and to act as a restraining influence on the professional judiciary. It should be noted that trial by jury is now only a very small part of our criminal justice system – 98 per cent of all criminal trials take place summarily in the magistrates' court. Nevertheless, since jury trial as a rule involves serious crime offences and since trial by jury is usually held out as the ideal mode of trial, its performance must be judged according to high standards.

It is generally agreed that trial by jury is an arbitrary and unpredictable business but those involved in research have on the whole concluded that the institution should NOT be abolished.

It is true to say that discussion of the jury is often heated and certainly does appeal to the emotions. Perhaps the main reason for this is due to the symbolic image accorded to the jury – it is regarded by most as a cornerstone of a free, liberal and democratic state. It is the medium through which the common man can partake in the legal system. Furthermore, only a fool would attempt to minimise the importance of its political and constitutional independence. Blackstone called it 'The glory of English Law', 'The most transcendant privilege which any subject can enjoy'. Devlin said of the jury that it is 'The lamp that shows freedom lives'. Atkin said 'The bulwark of our liberty'. However, many no longer regard the jury with the sort of reverence with which it is customarily bestowed. It is often seen as inviolate but sound research has shown that the institution is not sacrosanct and that such reverence has become increasingly difficult to defend.

The mainstay of contemporary research has been carried out by Zander (1974), McCabe and Purves (1972) and more recently by Baldwin and McConville (*Jury Trials* (1979)). Their work is highly regarded but it should be emphasised that it is limited in two main ways. Firstly, the research is not strictly relevant to some of the issues in the jury debate (in particular, the jury's political function) and secondly that the material gathered is susceptible to differences of interpretation.

The researchers' findings do, all the same, merit considerable attention. The question asks purely for the discoveries as to juries' decisions but the present writer submits that the following points are inextricably linked to the question.

The 'professional criminal' is universally referred to in the aforementioned research projects. Observers allege that the professional criminal, sometimes abetted by dishonest lawyers, is best able to secure an acquittal. The present writer suggests, however, that the success of professional criminals is more apparent than real. Further research has revealed that professional criminals are not acquitted with any frequency and that they were only acquitted in questionable circumstances. On conviction they did, of course, receive heavier sentences than other groups.

Evidence relating to jury composition and the effect on the decision is less clear-cut. Baldwin and McConville take Birmingham as their example. They point out that the ideal of the jury being a cross-section of the community at large is only partially achieved. The jury is broadly representative of the community in terms of age and social class but unrepresentative in terms of sex and race. The problem here is that justice must be seen to be done. Where the jury panel is manifestly unrepresentative of the wider community doubts can be quite reasonably raised. Empirical evidence has been forwarded to show that juries have reached wrong or questionable verdicts with a surprising frequency. Research shows that questionable acquittals may be the result of sympathy for the defendant or antipathy for the victim. Most disturbing is evidence as to questionable convictions. It is well known that despite the high burden of proof upon the prosecution in criminal cases, the operation of the judicial system occasionally results in the conviction of innocent defendants. As Williams put it, 'It is unpalatable to contemplate the conviction of a simple innocent defendant. But some risk must be run because you cannot have a system of criminal trial without running some risk of a miscarriage of justice.'

According to statistics proferred by Baldwin and McConville five per cent of those convicted by jury were said to have been convicted in doubtful circumstances. It is of course no answer to point to current appeals procedure since this inhibits, except on technical grounds, an effective review of the question of guilt. It is true that if there is to be any bias, it is better to err on the side of acquitting the guilty – the wrongful acquittal of some defendants is a small price to pay for safeguarding the overwhelming majority.

Research has not been forthcoming on the political function of the jury, but these functions are no less important. Because of that the jury is, for instance, a good barometer of public feeling. The acquittal of Clive Ponting on a charge under the Official Secrets Act 1911 demonstrates the public's dislike of the oppressive use of these laws by the state; a robust view of the police evidence and unwisdom of the bringing of the prosecution against Mrs Cynthia Payne on charges of running a brothel resulted in her acquittal. There is reason to believe that the English jury does embody commonsense and fairplay.

Researchers do not rally towards abolition of the institution but rather its reform. Lord Justice Sir Sebag Shaw gives a powerful and articulate defence of the jury. Other senior legal personalities of differing views, such as Lord Denning and Lord Hailsham, criticise the jury but in the end they accept the enormous value of the jury trial in serious criminal cases.

The Roskill Report in 1986 recommended that the jury should be replaced by professional assessors. This suggestion has not been taken up, instead the Government has reformed the nature of fraud trials – Criminal Justice Act 1987.

Six-member juries have been suggested but on the whole such 'mini-juries' have certainly been unfavourably received in the US.

The proposals of the James Committee 1975 to restrict a defendant's right to opt for trial by jury in certain cases involving theft were severely criticised and rejected.

Lord Denning has proposed that jurors should be recruited in the same fashion as magistrates are presently appointed – but the basic qualifications remain unaltered.

Radical reform seems unlikely – the jury enjoys the considerable confidence of the public; it appears to return verdicts that are generally deemed reasonable by judges, lawyers and the police; it successfully maintains its political and constitutional independence. In the words of Denning, 'Trial by jury has no equal.'

Question 3

Should juries have to give reasons for their verdicts, if asked to do so a) by the judge or b) by a party convicted of an offence?

University of London LLB Examination
(for External Students) English Legal System June 1991 Q4

General comment

This question is easily compartmentalised and gives a fresh slant on the jury system. Requires some thought in advance but if you ask yourself the right questions the subject falls open. You have to understand the justifications for the jury system and be able to incorporate them in your answer. Be sure to answer both parts but do not separate them with (a) or (b) – they are part of the same theme; be fluent and cohesive.

Skeleton solution

- What is the justification for not giving reasons in the present system?
- Notions of the adversarial system? What do we want to achieve with a jury?
- Why might a judge want reasons?
- Why might the defendant (or even the prosecution) want reasons?
- Are there any circumstances where giving reasons would be useful, or any other reforms?
- Conclusion.

Suggested solution

In order to consider whether and in what circumstances the jury should be required to give reasons for its decision in an English trial we must first examine the justifications for the present situation.

Traditionally the decision-making process of the jurors has been secret and free from public scrutiny. There would be little purpose in the secrecy of the jury's deliberations if the reason for its eventual decision were made known. The secrecy ensures that the decision is free from outside influences which might prejudice the fairness of the verdict. The question suggests that the secrecy would be breached only when a judge or a party desire it but it is submitted that this would be frequent enough to open the door to prejudicial influences. It would be hard for jurors to justify their decision in court before the person they had convicted, or the authority of a judge or the pain of a victim. The adversarial system seeks to insulate the jury from too great an emotive pressure in the court-room so as to promote a considered choice. The requirement for reasoned decisions would expose the jurors to unfair pressures and imperil the quality of the verdict.

Furthermore the principle of the independence of the jury would be threatened by making jurors answerable to some degree for their actions. The nature of trial by one's peers means putting faith in the moral judgment of the jurors and not requiring a legalistic reasoned response from them. They have the right and duty to reach the decision they feel is correct and base it on a subjective appreciation of the evidence before them. There is a balance to be struck between the formality and objectivity of the court process and the role of the jury in assessing the intangible credibility of the facts before it. Requiring a justification of the jury's decision would lead to greater formality at the expense of the human element of the legal process. If we are to have a jury system we must trust the people to reach a carefully thought out decision based on their impressions and not ask them to give the often inexplicable reasons for that decision.

Obviously this system has its flaws and it is possible that the giving of reasons may alleviate these. It is often alleged that the jury give inconsistent decisions though studies by McConville & Baldwin and Zander belie this. The giving of reasons would not necessarily avoid any inconsistency that may exist but it would encourage the jury to give structured opinions which would encourage uniformity. Further if reported (as judges' decisions are) the pressure to treat like cases alike would increase. Uniformity of treatment of defendants in the system is desirable, promoting certainty and equality of treatment between defendants. However the question poses two other reasons for the giving of reasons by the jury.

Judges would be aided in sentencing defendants were they to ask the jury to give reasons or if they asked the jury salient questions. The jury is told to deliver a verdict in accordance with the law as explained by the judge. They do not have a ready forum to express a feeling that the defendant was legally guilty but morally not so culpable as to deserve a heavy punishment or vice-versa. Judges would also be able to establish the reasons behind a 'perverse' verdict – understanding what moral considerations led the jury to decline to follow which element of law. Furthermore in defamation, questioning the jurors as to the basis for the monetary award they make would perhaps stop damages escalating quite so rapidly. Such a power would be open to abuse if the judge could then overturn or interfere in another way with the jury's verdict. However it seems sensible to permit the moral aspects of a jury's verdict to be communicated to the judge to assist in sentencing; or even to recommend a conviction for a lesser offence where possible (the prosecution often charge only the most severe offence sustainable to ensure their credibility).

Secondly a party may wish to know the basis for the jury's decision in order to appeal the verdict. The appeal courts are loath to overturn a jury's verdict unless there is evidence of a mistrial or gross misdirection that would clearly have changed the verdict. As we have seen recently even proof of faulty evidence does not incline the appeal courts to swiftly rectify an error. If the evidence on which the jury relied was stated by them, it would make such appeals easier as the jurors are effectively saying 'on this basis, this verdict' and where the basis is subsequently disproved we can assume the jury would wish their decision altered. However as suggested above, there are intangibles which cannot be explained and if we have faith in the jury system should perhaps not be explained. Would it be fair for the prosecution to be able to question the jury in a case such as *R* v *Ponting* (1985) (such a right would have to be given to both parties)? Surely such a practice would inhibit the jury from returning a verdict contrary to the law and thus remove a vital element of public participation in the legal process. It is submitted that the jury's verdict is correctly viewed as a decision that should only be tampered with in exceptional circumstances (though this should not be used to hide prosecution, police or judicial malpractice).

In conclusion we should strengthen the jury system not undermine it by pressuring the jurors into a purely rational verdict. Nor should we make the jury answerable to a higher power – its decision is the voice of the public in our system for good and ill. Perhaps with more explanation and education the jury could volunteer reasons where (as suggested) they reflect on sentence or avoid the blunt instrument of a perverse verdict by openly recommending the charge dropped. If we believe in the jury system we should encourage its representative autonomy.

Question 4

What arguments may be advanced to abandon the random selection of juries and to institute a selection procedure based upon jurors' gender, race and professional knowledge?

University of London LLB Examination
(for External Students) English Legal System June 1992 Q2

General comment

This question requires some imagination and considerable original thought on the part of the student, and so it is not as straightforward as might at first appear.

Skeleton solution

- Selection process and function of jury.
- Theory of random selection.
- Specific problem areas:
  - ethnic;
  - gender;
  - professional knowledge.
- Conclusions and alternatives.

Suggested solution

The English jury system is regarded by many as one of the most essential and central features of the legal process: 'the bulwark of individual liberties'. However, both the jury selection process and the value of decision-making by juries are frequently criticised. Before one can validly discuss the arguments for or against random selection, the process of that selection and the role of the jury must first be considered.

The Juries Act 1974 provides the criteria of eligibility for jury service. Broadly, anyone aged between 18 and 70 years old who is on the electoral register may be eligible. There are also provisions as to those who are disqualified, ineligible or may be excused from jury service, which range from a person with a criminal record to a practising lawyer or member of the clergy. But the central feature of the whole process is that it should be a totally random selection, from the moment the first panel is picked through to the swearing-in of 12 jurors.

This random selection is considered key to the maintenance of an effective jury system. A man (or woman) has a right to be tried by his peers, 'twelve men good and true', who will decide his fate. This lay involvement is supported as the fairest way to make the decisions as to fact in a case, and an important way to see that society's views and current thinking are expressed, whatever the influence of the judge (eg the Clive Ponting trial where the jury refused to follow the judge's direction to convict).

But if this lay involvement is so crucial, why is it that juries deal with less than five per cent of criminal cases and only the rarest of civil cases? In civil trials they have been all but abolished, partly because they seemed to be anything but in touch with the realities of society in the huge damages awards they gave, as can still be seen in libel cases. The great majority of criminal trials are dealt with summarily in the magistrates' courts. Where juries are used they are frequently accused of giving perverse verdicts (although some regard this as their essential feature), and the recently publicised miscarriages of justice have also called into question their value as arbiters of fact.

Many feel that juries do not truly represent a cross-section of society, and also, in the case of complex fraud trials, that they are out of their 'depth'. So one can begin to see where the arguments for abandoning random selection find their support.

It is also questionable how far the final selection is random and therefore a true cross-section of society and trial by peers. It has been argued that with the introduction of the poll tax, many potential jurors are not in fact registered on the electoral roll, and so already the pool of selection is restricted. The possibility in some cases of allowing the prosecution to vet potential jurors and the general process of challenging further narrows the chances of getting 12 unbiased jurors. It has been suggested that it is too easy for the prosecution to use these powers to tailor the jury, while the defence is at an unfair disadvantage.

Some have tried to use the process of challenging to gain a jury that is better balanced in its ethnic membership. Studies have shown that there is an under-representation of racial minorities in proportion to their representation in society. In 1976 Baldwin and McConville found that less than 0.7 per cent of jurors were of Afro-Caribbean or Asian origin. Throughout the 1980s there was a series of cases where counsel attempted to redress the balance using their power to ask jurors to 'stand by' – and judges were also prepared to 'step-in' (ie become involved in the selection process). In *R* v *Binns* (1982) prosecuting counsel was allowed to use this power, with the defence's agreement. In the trial of *Newton Rose* (1981) (a black defendant) for murder, the judge advised jurors to disqualify themselves if they had strong views against blacks or supported extreme left-wing or right-wing political parties. Certainly, there seemed to be some judicial sympathy for the problem. The Court of Appeal finally considered the matter in *R* v *Ford* (1989) and Lord Lane CJ emphasised that the principle of fairness of a jury is based upon its random selection, and it was the duty of trial judges to ensure that the jurors were selected randomly. In favour of preserving the status quo there is a strong argument to say that while ethnic minorities might be under-represented, it is not appropriate to assume that all whites are prejudiced, nor indeed should any defendant be allowed to select a more sympathetic jury. But calls remain from the Commission on Racial Equality and similar bodies for a trial judge to have a statutory right to ask jurors to 'stand by' to achieve the correct racial mix.

Baldwin and McConville also found (in 1976) that women were under-represented. Seventy-two per cent of jurors were male. The reasons for this, it was suggested, were that more women than men asked for excusal (perhaps because of family commitments) and, more worryingly, that there had previously been an unofficial policy of calling twice as many men as women. Certainly, the problem of under-representation of women is far less severe than when the basis of selection was 'householders' (usually men) rather than the electoral register, but it nevertheless remains an issue. How far it is a problem again depends upon whether one assumes that men are more likely to be biased than women.

The most detailed studies and discussions have surrounded the intellectual ability of juries to deal with the complexity of evidence and issues before them. It has been argued that the present law of evidence is in practice much distorted by the need to accommodate the bias and inexperience of juries. In response, the Criminal Justice Act 1987 changed some of the procedural matters on evidential points to simplify the rules on admissibility. Another frequent criticism is based on the very fact that jurors are lay men, uneducated in the law and too easily influenced by clever advocacy. In 1986 the Roskill Committee investigated the role of juries, in particular in complex fraud trials. It came firmly to the conclusion that they were unable to understand the lengthy and complicated evidence before them. Furthermore, the sheer length of these trials meant it was impractical to use a jury and expect people to be away from their jobs for many months. The Committee came to the conclusion in such cases that it would be far more appropriate for a judge to sit with two experts, ie with business or accounting skills. While this proposal is much talked about, it still remains only a proposal and it is not itself without flaws. It might be more difficult for two City professionals to remain unbiased in the large City fraud trials. Nor are these experts legally trained and therefore better able to understand the complexities of the rules of evidence, and they might still be swayed by good oratory from counsel. It is also worth noting that public criticism of the recent Guinness and Blue Arrow trials has been directed not at the juries' guilty verdicts, but at the sentencing and appeal decisions adopted by the judges.

As long as the jury system remains it will always have its defenders and its critics. But if the principle of random selection is paramount to the ideal of trial by peers then moulding juries so that counsel and defendants see the 'right' faces before them undermines that principle. To say that we need to select juries on the basis of gender, race or expertise assumes that people are unable to be objective and unbiased, and, further, at what point does a minority become too small to be represented? Should we not also consider selection on the basis of social background, moral or religious upbringing or political persuasion? If one remembers that trial by jury is the exception rather than the rule, perhaps the discussion should be not on how we should select our juries, but should we be using them at all?

12 CIVIL PROCEDURE IN THE HIGH COURT

12.1 Introduction

The High Court consists of three divisions and the procedure that governs proceedings in these courts is to be found in the Rules of the Supreme Court (RSC). The jurisdiction of the High Court is not limited geographically.

12.2 Key points

a) *Commencing an action*

A civil action may be commenced in the High Court in four main ways.

i) Originating summons

This method of commencement is used mainly in the Chancery Division. This type of summons is a means used to bring the questions to be determined to the court's attention.

ii) Originating motions

This mode of commencing proceedings is also used mainly in the Chancery Division. This is usually made by oral application to the court with written notice to the parties.

iii) Petitions

This method may only be used where authorised by the Rules of the Supreme Court or by statute in actions that deal with eg the winding up of companies or divorce, amongst other actions.

iv) Writ of summons

This mode of commencement is generally used in tortious claims for death, personal injuries, or other breaches of duty. This formal document informs the defendant that proceedings against him have commenced and will explain the need for him to acknowledge service. The writ must contain:

- the names of all the parties;
- their status;
- the relevant division of the High Court in which the plaintiff is suing.

The back of the writ must be indorsed by the plaintiff with:

- the nature of the claim;
- the relief required;
- sufficient particulars to allow the defendant to identify the cause of action;
- the name and address of the plaintiff or his solicitor.

b) *Service of writ*

Once issued the writ must be served within four months from date of issue (RSC Ord 6 r8(1)). The court may however renew a writ, thereby extending its validity, if there is some good reason for justifying renewal: *Waddon* v *Whitecroft-Scovill Ltd* [1988] 1 WLR 309. The rules permit the following methods of service:

i) personal service;

ii) service by post to the defendant's last known address;

iii) service to the defendant's solicitor;

iv) substituted service (where other means impracticable).

c) *Acknowledgment of service*

Once served, the defendant takes his first step in the action by completing his acknowledgment of service. He must do so within 14 days of service to indicate if he intends to defend the claim. This must be sent to the court from which the writ was issued.

d) *Judgment in default: RSC Ord 13*

i) The plaintiff may seek judgment in default where the defendant has acknowledged service but failed to give notice of intention to defend or where the defendant fails to acknowledge service altogether.

ii) The plaintiff must put into the court office the original writ, a copy of the judgment required and an affidavit of service. Where the claim is for liquidated damages, judgment is final and may be enforced immediately. For unliquidated claims, however, judgment is only interlocutory, that is to say, it is final as to liability but not as to quantum. In order to obtain final judgment, the plaintiff must issue and serve an inter partes summons returnable before the Master for assessment of the quantum of damages.

iii) The defendant may, if he wishes, apply to have the judgment in default set aside according to the procedure in RSC Ord 13 r9.

e) *Summary judgment: RSC Ord 14*

Once the defendant gives notice of intention to defend, judgment under Ord 13 is unavailable to the plaintiff. Instead, he may seek summary judgment, on the basis that the defendant has no real defence to the claim. The following procedure must be followed:

i) the plaintiff must serve a full statement of claim on the defendant;

ii) the application for summary judgment is made by inter partes summons returnable before a master in chambers and must be accompanied by a verifying affidavit stating the belief that there is no defence;

iii) this summons and affidavit must be served 10 clear days before the return date;

iv) the defendant will generally serve an affidavit in opposition, setting out all the grounds of his defence with supporting evidence;

v) should the defendant fail to serve an affidavit in opposition, summary judgment will be awarded against him;

vi) should summary judgment be given against the defendant, he may appeal either to a judge in chambers (see RSC Ord 58 r1) or to the Court of Appeal (see RSC Ord 58 r2).

RSC Ord 14A makes provision for the speedy determination of questions of law or construction.

f) *Payment into court: RSC Ord 22*

The defendant may make a payment into court where he admits liability but disputes the size of the plaintiff's claim. The procedure is as follows:

i) the defendant pays in the sum to the Accountant General of the Supreme Court;

ii) the defendant must serve due notice on the plaintiff;

iii) the plaintiff must acknowledge receipt of notice in three days;

iv) should the plaintiff wish to accept he must do so within 21 days;

v) the plaintiff then serves notice of acceptance on the defendant;

vi) there then follows an automatic stay in proceedings.

The consequences of rejecting a payment in are serious for the plaintiff as he stands to pay the parties' costs from the date of payment in, should he be awarded a lesser sum in damages.

g) *Injunctions: RSC Ord 29 r1*

Interlocutory injunctions are orders made by the court before trial or before the commencement of proceedings to keep matters static until the issue is decided at trial. Injunctions can be either mandatory or prohibitory. In general injunctions are only a temporary measure and their grant depends on whether there is a serious question to be tried and on the balance of convenience: *American Cyanamid Co* v *Ethicon* [1975] AC 396.

h) *Interim payments: RSC Ord 29 r9*

Applications for interim payments are generally made with Ord 14 claims for damages to be assessed. Interim payments will generally not amount to more than two-thirds of the total sum claimed. Interim payments of damages are an effective means of allowing some compensation to victims of accidents before final points are decided at trial.

i) *Pleadings: RSC Ord 18*

i) Statement of claim

This document is issued by the plaintiff and is an outline of his claim against the defendant. If not indorsed on the back of the writ, the statement must be served separately within 14 days.

ii) Defence and counterclaim

The defendant must serve his defence on the plaintiff within 14 days of the service of the statement of claim.

- The defendant must ensure that he deals with each of the allegations made by the plaintiff, as he is taken to admit any allegations not dealt with.
- Where the defendant has a separate claim against the plaintiff, it may be pleaded along with his defence. The counterclaim puts the defendant in the position of plaintiff with regard to the counterclaim.

iii) Reply and defence to counterclaim

- The plaintiff may if he wishes serve a reply to deal with some of the matters raised by the defence.
- Where the defendant has made a counterclaim and the plaintiff wishes to defend it, he must do so within his reply.

j) *Procedure from close of pleadings to trial*

i) Discovery and inspection of documents: RSC Ord 24

In most civil actions, general discovery of documents occurs automatically within 14 days after close of pleadings. The plaintiff and defendant will exchange lists of all relevant documents.

ii) Security for costs: RSC Ord 23

The plaintiff may be required in certain cases to deposit a sum of money as security for the costs of the action. This procedure exists to protect the defendant, generally where the plaintiff resides outside of the jurisdiction.

iii) Summons for directions: RSC Ord 25

This procedure should be taken out by the plaintiff within one month from close of pleadings. A variety of issues are dealt with in the summons for directions, including place and mode of trial and presentation and use of evidence.

iv) Exchange of witness statements: RSC Ord 38 r2A. The court may order this at any stage, with a view to saving costs.

k) *The trial*

i) In general, the plaintiff's case is heard first including witness evidence. Once examined, the plaintiff's witnesses will be cross-examined by the defence counsel and re-examined by the plaintiff's counsel. At the close of his evidence counsel for the plaintiff will make submissions on law to support his case.

ii) Counsel for the defence will then call his evidence and witnesses, who will go through the same procedure as the plaintiff's witnesses, and the defence counsel will make similar closing submissions.

iii) The plaintiff's counsel may make a closing speech where the defence called evidence, and may exceptionally call evidence in rebuttal.

l) *Costs: RSC Ord 62*

The general rule is that 'costs follow the event', ie the successful party has his costs paid by his opponent. Costs if not agreed upon will be assessed by the taxing master. See also s51 of the Supreme Court Act 1981, as substituted by s4(1) of the Courts and Legal Services Act 1990.

12.3 Recent statutes

Courts and Legal Services Act 1990.

12.4 Analysis of questions

Past examination questions in this area have concentrated on possible reforms to the system. With the introduction of the Courts and Legal Services Act 1990, examiners are now likely to dwell on the effectiveness of the reforms which have been made. In view of this the statute and its implications must be thoroughly revised.

12.5 Questions

Question 1

'The present structure and organisation of the civil courts in England and Wales requires reform.' Discuss.

University of London LLB Examination
(for External Students) English Legal System June 1989 Q1

General comment

A reasonably straightforward question which requires a good knowledge of the court system.

Skeleton solution

- Choice of court.
- Impact of the Courts and Legal Services Act 1990.
- New financial limits.
- Costs.
- Appeals – a fair system?
- Utility of the House of Lords for civil appeals.

Suggested solution

The choice of court in which to commence a civil action is generally not dictated by subject matter (except in certain cases) but by the amount of damages claimed or value of the subject matter.

Magistrates' courts, while primarily known as courts of criminal jurisdiction, have a very varied civil jurisdiction. They have jurisdiction over domestic proceedings. Appeals on family matters go to the Divisional Court of the Family Division.

The county courts, established by statute in 1846, offer a relatively comprehensive speedy and cheap procedure and deal with the bulk of civil litigation. There are about 400 county courts in England and Wales. Some of these are specially designated divorce county courts which deal with undefended divorces and related matters; their jurisdiction is not geographically limited. They are staffed by circuit judges.

The High Court in its present form dates only from the Administration of Justice Act 1970. It has three divisions, Chancery, Queen's Bench and Family. Before the Courts Act 1971 the High Court sat solely in the Law Courts in the Strand, although High Court judges also tried civil cases on assize. The Act provided that the High Court could sit at other locations.

In his highly-regarded book on the workings of the English civil justice system, Master Sir Jack Jacob suggested that there should be a single 'Court of Civil Judicature', incorporating the current civil jurisdictions of magistrates' courts, county courts and High Court. This would avoid the disparity in waiting times that exists at present. The delay varies from area to area and the county court hears cases after some months whereas the High Court can take years.

The Civil Justice Review looked at this idea but rejected it, emphasising the need for the greater experience of High Court judges to be used for the more important cases. However, the CJR considered that improvements could be made to the present structure of the courts by re-organising the workload of the High Court and county court. This has since been implemented by the Courts and Legal Services Act 1990 by raising the financial jurisdiction of the county court.

The High Court should be reserved for cases of special importance, instead of being over-burdened with cases that could be adequately dealt with in the county court. Therefore the CJR recommended that public law cases, specialist cases and substantial cases, ie those involving more than £25,000 should be heard in the High Court: see Article 7(3) CLSA 1990. All other cases would be dealt with by the county court, and all personal injuries cases would have to commence in the county court.

It may well be wondered whether small claims should be dealt with at all in the adversarial court system. At present small claims of £1,000 or less in the county court are automatically referred to arbitration before a district judge and a more inquisitorial approach may be adopted. Lawyers are rarely present and costs cannot usually be awarded against either party.

Appeal from the High Court is to the Court of Appeal although it is possible to go straight to the House of Lords on a point of law. The civil division of this court is composed of ex officio judges who are the Lord Chancellor, the Master of the Rolls, the President of the Family Division, the Lords of Appeal in Ordinary and former Lord Chancellors, the Vice-Chancellor and the Lords Justices of Appeal. In practice only the Master of the Rolls of the ex officio judges sits with the Lords Justices of Appeal.

Interlocutory appeals may now be heard by a single judge sitting in chambers (in private). Appeals from county courts are now usually heard by two judges. Under the direction of Sir John Donaldson MR the procedure of the Court of Appeal has undergone several changes, designed to speed up procedure and clear a backlog of cases, the most notable of which has been the introduction of skeleton arguments.

From the Court of Appeal, appeal lies to the House of Lords, provided that leave to appeal has been obtained from either the Court of Appeal or the Appeals Committee of the Lords. The House of Lords consists of at least three, and usually five judges who must be drawn from the Lords of Appeal in Ordinary, the Lord Chancellor and any other peer who has held high judicial office.

It may be asked whether the existence of a second appeal court is justifiable. Only a very small number of cases proceed from Court of Appeal, which thus acts as a filter. The extra delays and costs of an appeal to the House of Lords can be great, and are often in practice only available to the Inland Revenue, Government departments and large corporations. A litigant may feel unfairly treated if he loses a case in the Lords by a bare majority of 3:2 when he had won at first instance and unanimously in the Court of Appeal; a total of three judges out of nine against him.

In their study of the Lords, *Final Appeal*, Blom Cooper and Drewry suggest that the issue is not so much one of efficiency or speed in the conduct of an appeal, but one of social utility: what is the function of the House of Lords? As the second appellate court, the Lords is in a good position to supervise and direct major developments in the law, as well as correcting faulty decisions of the Court of Appeal. Yet it does not really justify its presence in these areas. It has eschewed an active law-making function, declaring that such matters must be left to Parliament. It is too concerned not to upset the status quo, most particularly in its reluctance to depart from its own previous decisions (unlike the Court of Appeal, the House of Lords, under the terms of its *Practice Statement* of 1966, is not bound by its own previous decisions). But even if the House of Lords should be more active in developing the law, it is only able to act on the cases that come before it.

A sensible solution would be to abolish either Court of Appeal or House of Lords, and allow the remaining body to depart from its own previous decisions.

Question 2

Why is English civil procedure often characterised as 'trial by ambush'? What effect will changes recommended by the Civil Justice Review have on the disclosure of information by the parties and the progress of a civil case?

University of London LLB Examination
(for External Students) English Legal System June 1991 Q3

General comment

A rather out-dated question; civil procedure has moved very far away from 'trial by ambush'. Once again, merely cataloguing the Civil Justice Review will not gain good (or even pass) marks. Knowledge of the details of civil procedure is needed to answer well; there is little room for long discussion of principles.

Skeleton solution

- What is civil law? What is effect of *non*-disclosure of information and progress of case on people?
- What has already been done. Its relation to CJR.
- Disclosure rules. Their effects. Link to progress of case by time, rules for exchange, etc.
- Progress of case. Effects.
- What other changes could be made? CJR or not?
- Conclusion

Suggested solution

The civil law category in the English legal system governs the rights and duties that exist inter partes. It enables the social and business intercourse of individuals. This balance is reflected in the procedure for legal enforcement of these 'civilian' laws. The rules of court seek to give each party a fair and equal hearing and apply universal standards of behaviour in judging between them.

The ability to withhold information from another party in the preparation for trial alters this balance of fairness. The principles of natural justice taken to their logical conclusion preclude such surprise attacks and gradually the rules of court have changed to reflect this view. The powers by which a party can extract information from his opponent prior to the trial are now very strong and well developed (if weighted in favour of the plaintiff). Rules governing advance disclosure of documents, reports and even witness statements have become more strict in the last few years as civil justice procedure has moved away from trial by ambush. The catch-phrase of the present is the 'cards-on-the-table approach'.

In many respects the Civil Justice Review (CJR) has been ignored yet implemented. The Review's report in June 1988 now seems dated as many of its provisions have become law, by changes to the Rules of the Supreme Court and small items slipped into Acts of Parliament, in particular the Courts and Legal Services Act (CLSA). As Lord Lane has commented: 'Many of the proposals in Part I (of the CLSA) have already been pre-empted by what judges have done by way of distributing work.' It is the judges who changed the Rules of the Supreme Court to reflect many of the recommendations of the CJR. So without any fanfare the procedure of civil justice has evolved in an attempt to improve the efficiency and fairness of the system.

Taking the two specific areas in turns, the rules governing discovery and exchange of information between parties have been altered beyond the suggestions of the CJR. Police accident reports and medical reports are now released earlier to the plaintiff but moreover a medical report must be included with the Particulars or Statement of Claim that commence the proceedings. This advance disclosure enables the defendant to assess the value of the claim and decide whether it is cost effective to contest the case. As suggested by the CJR but pre-empted by the Official Referee's Court, witness statements must now be exchanged, prior to trial, by RSC Ord 38 r2A (and CCR Ord 20 r12A). The benefits are considerable, preventing surprise evidence being adduced and enabling the parties to assess the strength of the case against them.

In addition the general move in favour of openness has led to a change in the attitude of Registrars and Masters towards parties who may be prevaricating about the disclosure of documents or not admitting to the possession of relevant evidence. The penalties are harsher and the time limits more rigid which together have reduced the abuses of the procedure which were commonplace. The imposition of stricter time limits has affected the progress of all civil cases. In an effort to reduce the delays which damage the quality of evidence and postpone justice, a firm time-table is drawn up earlier in the litigation and monitored by the Master or Registrar concerned. In many cases (all County Court matters and all personal injury cases in the High Court) this time-table is now automatic, as recommended in the CJR, enabling parties to prepare in advance for the stages of the litigation. The progress of civil cases is now quicker, more logical and more adequately balanced between the parties.

Many aspects of the CJR have slipped into the process of civil justice in England and Wales without disturbing the natural evolution of the rules of court. In many respects this is a tribute to the sensible nature of the recommendations of the Review, which sought to improve rather than radically alter the fabric of civil procedure. Suggestions such as amending the Limitation Act to force proceedings to be issued and served within the limitation period may yet be adopted as may the more challenging unification of County Court and High Court procedures. However, reforms of the administration of the courts system (especially the County Court) are unlikely to be implemented because there is insufficient money, or political will to extract finances from the Treasury, to carry out the suggestions. Notwithstanding the efficiency programmes instituted by these changes and the Lord Chancellor's Department, the County Court will continue to offer a sub-standard level of justice unless ways can be found to clear the backlog of cases that have been passed to that court.

In conclusion, there has been a general movement towards an open system of civil litigation and away from the combative style of previous decades. In that respect the CJR reflects the trend towards a realisation of the principles of natural justice. All the changes caused by the CJR and/or instituted by the judges and Acts have reduced the ability of a party to take advantage of the rules of court. There is little scope for ambush as the process of litigation turns from a bloody war into a game of chess.

13 CIVIL PROCEDURE IN THE COUNTY COURT

13.1 Introduction

The County Courts Act 1984 (CCA 1984) and the County Court Rules (CCR) govern procedure in the county courts. The Courts and Legal Services Act 1990 has added to the jurisdiction of the county court.

13.2 Key points

For a full list of the changes made by the Courts and Legal Services Act 1990 see the suggested solution to the first question in this chapter.

a) *Jurisdiction*

Although the county court is in general governed by the CCA 1984, many other statutes give special jurisdiction to the county courts. The most recent changes to jurisdiction can be found in the Courts and Legal Services Act 1990 (CLSA 1990).

The CLSA 1990 empowers the Lord Chancellor to allocate business between the High Court and county courts. The High Court and County Courts Jurisdiction Order 1991 has increased the jurisdiction of the county court as follows:

i) actions worth less than £25,000 must be tried in the county court;

ii) actions worth £50,000 or more must be tried in the High Court;

iii) actions worth between £25,000 to £50,000 may be tried in either way;

iv) however, personal injuries claims worth less than £50,000 must be commenced in the county court.

As a general rule, the enforcement of county court judgments worth £5,000 and above must be undertaken in the High Court. County court enforcement must be used for judgments worth up to £2,000. Between these figures either court may be used.

b) *Commencement*

i) Proceedings must commence in one of the following districts (Ord 4 r2):

- the district in which the defendant resides; or
- where the defendant carries on his business; or
- the district in which the cause of action arose.

ii) Proceedings in the county court are either actions or matters. Actions may be either default actions or fixed date actions.

- A default action is generally used in claims for debt and damages. Should the defendant fail to file a defence or counterclaim within 14 days, judgment in default will be awarded against him. The defendant also has the option of making a payment to satisfy the plaintiff's claim, within 14 days. This would end proceedings.
- Fixed date actions are used in claims which are not to do with money, for example, claims for possession of land, injunctions or declarations.
- Matters are proceedings in all other areas. Such proceedings may be in the form of originating applications, petitions and entries of appeal.

iii) In order to begin proceedings the plaintiff must:

- file a formal request for summons;
- along with the request, put in two copies of the particulars of claim;
- give an undertaking as to costs if he is under disability as defined in CCR Ord 10;
- if he is legally aided, submit his legal aid certificate;
- where the action concerns a personal injury claim, file a medical report.

iv) Once the plaintiff has completed the above the court will issue the summons, which will be served on the defendant. The plaintiff will receive a plaint note from the court.

c) *Pre trial review*

i) Pre trial review is held by the district judge to consider any directions for just and quick disposal of the action, any admissions and agreement and any other relevant directions, including those for discovery.

ii) Should the defendant fail to appear the district judge may enter judgment if the plaintiff can prove his claim. Judgment may also be given if in a fixed date action the defendant has not delivered an admission or defence.

iii) In default, fixed date and personal injury actions, there may be automatic directions for discovery. The following procedure should apply:

- within 28 days from close of pleadings the lists of documents must be served;
- these documents on the list are to be inspected within seven days;
- within 10 weeks of the close of pleadings, the experts' reports are to be disclosed;
- within six months of close of pleadings the plaintiff must request a date for hearing. Should he fail to do so within 15 months, his action will be automatically struck out.

iv) Summary judgment is available in the county court for default actions where the plaintiff's claim is for £500 or more.

d) *Pleadings*

The process of pleadings is much the same as in the High Court and the pleadings must be filed at the court office.

e) *Interlocutory proceedings*

Nearly all the same interlocutory proceedings are available in the county court as in the High Court.

f) *Trial*

The trial proceeds in the same way as in the High Court, although the judge may direct the order of speeches and dispense with opening speeches

g) *Small claims procedure*

The small claims procedure is used when the plaintiff's claim does not exceed £1,000. Proceedings are generally begun by default summons:

i) Where no defence or counter is filed, judgment in default will be awarded.

ii) The amount awarded is assessed by the district judge.

iii) Should a defence be filed, the claim may be referred to arbitration by the district judge: CCR Ord 19 r2.

iv) Arbitration has many advantages for the litigant. In particular:

- informal proceedings;
- relaxation of evidential rules;
- there is no necessity for lawyers;
- there is a no costs rule.

13.3 Recent statutes

Courts and Legal Services Act 1990.

13.4 Analysis of questions

Questions on county court procedure were, in the past, generally combined with High Court procedure questions. However, as the Courts and Legal Services Act 1990 is now in force, questions are likely to arise on the allocation of High Court work to the county court. Furthermore, some consideration of the small claims procedure and alternative dispute resolution may be required.

13.5 Questions

Question 1

List the changes made to civil procedure in the county court by the Courts and Legal Services Act 1990.

Written by Editor

Skeleton solution

- Jurisdiction.
  - jurisdiction – Articles 2–4.
  - exercise of jurisdictional powers – Article 5.
  - allocation and enforcement – Articles 7 and 8.
  - value of actions – Articles 9 and 10.
- Cost penalties – s4(1) CLSA 1990.

Suggested solution

Jurisdiction:

a) Section 1 of the Courts and Legal Services Act 1990 gave the Lord Chancellor power to make orders dealing with the allocation of civil cases between the High Court and the county courts. However, before exercising that power, he is required to consult the Lord Chief Justice, the Master of the Rolls, the President of the Family Division, the Vice-Chancellor and the Senior Presiding Judge: s1(9) of the 1990 Act. The Senior Presiding Judge is one of the Lords Justices of Appeal appointed to this office by the Lord Chief Justice with the agreement of the Lord Chancellor: ibid, s72(2), (3). It should be noted that the Lord Chancellor's power, conferred by s1 of the 1990 Act, does not enable him to confer jurisdiction on any county court to hear any application for judicial review: ibid, s1(10).

   In exercise of the power conferred on him by s1 of the 1990 Act, the Lord Chancellor made the High Court and County Courts Jurisdiction Order 1991 and it came into force on 1 July 1991. The order reflects proposals made in the Report of the Review Body on Civil Justice (Cm 394, 1988). In general terms, the order enlarges significantly the jurisdiction of county courts, although it does not apply to family proceedings within the meaning of Part V of the Matrimonial and Family Proceedings Act 1984 or to proceedings to which s27(1) of the County Courts Act 1984 (Admiralty jurisdiction) applies: art 12 of the 1991 order.

b) The other principal provisions of the 1991 order as to jurisdiction are on lines as follows:

Article 2

(1) A county court has jurisdiction under, inter alia, ss15 (contract and tort), 21 (recovery of land) and 25 (Inheritance (Provision for Family and Dependants) Act 1975) of the County Courts Act 1984, 'whatever the amount involved in the proceedings and whatever the value of any fund or asset connected with the proceedings.'

(2) A county court has jurisdiction under certain provisions relating to local land charges and rent charges where the sum concerned or amount claimed does not exceed £5,000.

(3)-(6) A county court has jurisdiction under certain provisions of, inter alia, the Law of Property Act 1925 and the Land Charges Act 1972 where, generally, the value of the land does not exceed £30,000.

(7) A county court has jurisdiction under certain provisions of the Solicitors Act 1974 where a bill of costs relates wholly or partly to contentious business done in a county court and the amount of the bill does not exceed £5,000.

Article 3 – Injunctions

The High Court has jurisdiction to hear an application for an injunction made in the course of or in anticipation of proceedings in a county court where a county court may not grant such an injunction.

Article 4 – Allocation – Commencement of proceedings

Subject to articles 5 and 6, proceedings in which both the county courts and the High Court have jurisdiction may be commenced either in a county court or in the High Court.

Article 5

(1) Proceedings in which county courts have jurisdiction and which include a claim for damages in respect of personal injuries must be commenced in a county court, unless the value of the action is £50,000 or more.

(2) In this article 'personal injuries' means personal injuries to the plaintiff or any other person, and includes disease, impairment of physical or mental condition, and death.

As to the indorsement of writs as to value in such cases, see *Practice Direction* [1991] 3 All ER 352.

Article 7 – Allocation – Trial

(1) Subject to the following provisions of this article, proceedings in which both the High Court and the county courts have jurisdiction may be tried in the High Court or in a county court.

(2) The following provisions of this article apply (with certain exceptions) to proceedings in which both the High Court and the county courts have jurisdiction, save that paras (3) and (4) do not apply to proceedings which have no quantifiable value.

(3) An action of which the value is less than £25,000 must be tried in a county court unless –

(a) a county court, having regard to the criteria set out in sub-paras (a) to (d) of para (5), considers that it ought to transfer the action to the High Court for trial and the High Court considers that it ought to try the action; or

(b) it is commenced in the High Court and the High Court, having regard to the said criteria, considers that it ought to try the action.

(4) An action of which the value is £50,000 or more must be tried in the High Court unless –

(a) it is commenced in a county court and the county court does not, having regard to the criteria set out in sub-paras (a) to (d) of para (5), consider that the action ought to be transferred to the High Court for trial; or

(b) the High Court, having regard to the said criteria, considers that it ought to transfer the case to a county court for trial.

(5) The High Court and the county courts, when considering whether to exercise their powers under ss40(2), 41(1) or 42(2) of the County Courts Act 1984 (Transfer) must have regard to the following criteria –

(a) the financial substance of the action, including the value of any counterclaim,

(b) whether the action is otherwise important and, in particular, whether it raises questions of importance to persons who are not parties or questions of general public interest,

(c) the complexity of the facts, legal issues, remedies or procedures involved, and

(d) whether transfer is likely to result in a more speedy trial of the action, but no transfer can be made on the grounds of sub-para (d) alone.

Article 8 – Enforcement

(1) A judgment or order of a county court for the payment of a sum of money which it is sought to enforce wholly or partially by execution against goods –

(a) must be enforced only in the High Court where the sum which it is sought to enforce is £5,000 or more and the proceedings in which the judgment or order was obtained did not arise out of an agreement regulated by the Consumer Credit Act 1974;

(b) must be enforced only in a county court where the sum which it is sought to enforce is less than £2,000;

(c) in any other case may be enforced in either the High Court or a county court.

(2) Section 85(1) of the County Courts Act 1984 (Execution of judgments or orders for payment of money) is amended by the insertion, at the beginning of the subsection, of the words 'Subject to article 8 of the High Court and County Courts Jurisdiction Order 1991'.

Article 9 – Definition of value of action

(1) For the purposes of arts 5 and 7 –

(a) the value of an action for a sum of money, whether specified or not, is the amount which the plaintiff or applicant reasonably expects to recover;

(b) an action for specified relief other than a sum of money –

i) has a value equal to the amount of money which the plaintiff or applicant could reasonably state to be the financial worth of the claim to him, or

ii) where there is no such amount, has no quantifiable value;

(c) an action which includes more than one claim –

i) if one or more of the claims is of a kind specified in paragraph (b)(ii), has no quantifiable value,

ii) in any other case, has a value which is the aggregate of the values of the claims as determined in accordance with paras (a) and (b)(i).

(2) In determining the value of an action under para (1), claims for –

(a) unspecified further or other relief,

(b) interest, other than interest pursuant to a contract, and

(c) costs,

must be disregarded.

(3) In determining the value, under para (1), of an action which is brought by more than one plaintiff or applicant, regard is to be had to he aggregate of the expectations or interests of all the plaintiffs or applicants.

(4) In determining the value of an action under para (1)(a) –

(a) the sum which the plaintiff or applicant reasonably expects to recover is to be reduced by the amount of any debt which he admits that he owes to a defendant in that action and which arises from the circumstances which give rise to the action;

(b) no account is to be taken of a possible finding of contributory negligence, except to the extent, if any, that such negligence is admitted;

(c) where the plaintiff seeks an award of provisional damages as described in s32A(2)(a) of the Supreme Court Act 1981, no account is to be taken of the possibility of a future application for further damages;

(d) the value is to be taken to include sums which, by virtue of s22 of the Social Security Act 1989, are required to be paid to the Secretary of State.

Article 10

The value of an action is to be determined –

(a) for the purposes of art 5, as at the time when the action is commenced, and

(b) for the purposes of art 7, as at the time when the value is declared in accordance with rules of court.

c) Further particular points in relation to county court jurisdiction should be noted as follows:

i) County courts do not normally have jurisdiction to hear and determine any action for libel or slander: s15 of the 1984 Act as amended by the 1991 order.

ii) Where a plaintiff has a cause of action for more than the county court limit, he may abandon the excess and so give the county court jurisdiction: s17 of the 1984 Act.

iii) The parties may agree, by signed memorandum, that a specified county court shall have jurisdiction in the matter: ss18 and 24 of the 1984 Act, as amended. However, this power is subject to specified exceptions (ibid) and, in any case, it must now be read subject to the 1991 order.

iv) County courts have jurisdiction, subject to the 1991 order, to hear and determine –

- actions for the recovery of land and as to the title to any hereditament: s21 of the 1984 Act;
- equity proceedings, eg for the administration of a deceased's estate: s23 of the 1984 Act;
- applications under s2 of the Inheritance (Provision for Family and Dependants) Act 1975: s25 of the 1984 Act;
- probate proceedings: s32 of the 1984 Act.

v) It is not lawful for a plaintiff to divide a cause of action for the purpose of bringing two or more actions in one or more of the county courts: s35 of the 1984 Act.

vi) A county court does not have power to order mandamus, certiorari or prohibition: s38(3)(a) of the 1984 Act, as substituted. See also the County Courts Remedies Regulations 1991 made under this section.

d) Where the High Court is satisfied that any proceedings before it are required by any enactment, including s1 of the 1990 Act, to be in a county court, it must order the transfer of the proceedings to a county court or, if it is satisfied that the person bringing the proceedings knew, or ought to have known, of that requirement, order that they be struck out: s40(1), (8) of the 1984 Act as substituted by s2(1) of the 1990 Act. Subject to any such requirement, the High Court may order the transfer of any proceedings before it to a county court: s40(2) of the 1984 Act, as substituted. For procedure on transferring cases to a county court, see *Practice Direction* [1991] 3 All ER 349.

   Conversely, subject to any enactment, including s1 of the 1990 Act, if the High Court thinks it desirable that any proceedings commenced in a county court should be heard and determined in the High Court, it may order that the proceedings be so transferred: s41(1), (3) of the 1984 Act, as amended by s2(2) of the 1990 Act.

   By virtue of s42 of the 1984 Act, as substituted, a county court enjoys powers of transfer to the High Court similar to those enjoyed by the High Court by virtue of s40 of the 1984 Act, as substituted. For procedure on transfer to the High Court, see CCR O16, rr9-11.

   As to costs in transferred cases, see s45 of the 1984 Act.

Cost penalties:

By virtue of s51(8), (9) of the Supreme Court Act 1981, as substituted by s4(1) of the Courts and Legal Services Act 1990, where a person has commenced proceedings in the High Court but those proceedings should, in the opinion of the court, have been commenced in a county court in accordance with any provisions made under s1 of the 1990 Act or by or under any other enactment, the person responsible for determining the amount which is to be awarded to that person by way of costs is required to have regard to those circumstances. Where, in complying with this requirement, the responsible person reduces the amount which would otherwise be awarded to the person in question, the amount of that reduction must not exceed 25 per cent. On any taxation of the costs payable by that person to his legal representative, regard must be had to the amount of the reduction.

Question 2

Why is it considered necessary to have a special procedure for small claims in the English civil justice process? How well does the procedure work in practice?

University of London LLB Examination
(for External Students) English Legal System June 1992 Q6

General comment

This essay clearly requires more than an outline knowledge of the procedure for small claims. There must also be evidence of a good knowledge of the research and arguments about the system.

Skeleton solution

- History of small claims.
- Process today.
- Criticisms in general.
- 'Official' research.
- Government response.
- Conclusions.

Suggested solution

While being the envy of many, the English court system is also the fear of many. It has always been a difficulty that those with a problem either do not recognise it as one with a potential legal remedy or the fear of costs and confusion of starting litigation prevents them from seeking that remedy. It is against this background that the idea of a separate small claims procedure was introduced.

The original County Courts Act 1846 sought to create a cheap, accessible and simple forum for the recovery of small debts (originally less than £20) and demands. However, criticism as to costs and complexity, especially in small claims, remained and led to further calls for change. One of the most convincing and forceful came in the Consumer Council's document, *Justice Out of Reach*. In 1973 the government responded with the introduction of separate rules for small claims.

Initially changes were made to the existing procedure and were intended to make the system more approachable and less expensive. Changes included the introduction of a pre-trial review to assist the litigant in person, the encouragement of the use of arbitration rather than trial, and the introduction of the policy of no costs being awarded where the claim was less than £100. In 1981, more changes were made and arbitration became the normal method of settling disputes for claims less than £500. In October 1991, this threshold was raised to £1,000, perhaps reflecting the success of the process, as well as continued recognition of the need for a special procedure.

The aim, then, of the small claims procedure was to make the system more approachable to the litigant in person. The District Judges (formerly Registrars) operate whatever method of procedure they feel is convenient or fair. In trying to achieve this aim there are generally no legal representatives, no strict rules of evidence or procedure are applied, and claims are dealt with by means of arbitration in informal surroundings. However, in practice there continue to be problems as well as successes.

To refer a matter to the small claims arbitration is now an automatic process. But there is an element of flexibility, for example where the District Judge feels one of the specified grounds exist, such as there being a complex point of law or facts, or an allegation of fraud, he will recommend that the case goes to the normal trial process. Similarly, if the parties agree, the case can instead be dealt with in the county court. In *Pepper* v *Healey* (1982) the Registrar rescinded the case on the grounds that it would be unreasonable to use the arbitration process having regard to the circumstances of the parties. Following a road traffic accident, the parties came to court; the defendant (Mrs Healey) was represented by her insurers and therefore had all her legal expenses covered, including the cost of an expert witness. The Registrar felt that the plaintiff needed legal representation in order to present her case properly and the cost burden upon her would be unfair as against a fully insured defendant, whereas at least if she won at county court, her costs would be awarded. The Court of Appeal upheld this approach, although it took three hearings in all to come to this decision!

The Consumer Council was against legal representation being permitted at all in the small claims procedure, but it is argued that in any event the no costs rule strongly discourages the presence of paid representatives. However, *Pepper* v *Healey* shows that it is perhaps not a strong enough deterrent where insurance companies are involved, which is likely to be an ever increasing situation in modern society. There are also inconsistencies in approach and procedure from area to area. While District Judges are all agreed that they value informality, the hearings vary considerably between adversarial and inquisitorial approaches and in their adherence to the rules of evidence. It has been argued that this is both a useful aspect of the system (flexibility) and a negative aspect in terms of fairness. Whatever approach is adopted, the fundamental principles of the adversarial system cannot be set aside. This was confirmed by the Court of Appeal in *Chiltern* v *Saga Holidays plc* (1986) where the Registrar had refused to allow the defendants' solicitor to cross-examine the unrepresented plaintiffs, saying that all questions should come through him. On appeal, the Master of the Rolls confirmed the informality of the small claims process, but added that it was fundamental to the adversarial system 'that each party shall be entitled to ask questions designed to probe the accuracy or otherwise, or the completeness or otherwise, of the evidence which has been given'.

Studies have shown that although it was intended to be for individuals, at least half the plaintiffs using the small claims procedure are companies or firms. While this is an encouraging sign that the system is being used, when taken with cases like *Chiltern* and *Pepper* v *Healey* it perhaps suggests that there is too much involvement by bodies likely to be legally represented, reducing the scope for informality and the approachability for individuals. Further, it remains a criticism of the procedure that it is inaccessible to the private citizen unsure how to start proceedings without legal assistance. Nevertheless, the use of the small claims procedure has expanded. Although they form only a small part of the vast number of cases handled in the county courts, in 1989 cases involving small claims represented just under 50,000 of the total number of cases dealt with (this figure was 5,000 in 1974).

The most thorough recent review of the procedure was that carried out by the Civil Justice Review which reported in 1986. This found that most litigants were more than satisfied with the process and would be happy to use it again. It was praised for being able to produce results with the minimum of delay and costs and for being an 'easier' process. But there were criticisms, such as the lack of uniform procedure (discussed above) leading to prejudice. It was also proposed that the pre-trial hearing should be abolished and instead everything should be dealt with at one hearing, the date being fixed by the courts rather than waiting for the parties to declare their readiness.

Although this might have the practical effect of allowing minimum time in court and therefore minimum expense for the parties, it also suggests moves towards a more rigid administrative procedure, which would defeat the original objects of the system. Another suggestion was that while the right to representation should remain, representation should be able to be by anyone, not just a lawyer. Again, this offers scope to the litigant, but may also encourage and worsen the kind of problems encountered in *Chiltern* and *Pepper*. The major problem the Review found with small claims arbitration was, in fact, the lack of enforcement procedures within the system. While many plaintiffs were 'successful' before the judge, they never received the remedy awarded unless they commenced new and separate county court enforcement proceedings.

The National Association of Citizens' Advice Bureaux (NACAB) felt the Review had been too complacent in its report. It said that the machinery of justice, even in small claims procedure, remains too slow and cumbersome. It felt that there were not just slight variations in procedure between courts, but huge differences with some allowing lay representatives, some not. NACAB also criticised the training, or lack of it, of the District Judges. It suggested that the use of experienced, outside arbitrators should be encouraged and there should be unrestricted rights of audience, ie lay or legal representatives should be allowed. It also said that costs still remained a severe deterrent.

Similarly, the National Consumer Council was not without criticism for the system it had been instrumental in bringing about. It found the county courts still had a forbidding and unapproachable image, and many people with unresolved disputes did not use the system. It confirmed that the process was not in fact as informal as it should be and agreed that litigants should be allowed access to any representative. It also proposed a new arbitration code written in clear, layman's English.

The government's response to the Review has been limited. The Courts and Legal Services Act 1990 attempted to answer some of these complaints. New rules will be allowed to prescribe the procedures and rules of evidence to be followed, and it is envisaged that any new rules will allow a District Judge to take a more inquisitorial approach as recommended by the Civil Justice Review. A statutory right to have a chosen lay representative has also been introduced under the Act.

However, these new proposals leave many problems unresolved. Lack of enforcement of judgments remains a problem; those still fearful of the courts have been given nothing to reassure them, and the potential introduction of rules on procedure may detract from the informal (and theoretically inexpensive) process originally envisaged. While reforms may be introduced, the criticisms seem to suggest that, in practice, small claims procedure is not solving the problems it was introduced to remedy. The need for an informal and inexpensive process has still not been satisfied.

14 ENFORCEMENT OF JUDGMENTS

14.1 Introduction

There is a variety of methods available for enforcing judgments. The method chosen depends very much on the remedy the court has provided. The enforcement of judgments in both the High Court and the county court will be considered.

A HIGH COURT ENFORCEMENT

14.2 Key points

a) *Money judgments*

Where the court gives judgment in the form of money, it is recoverable as a debt. This debt is payable from the date of judgment. There are various methods of enforcing these judgments:

i) Fieri facias ('Fi fa')

This is a writ issued under Ord 47 of the Rules of the Supreme Court. It directs the sheriff to seize and sell the debtor's goods (see s15(1) of the Courts and Legal Services Act 1990) to pay the judgment debt. This writ is generally used to recover small amounts of money.

ii) Charging order

These orders may be absolute or conditional, the latter to allow the debtor to explain his failure to pay. The order gives the plaintiff the right to be paid his debt out of specific property: see RSC Ord 50.

iii) Garnishee proceedings

A garnishee order operates to assign debts of the debtor to the creditor. The most common debt which is garnisheed is the debtor's bank account: see RSC Ord 49.

iv) Appointment of a receiver

A receiver is appointed to obtain profits arising out of the debtor's assets to pay the judgment creditor: see RSC Ord 51.

v) Bankruptcy proceedings

The creditor may serve a notice on the debtor requiring him to pay the debt by a certain date. If he does not he commits an act of bankruptcy. After this a petition of bankruptcy may be filed. Generally used as a last resort.

b) *Other judgments*

i) Writ of delivery

This writ can either be general or specific.

- General: judgment orders delivery of goods with an alternative of payment of the value of the goods.
- Specific: here there is no alternative and the specific goods can be seized by the sheriff and delivered to the creditor.

See RSC Ord 45.

ii) Writ of possession

Used to allow the plaintiff to take possession of land.

iii) Sequestration

Where a judgment orders a time limit to be complied with to perform or refrain from acting, the plaintiff may issue a writ of sequestration if the defendant does not comply. The writ allows sequestrators to enter the property and to take its profits and to detain the property until the order is obeyed.

The plaintiff cannot issue such a writ without leave of the court. Before leave will be granted:

- a copy of the judgment or order must be served on the defendant;
- this will be endorsed with a penal notice, which informs the defendant of the consequences of non-compliance.

See RSC Ord 45.

iv) Committal

The court may imprison or fine a defendant for failing to obey an order. The defendant is said to be committed for contempt.

B COUNTY COURT ENFORCEMENT

14.3 Key points

Enforcement in the county court is very similar to High Court enforcement. There are however some differences in the manner in which the orders function.

a) In the county court, the debtor has 14 days from judgment to pay his debt.

b) The county court may permit payment by instalments: CCR Ord 22.

c) The warrant of execution which is carried out by the bailiff is equivalent to 'fi fa' in the High Court: see CCR Ord 26.

d) Attachment of earnings is provided for by the CCR Ord 27. This order requires the debtor's employers to make deductions from his salary to satisfy judgment.

14.4 Analysis of questions

Past examination questions in this area have all tended to be straightforward. They have required students to list and explain the enforcement procedures available in each court and to distinguish them. The impact of the Courts and Legal Services Act 1990 is likely to feature in future questions.

14.5 Question

How can judgments of the High Court and county courts be enforced? What methods are unique to each jurisdiction?

University of London LLB Examination
(for External Students) English Legal System June 1986 Q4

General comment

This is a very straightforward question which appears on the External LLB paper at regular intervals. Your answer needs to be arranged logically and to examine the various methods of enforcing judgments in both the High Court and the county court. You need to consider the means of enforcing judgments for money first, and then proceed to discuss the range of remedies for non monetary judgments. Unlike many previous questions of this type which have required simply a discussion of the different methods of enforcing judgments in the High Court and the county court, this question specifically asks the student to point out which methods are unique to each jurisdiction. Students should take care to answer every part of the question and must therefore make sure that the answer to the latter part of the question is provided. Extra marks may, perhaps, be awarded to students who remember the order numbers of particular rules, but this is probably not essential.

Skeleton solution

a) Enforcement of money judgments

- Fieri facias (High Court): RSC Ord 47; execution by sheriff; exempt property; disadvantages.

- Warrant of execution (county court): CCR Ord 26; execution by bailiff; discretionary.
- Garnishee: available in both courts – RSC Ord 49, CCR Ord 30; charge over debts; financial limits.
- Charging orders: RSC Ord 50, available on both courts; effect, charge on property.
- Attachment of earnings: Attachment of Earnings Act 1971 and CCR Ord 27; protected earning rate; payment by employer; disadvantages.
- Bankruptcy proceedings: mainly High Court jurisdiction; vesting of property in trustees; order of payments.
- Equitable receiverships: RSC Ord 52, CCR Ord 29; effect of legacies, trust funds, etc; advantages.

b) Non-monetary judgments

- Committal orders: available in both courts – Contempt of Court Act 1981 s14; used to enforce injunctions; effect – imprisonment or fine.
- Writ of delivery (High Court); warrant of delivery (county court): sheriff to seize goods for delivery to plaintiff.
- Writ of possession (High Court); warrant of possession (county court): effect to give plaintiff possession of land.
- Sequestration RSC Ord 46: only available in the High Court; effect – sequestrators to take possession of the defendant's real and personal property.

Suggested solution

Obviously not all judgments need enforcing. Some judgment debtors will settle up with good grace, particularly if the judgment debtor is insured and the defence has been conducted by his insurers. Unfortunately, however, this is not always the case, and the successful party must decide how best to enforce the judgment which has been entered in either the High Court or the county court.

Assuming therefore that enforcement has not been stayed pending an appeal against that judgment, the 'judgment creditor' (as the successful party is now called) has a wide variety of methods of enforcing the court's order. We will first consider the methods for enforcing judgments for money, and then the methods for enforcing judgment for specific relief such as injunctions.

a) *Enforcement of money judgments*

A money judgment will attract interest at the rate prescribed for the time being under the Judgments Act 1838 on any outstanding unpaid amount. The judgment bears from the date it is entered in the court records until the date it is finally satisfied.

Writ of fieri facias (High Court): warrant of execution (county court):

The writ of fieri facias is a remedy granted under Ord 47 of the Rules of the Supreme Court 1965. It is a form of enforcement against the debtor's goods and chattels, and is issued to the sheriff of the county in which is situated the property which it is proposed to seize.

The writ commands the sheriff to cause to be made (fieri facias) out of the debtor's goods and chattels a sum sufficient to satisfy the judgment debt and interest plus the costs of execution. The sheriff is entitled to enter land not only of the judgment debtor, but also of a third party if the debtor's goods are to be found there, and seize and sell goods and chattels including choses in action (ie bank notes and cheques) and even a lease belonging to the judgment debtor. The sheriff may not, however, effect a forcible entry (*Vaughan* v *McKenzie* (1969)), although once inside he may break down internal doors to reach the goods.

Certain property is exempt from execution and cannot be seized, for example, a freehold interest in land, equitable interests in land or chattels, fixtures attached to land, clothing and tools of the judgment debtor's trade to a certain value (Small Debts Act 1845 s8 as amended) and goods which are the property of a third party.

The sheriff is normally an auctioneer and valuer appointed by the court, and he must make arrangements for the sale of the property seized. It is usually sold by public auction and the sale should not take place on the judgment debtor's premises: Ord 47 r6.

Often the goods are left in the possession of the judgment debtor subject to periodic inspection by the sheriff's officers. This arrangement, which is termed 'walking possession', is a good idea in practice since very often the judgment debtor will pay the debt to avoid sale of his property.

Leave of the court is unnecessary in order for this writ to be issued if it is issued within six years of the judgment order. Thereafter, leave of the court is necessary: Ord 45 r2(1)(a).

The biggest problem with the writ of fieri facias is that goods rarely fetch their full value at a forced sale by auction and a second writ becomes necessary.

This method is not unique to the High Court since the county court has a near equivalent remedy under Ord 26 of the County Court Rules 1981, the warrant of execution. However, it is generally agreed in practice that execution by a sheriff's officers in the High Court is more effective than execution by a bailiff in the county court. This is probably because sheriff's officers are paid to some extent on commission and are consequently more persistent than the county court bailiffs. Sheriffs often end up persuading the debtor to pay, thus avoiding the expense and delay of seizure and sale, whilst the bailiff is often inexperienced in valuing goods and seizes too little to satisfy the judgment debt.

The issue of the warrant of execution is at the discretion of the court.

Garnishee proceedings:

This is another remedy which is available in both the High Court and the county court. It may be used as an alternative, or an addition to execution against goods, and is available if the judgment debtor is himself the creditor of another. A garnishee order is an order that the debtor of the judgment debtor should pay the amount owed to the judgment creditor. In the High Court this is governed by Ord 49 of the Rules of the Supreme Court 1965, and in the county court by Ord 30 of the County Court Rules. Garnishee proceedings cannot be taken in the High Court on a judgment for a sum less than £50 or its foreign equivalent, and in the county court the minimum judgment sum is £25.

The judgment debtor may have to attend before a master for oral examination as to what debts are owing to him. After this, the judgment creditor may apply ex parte by affidavit for an order nisi which is served on the garnishee and on the judgment debtor. The order binds the debt specified in the order from the moment of service of the order. The order commands the garnishee to pay the debt to the judgment creditor. The order nisi makes it a contempt of court for the garnishee to pay it to the judgment debtor.

At a second hearing the order will be made absolute unless the garnishee or judgment debtor show cause why it should not be so. Once the order is made absolute, execution will issue against the garnishee if the attached debt is not paid to the judgment creditor (ie the judgment creditor may sue the garnishee for it as if it had always been owed to him).

The remedy of a garnishee order is also available in the county court and the proceedings differ from the High Court in that the hearings are before the registrar rather than the master.

This kind of proceeding is useful if the judgment debtor is solvent, a bank account being the obvious target, or if he at least has debts owed to him. If he is not solvent there are further options open to the judgment creditor.

Charging order: RSC Ord 50:

Charging orders are available in both the High Court and the county court and the differences between the two procedures are very few.

The judgment creditor may apply ex parte on affidavit for an order imposing a charge on property of the kind specified in s2 Charging Orders Act 1979. This includes things like any interest held by the debtor beneficially in land and securities of various kinds and any interest under a trust. An order may also be made charging a partnership interest. There is a hearing for an order nisi and a subsequent hearing for order absolute.

The effect of such orders is to give the judgment creditor priority over unsecured creditors of the judgment debtor. The order charges the debtor's interest in the relevant property, giving the creditor security for the judgment, but no immediate money. If granted over interests in land, the charge so created is a general equitable charge and the judgment creditor should register it in the Land Charges Registry under the provisions of the Land Charges Act 1925. A land charge may be enforced by an order for sale in the Chancery Division: Ord 31 r1, ie he may wish to turn it into cash. The court is wary of ordering sale of land if it comprises the matrimonial home in which the debtor's family and children are still living. If sale is delayed, however, interest on the judgment debt will continue to accrue.

Attachment of earnings:

This is governed by the Attachment of Earnings Act 1971 and County Court Rules, Ord 27. It has been described as a kind of garnishee proceedings to attach 'future debts' payable by an employer.

Attachment of earnings is available both in the High Court and the county court, but the order is limited in the High Court to judgment for the payment of periodic maintenance in domestic proceedings in the Family Division. For all other High Court money judgments, transfer to the county court is necessary before the order can be obtained.

To obtain an attachment of earnings order the judgment creditor must apply to the county court for the district in which the debtor resides. A questionnaire is sent to the judgment debtor, and sometimes to his employer, which must be completed, giving details of his employment, pay and financial liabilities. This information will enable the court to calculate what sum he should pay per week or per month from his net earnings. This sum is called the 'normal deduction rate'.

The court will also specify a 'protected earnings rate' which is the amount which the court decides the debtor must be allowed to retain out of his earnings in any event. It will normally be a sum equal to the sum the debtor would receive for himself and his family if he were on supplementary benefit.

The normal deduction rate will be paid into court by the employer unless in any period the debtor's earnings fall below the protected earnings rate, in which case only so much as will leave the debtor with that sum in his hands is paid in.

Both the debtor and the employer have a duty to notify the court of any cesser or change in the debtor's employment.

The major drawback of this remedy is that the creditor may have to wait a considerable time for the full amount of the debt to be paid. Obviously, the larger the debt, the longer the judgment creditor may have to wait.

Bankruptcy proceedings: Bankruptcy Act 1914; Companies Act 1985:

This is probably the least satisfactory method of enforcement, although often the mere threat of bankruptcy proceedings may cause the judgment debtor to pay up. In the case of a debtor who is a company registered by the English Companies Act the appropriate procedure is a winding-up by the court.

The High Court has jurisdiction in all cases, but not all county courts have bankruptcy jurisdiction. It is, however, possible to bring the proceedings in a court other than that in which the judgment was obtained.

The procedure is that a bankruptcy notice must be issued by the court for the bankruptcy district in which the judgment debtor resided or carried on business for the most part of the six months immediately preceding the notice. If payment is not forthcoming, a bankruptcy or winding-up petition may be presented. If granted, the property vests in a trustee in bankruptcy or a liquidator, and is applied first in paying the secured creditors, the costs of the administration of the assets, the preferential creditors, the secured creditors and then the shareholders.

Equitable receiverships: RSC Ord 52; CCR Ord 29:

This remedy is available in both the High Court and the county court. It is a particularly useful method since it reaches property other methods cannot reach, such as a legacy, income under a trust fund, or income from a business the debtor owns in partnership with others. The application in the High Court is under the Rules of the Supreme Court, Ord 51 and in the county court under the County Court Rules, Ord 32.

This remedy is of great value against judgment debtors who do not presently have funds to pay the debt, but who may well have at some future date.

The court may appoint a receiver to wait until the future property falls due, to step in and receive it instead of the debtor, and to pay the amount of the judgment debt out of it to the creditor, remitting any balance to the debtor. This procedure prevents the debtor being tempted to squander the money to the detriment of the creditor.

It will be noticed that whilst some of the methods of enforcement of judgments discussed above differ slightly between the High Court, and the county court, none of them is unique to either jurisdiction.

b) *Non-monetary judgments*

There are methods of enforcement of judgments where the judgment is for the doing or refraining from doing some specific act.

Committal orders:

A committal order is an order committing a person to prison for contempt of court. An order may be made where a person required by a judgment or order to do an act within a time specified refuses or neglects to do it in time, or a person disobeys a judgment or order requiring him to abstain from doing an act.

The order must be made by a judge. Examples of situations in which such an order might be made are if the judgment consists of an injunction to abate a nuisance or to refrain from breaching a contract.

The order, when served on the defendant, must be endorsed with a 'penal notice' warning him of the consequences of disobedience. He will be brought before the court on a motion for committal which will lay him open to an unlimited fine and up to two years' imprisonment: Contempt of Court Act 1981 s14.

This remedy is available in both the High Court and the county court.

Writ of delivery (High Court); warrant of delivery (county court):

This is appropriate where the judgment orders the delivery of goods with an alternative provision for payment of their assessed value. The writ directs the sheriff to seize the appropriate goods and deliver them to the plaintiff, and if this is not possible, to levy execution upon goods and chattels of the defendant to realise the assessed value of the goods.

Writ of possession (High Court); warrant of possession (county court):

This writ directs the sheriff to enter the land and cause the plaintiff to have possession of it. Sometimes there are penalties for contempt in refusing the court's officer entry to premises or access to property.

Sequestration: RSC Ord 46:

This remedy is unique to the High Court, and it will be noticed that it is the only remedy so far discussed which is not available in some form in the county court as well as the High Court.

This is a form of contempt proceedings which will result in a sequestration order if the defendant has repeatedly and wilfully disobeyed a specific order.

Application is made to a judge by motion for leave to issue a writ of sequestration which is a writ appointing four sequestrators, and directing them to take possession of all the defendant's real and personal property, and to keep it until the contempt is purged. The court may apply the property for the benefit of the judgment creditor: RSC Ord 45 r5.

15 CRIMINAL AND CIVIL APPEALS

15.1 Introduction

Decisions of lower courts may in certain circumstances be challenged in the higher courts. This chapter will deal with appeals from the magistrates' and Crown Courts and with appeals from the county and High Courts.

A CRIMINAL APPEALS

15.2 Key points

a) *Appeals from the magistrates' court*

i) Appeals to the Crown Court

The defendant may appeal as of right, if he pleaded guilty, against his sentence and if he pleaded not guilty, against his conviction. The prosecution may not appeal against an acquittal.

The procedure:

- notice of appeal must be given within 21 days of decision or sentence;
- the notice must contain the grounds of appeal;
- an appeal is treated as a re-hearing.

The powers of the Crown Court – it may:

- confirm, reverse or vary the decision;
- remit the case with an opinion to the magistrates' court;
- make any order it thinks just.

ii) Appeals to the High Court

These may be made by way of case stated by any party to the proceedings or any aggrieved party. The appeal may be made on the grounds that the decision was wrong in law or made in excess of jurisdiction.

The procedure:

- application is made to the justices' clerk to state a case for the opinion of the High Court;
- the application must be made within 21 days and once made, any rights of appeal to the Crown Court are lost;
- the justices' clerk can refuse to state a case where it is frivolous;
- a draft is sent to all parties and it must state the question of law or jurisdiction on which guidance is sought.

The powers of the High Court – on appeal it may:

- reverse, affirm or amend the decision;
- remit to the magistrates' court for reconsideration in the light of the court's opinion;
- make such order as it thinks fit, eg, order a re-hearing by the same or a different bench: *Griffith* v *Jenkins* [1992] 1 All ER 65.

iii) Appeals from the High Court to the House of Lords

The defence or prosecution may appeal to the House of Lords on a point of law or an issue of general importance. Leave must be obtained from either court. The House of Lords can make whatever order it thinks fit, including remitting the case to the High Court.

b) *Appeals from the Crown Court*

The prosecution has no right of appeal against an acquittal by a jury, however perverse the verdict. The defendant tried on indictment may appeal to the Court of Appeal. The appeal may be made against the conviction and/or sentence.

i) Appeals against conviction

Where the ground of appeal is in relation to a question of law alone, appeal is as of right. The following procedure must be followed:

- notice of appeal must be given within 28 days of conviction to the registrar of criminal appeals;
- the notice must contain the grounds of appeal;
- the registrar may refer the appeal for summary determination if he finds there are no substantial grounds for appeal;

- a court may dismiss an appeal if it considers it to be frivolous or vexatious.

Where the appeal against conviction is based on fact alone or mixed law and fact a certificate from the trial judge must be obtained as must leave from the Court of Appeal:

- the certificate and notice of appeal must be served on the registrar;
- this will be considered by a single judge;
- if refused the application can be renewed in 14 days.

The powers of the Court of Appeal are provided for by s2 of the Criminal Appeal Act 1968. The court can allow the appeal if it thinks that:

- the verdict of the jury is unsafe and unsatisfactory (see *R* v *Lee* [1984] 1 All ER 1080);
- the decision is wrong on a question of law; or
- there was some material irregularity in the course of trial.

The court may also dismiss an appeal if no miscarriage of justice has actually occurred: see s2(1) Criminal Appeal Act 1968.

The Royal Commission on Criminal Justice has proposed:

- that legal aid should be available for drafting grounds of appeal;
- the present grounds should be replaced by a single broad ground, eg 'that the conviction is or may be unsafe'. This would give the court flexibility to consider all categories of appeal.

ii) Appeals against sentence

A person convicted may appeal against sentence (other than a sentence fixed by law) provided that leave is obtained from the Court of Appeal or from the judge who passed the sentence: see ss9, 11 Criminal Appeal Act 1968. The Court of Appeal will only alter a sentence if it is wrong in principle.

Section 36 of the Criminal Justice Act 1988 allows the prosecution to appeal to the Court of Appeal against an unduly lenient sentence. On review the Court of Appeal may:

- quash any sentence; and
- pass an appropriate sentence within the power of the Crown Court.

c) *Appeals from the Court of Appeal to the House of Lords*

i) Both the defence and prosecution may appeal to the House of Lords provided the Court of Appeal certifies a point of law of general public importance. Leave must be obtained from the Court of Appeal or House of Lords.

ii) The following procedure must be followed:

- the application for leave to appeal must be made 14 days after the Court of Appeal's decision;
- if the certificate is refused, the matter cannot be taken further;
- if the leave is granted the petition of appeal is generally made within three months;
- the House of Lords may exercise the powers of the Court of Appeal or remit the case to the Court of Appeal.

d) *Home Secretary's reference*

Where all rights of appeal have been exhausted, a case may be re-examined by the Home Secretary. This re-examination is aimed at the correction of alleged miscarriages of justice.

i) Following summary conviction

The only power available to the Home Secretary is the exercise of the royal prerogative of mercy. This is very rarely used.

ii) Following conviction on indictment

Section 17 of the Criminal Appeal Act 1968 may be used by the Home Secretary to refer a case to the Court of Appeal.

- This power is exercised when the Home Secretary 'thinks fit'.
- There must usually be fresh evidence or some other consideration of substance which was not previously before the court.
- Very few cases are referred in this way, but it was used in the 'miscarriage of justice' cases recently in the media, eg the Birmingham Six, the Guildford Four, etc.

iii) The Runciman Commission on Criminal Justice has proposed that the power should be taken away from the Home Secretary and given to a new independent authority. This body would be made up of lawyers, lay persons and specialist advisers, answerable to Parliament and have powers to direct investigations.

B CIVIL APPEALS

15.3 Key points

a) *Appeals from the county and High Courts to the Court of Appeal*

These will be discussed in conjunction as the procedure is similar.

i) Appeal is generally as of right and may be brought by any party to the proceedings. Appeal may be based on questions of fact, discretion or law.

ii) The procedure:

- the appellant must serve notice of appeal on all parties;
- the notice must specify grounds of appeal, and include the type of order which the appellant requires;
- this must be served four weeks from judgment date.

iii) The Court of Appeal is generally reluctant to disturb findings of fact. In relation to other discretionary matters, the court will only interfere if the judge erred in law and it is satisfied the decision was wrong.

b) *Appeals from the High Court to the House of Lords*

i) This process of appeal is also known as 'leap-frogging' as the Court of Appeal is being bypassed. This is only possible if the following conditions are fulfilled:

- the appeal concerns a point of law of general public importance;
- the point of law relates to the construction of a statute or the Court of Appeal is bound by its own decision or a later House of Lords decision;
- the parties all consent to this 'leap-frog'.

ii) The application for a certificate must be made within 14 days. If it is refused no appeal is allowable. Where the certificate is granted application for leave must be made within one month.

c) *Appeals from the Court of Appeal to the House of Lords*

i) Appeal lies from any judgment of the Court of Appeal. Leave must be obtained. No appeal lies if the Court of Appeal refuses leave; however, a petition for leave may be made to the House of Lords.

ii) The petition for leave may be made to the House of Lords. It will be heard by the Appeal Committee consisting of three Law Lords. This petition must be lodged within a month. If leave is refused no reason is given. Any appeal must be lodged in three months.

15.4 Analysis of questions

The emphasis of most past examination questions in this area has been on the effectiveness of the current appeal system to redress miscarriages of justice. In the light of recent cases concerning the Guildford and Birmingham pub bombings, it is unlikely that this pattern of questioning will alter.

15.5 Questions

Question 1

Is the present system of appeals in criminal cases designed to correct mistakes or to prevent injustice?

University of London LLB Examination
(for External Students) English Legal System June 1988 Q7

General comment

Your opinion is asked for; is the criminal justice system in this country, in relation to appeals, as foolproof as people say it is? There are many mistakes, as recent cases have shown, and you have to say why this is. Does the present system admit miscarriages of justice only where the defence show that mistakes have occurred, or does it truly extend to cases where the conviction appears unsatisfactory?

Skeleton solution

- Recent cases – Birmingham Six, Guildford Four.
- Role of the jury.
- Reluctance of Court of Appeal to interfere in jury decisions.
- Types of mistake – evidential and legal.
- System of available appeals.
- Impact of the Criminal Appeal Act 1968.
- Discretion of courts to overturn convictions or refuse appeals.

Suggested solution

There has been some dissatisfaction with the criminal appeals system recently, in particular, with cases such as the Birmingham and Guildford pub bombers. The 'Birmingham Six's' initial appeal was heard in 1987 and resulted in the Court of Appeal upholding the jury's guilty verdict. The subsequent reference back to the Court of Appeal has resulted in their release.

Lord Scarman lent his support to the 'Guildford Four' case and pressure was put on the Home Secretary to refer their case back to the Court of Appeal. They have also subsequently been released. In his article in *The Times* on Tuesday 5 March 1991, Lord Scarman made a number of suggestions for reform, one of which was the setting up of a court of review to deal with such cases. Furthermore, he indicated he was in favour of the establishment of greater judicial control in pre-trial investigations.

Behind all these cases is a doubt over the present appeals system, so does it work? One thing is clear and that is that juries are not infallible; they do make mistakes and research has shown that this may be in a higher percentage of cases than people would think. The question is; how good are the courts at recognising these mistakes? It is clear that under the present system heavy reliance is placed on the jury who are the sole judges of fact (unless part of the evidence is ruled inadmissible by the judge), and as they are the only people who have heard all the evidence and seen the witnesses give their evidence, the Court of Appeal will be very reluctant to interfere with their verdict. However, while this is true to a large extent, heavy reliance is also placed on the other components of a fair trial in our system; the judge in fairly summing up the evidence and excluding inadmissible evidence, and the prosecuting authorities and defence solicitors and counsel in ensuring that all witnesses are brought forward to give evidence and cross-examined about all aspects of their evidence with which the defence disagree. The need for all these components to be properly used means that there is a fair degree of scope for human error, if they are not.

Two types of mistake are covered by the present criminal appeals system, mistakes of evidence or law which are corrected by way of an appeal against conviction and mistakes of sentence which are of course corrected by an appeal against sentence. An appeal from conviction in the magistrates' court will lie to the Crown Court on the facts and will be dealt with by way of rehearing. Appeals against sentence also lie to the Crown Court. Appeals against a legal finding of the magistrates' court and against the lower court deciding a case on the wrong basis go to the High Court by way of 'case stated' and one of the prerogative orders will be issued if the appeal is successful. This will direct the lower court to rehear the case including some matter that they did not previously hear or direct them to consider the case on a basis other than on the one that they previously heard it on.

There is little dissatisfaction with appeals against sentence. Appeals against conviction from the magistrates' court are generally a fair airing of the defendant's grievance because the Crown Court judge hears the evidence again though in absence of a jury (although there may be concern in individual cases that the judge has allowed himself to be 'coloured' by the verdict of the lower court). The main concern is in the case of appeals to the Court of Appeal against conviction in the Crown Court.

In these cases appeals are under the Criminal Appeal Act 1968 and the rules made pursuant to that Act. Appeals are usually dealt with by way of submissions by counsel made on the basis of the transcript of the trial which is obtained prior to appeal. Such submissions will be based on the judge's exclusion of any defence evidence and more importantly the judge's summing-up. Also the Court of Appeal will consider any comments the trial judge made during the course of the trial tending to show bias to the prosecution rather than the defence, particularly any comments to the jury, as they are the sole triers of fact.

How well this system works can only be asked in individual cases and generalisation about how good the Court of Appeal are at preventing injustice are difficult to make. It would clearly not be possible to rehear the evidence in every case, or every convict would try and have a second go at getting the result he would have preferred to have seen in the first place. This would be a particularly strong temptation in criminal cases because in the large majority of cases the defendant is publicly funded. Such a procedure would be wasteful of the court's time and of public money therefore. What one can say by way of generalisation is that under the present system a very small number of appeals are successful and the Court of Appeal do appear to be mainly concerned with correcting specific mistakes by the trial judge. They generally take a robust view of appeals.

However, they do have a discretion in all cases to overturn a conviction in all cases where it is 'unsafe or unsatisfactory' and this is generally thought to mean cases in which they have a 'lingering doubt' in their minds: *R* v *Cooper* (1969).

But the court may still refuse the appeal where they believe no miscarriage of justice has occurred. However, in difficult cases, it ought to be the duty of the Home Secretary to either re-refer it to the Court of Appeal or release the convicts on the basis that on the evidence before him a real doubt exists over the veracity of the conviction. Perhaps greater vigilance should exist in cases of this kind by the Home Secretary. The Royal Commission on Criminal Justice (Cm 2263), chaired by Lord Runciman, which reported in July 1993, proposed that this duty should be transferred to a new independent body of lawyers, laymen and specialist advisers, answerable to Parliament.

The widely reported miscarriages of justice, which prompted the Commission's formation, may lead one to believe that the system is beyond repair. However, there are many less sensational cases, in which the Court of Appeal are successful in preventing injustice.

Question 2

'The system of appeals in criminal cases guarantees that no mistakes are left uncorrected, but is generally unconcerned with remedying injustices as such.'

Discuss.

University of London LLB Examination
(for External Students) English Legal System June 1990 Q1

General comment

This question requires a thorough knowledge of the basic appeal procedures, but in order to obtain a good mark candidates must also consider the second phrase of the question regarding injustice.

Skeleton solution

- Introduction – basic approach of appeals.
- Appeal procedures.
- Commentary and discussions:
  - problems of present system;
  - proposals for change.

Suggested solution

Broadly speaking, no man who has lost his case in the court of first instance is disposed to let the matter rest there, whether the court has got its law wrong or misinterpreted the facts. His discontent at being the loser in litigation is requited only by the fact that he can get the verdict rectified. Even the realistic 'loser', who is advised that the prospect of quashing the decision is remote, may cling to the vain hope of reversal of the decision.

The basic problem that faces any legislature in providing a criminal appellate system is twofold: (a) to ensure the correction of wrongful convictions and (b) that the due process at trial has been complied with. To rectify the improper conclusions of the trial court, that is to undo the miscarriage of justice, presents a straightforward issue of judgment about the validity of the trial product. But to quash a conviction due to errors in the trial procedure without any power to order re-trial, may produce results more favourable than many appellants actually deserve. Hence, appellate courts in the criminal field are inclined to condone some errors in the trial process so as to avoid what they perceive to be unjust acquittals of perfectly guilty offenders.

The system of appeals nevertheless offers some, though not perfect, relief from what some regard as injustice.

An appeal may lie from the Magistrates' Court to the Crown Court or, by way of case stated, to the Divisional Court of the Queen's Bench Division. If D pleaded guilty an appeal lies from the Magistrates Court to the Crown Court against sentence only. If D pleaded not guilty he can appeal to the Crown Court against either conviction or sentence or both (Magistrates Courts Act 1980, s108(1)). An appeal to the Crown Court takes the form of a complete rehearing of the case with witnessess but without a jury. The Crown Court has power to confirm, reverse, or vary the decision, and may impose a sentence which the Magistrates' Court could have imposed, whether more or less severe than that actually inflicted. It is anomalous that the Crown Court can increase sentence whereas the Court of Appeal cannot.

As an alternative to appealing to the Crown Court, an appeal may sometimes be taken direct to the Queen's Bench Divisional Court, by way of case stated from the Magistrates' Court. This procedure is only available where it is alleged that the decision is wrong in law or was given in excess of jurisdiction – note that a decision may be wrong in law because of a perverse finding on the facts (see post).

A further appeal to the House of Lords may be made from the Queen's Bench Division. In order to do so, leave from either court must be given *and* a point of law of general public importance must be involved.

Against conviction in the Crown Court, D may appeal as of right to the Court of Appeal on a question of law. But on a question of fact or a mixed question of fact and law, leave of the Court of Appeal is required.

Appeal against sentence of the Crown Court, D may appeal to the Court of Appeal with leave of the Court of Appeal. No appeal is possible against a sentence which is fixed by law (Criminal Appeal Act 1968, ss9 & 11).

However, s36 of the Criminal Justice Act 1988 allows the prosecution to appeal to the Court of Appeal against an unduly lenient sentence. This allows the Court of Appeal to quash the original sentence and replace it with an appropriate sentence for the facts. This power, known as an Attorney-General's reference, has been used in cases where there has been a public outcry at the lenience of the trial judge's decision. Such a reference in the case may go some way to remedy what certain people, if not D, would perceive as an injustice.

A further appeal from the Court of Appeal to the House of Lords lies if leave is granted and a question of law of general public importance is involved.

Our system of appeals is deficient in one important respect, which is unfortunately a necessary corollary of our trial system. Magistrates very seldom give any reasons when they decide to convict. Nor do a jury when delivering their guilty verdict. We are not told, although of course we can often infer, why the decision was guilty or not guilty.

Lewis Blom-Cooper QC in *The Changing Nature of the Appellate Process* (Lawson Lectures 1981-85) points out a further problem – TIME. The appeal process is very time consuming. He asks the question: should an appeal be by way of documentation, or an appeal by oral pleading? Foreign courts give a good deal of consideration to documents and written submissions drawn up and submitted in advance by Counsel. The English system has been habitually a process of oratory. A good deal of time is thus expended in developing arguments. Since 1983 the Court of Appeal has been encouraged to prepare a short document in advance of the hearing outlining the issues and the scope of the appeal. This has saved judicial time but perhaps does not save enough judicial time.

It should be noted that only one in three applications for leave to appeal in criminal cases is granted. In cases of appeal against conviction and sentence, less than 5 per cent are successful. Seventy five per cent of appeals against sentence only are wholly or partially successful.

Over the years the Court of Appeal has been criticised for failing to correct cases of apparent miscarriage of justice by taking an unduly restrictive view of its role and placing, in practice, far too great a burden on the appellant to prove his innocence. In particular, the Court has been attacked for being loath to accept that evidence unearthed since the trial might have influenced the jury towards acquittal if they had heard it – see for example the recent cases of the 'Birmingham Six' and the 'Guildford Four'.

Further, the appellant is at a great disadvantage because the Court will not interfere with a guilty verdict on the grounds that his lawyer handled the case badly, or used wrong tactics. So if for example his counsel failed to call a particular witness for the defence who should have been called, the accused is stuck with that decision.

There is also an unfortunate grey area between the functions of the Home Secretary, who can release prisoners before the end of their sentences and grant free pardons if convinced of their innocence, and the Court of Appeal with its different standards and procedures. Prisoners claiming their innocence can be shuttled between the two, gaining satisfaction from neither. Recently in the light of a number of cases of alleged miscarriage, there have been calls for a new body, or new procedures, to allow another look at questionable verdicts without the straitjacket of the present stringent criteria laid down by the Appeal Court.

Dissatisfaction with the facilities provided by English law for the correction of miscarriages of justice has been growing in recent years. Section 17 of the Criminal Appeal Act 1968 which confers a discretion upon the Home Secretary to refer a case for review by the Court of Appeal at any time, is a useful provision. However, it has two serious limitations. First, the Home Secretary appears reluctant to refer cases and whether he does so may depend too much on the amount of pressure exerted on him by people of influence. Secondly, the Court of Appeal appears reluctant to allow an appeal under s17 when it has already dismissed a normal appeal in the same case.

There is also disquiet over the absence of any entitlement to compensation on the part of those persons who have been wrongly convicted of over the lack of independence in the assessment of ex gratia awards. In 1982, Justice, the British section of the International Commission of Jurists, proposed that anyone who was granted a free pardon by the Home Secretary, or whose conviction was quashed by the Court of Appeal following a reference under s17, should have an automatic right to compensation. It was suggested, moreover, that the compensation should be assessed by an independent tribunal (the 'Imprisonment Compensation Board') operating on similar lines to the Criminal Injuries Compensation Board.

The House of Commons Select Committee on Home Affairs proposed several fundamental changes. The setting up of a review body to investigate alleged miscarriages of justice was recommended. The review body would be independent of the Home Office and would consist of up to twelve members, under a legally qualified chairman, appointed by the Home Secretary or the Attorney General.

More recently, the Runciman Commission on Criminal Justice (Cm 2263) which reported in July 1993 suggested that the Home Secretary's power should be transferred to a new independent authority made up of lawyers, lay persons and specialist advisers. It has also been suggested that the grounds of appeal should be simplified into one broad ground 'that the conviction is or may be unsafe'. However, such a broad approach would only be effective if the Court of Appeal judges were actually prepared to use such a new found flexibility.

It remains to be seen how far, if at all, the government will adopt these reforms. So far, there has been little comment on the Commission's proposals, though some have been completely contradicted by proposed legislation (eg the abolition of the right of silence in the current Criminal Justice Bill). However, pressure continues to grow, from all quarters, for change. Reform is, therefore, essential if the criminal appellate process is to retain some of the dignity conferred on it by the English legal system.

16 THE LEGAL PROFESSION

16.1 Introduction

The legal profession in England and Wales is a divided profession with both barristers and solicitors. There has been much debate as to whether the system should be retained in its present form or be fused. This chapter will consider in outline the functions of each branch profession and finally will consider the reforms to the system.

16.2 Key points

a) *Solicitors*

The Law Society is the controlling body of solicitors. It is the Law Society that has the power to make rules regulating professional practice and the conduct and discipline of solicitors. The nature of solicitors' work may require the enforcement of regulations. The Solicitors' Disciplinary Tribunal was set up by the Solicitors Act 1974.

i) Qualifying as a solicitor

Where a graduate has a law degree, he must follow this by completing the Legal Practice Course (formerly Law Society Finals). Once this has been passed the graduate must complete two years of articles as a trainee solicitor.

A non-law graduate is required to take the Common Professional Examination to convert his degree and after this he must pass the Legal Practice Course and complete two years of articles.

It is only after this process that the entrant will be admitted and his name put on the roll.

ii) Rights of audience

Solicitors have rights of audience in the following:

- magistrates' court;

- county courts;
- certain tribunals;
- Crown Court – where the proceedings are on appeal from the magistrates' court to the Crown Court or the case has been referred to the Crown Court for sentencing: see *Practice Direction* [1972] 1 All ER 608 and s12 Courts Act 1971;
- The European Court.

The Courts and Legal Services Act 1990 contains provisions that will affect the rights of audience. The Act sets up the Lord Chancellor's Advisory Committee on Legal Education and Conduct. It is this body that receives applications for rights of audience and offers advice on them to the Lord Chancellor.

- The Advisory Committee has considered an application by the Law Society for extended rights of audience, but has so far rejected any change.

iii) Liability of a solicitor

- A solicitor can be sued in tort or contract by third parties (in contract the action will be governed by the rules of agency).
- The solicitor owes contractual and tortious duties of care to his client.
- There is limited immunity from an action in damages where the solicitor is carrying out litigation work: see *Saif Ali* v *Sydney Mitchell & Co* [1978] 3 All ER 1033.
- A solicitor owes a fiduciary duty to his client which requires him to act in good faith: see *Lloyds Bank* v *Bundy* [1974] 3 All ER 757.

b) *Barristers*

The General Council of the Bar consists of representatives of all sections of the Bar and is responsible for the implementation of the Code of Conduct. Unlike solicitors, the Bar is not regulated by any statutory instruments.

i) Qualifying as a barrister:

- As with solicitors, a non-law graduate must take a conversion course (CPE).
- The next stage is termed as being the vocational stage of the course and graduates are required to become members of one of the Inns. All graduates wishing to practise in the UK must complete the Inns of Court School of Law Vocational Examinations and dine 18 times at their Inn! They can then be 'called' to the Bar.
- The final stage is the practical stage whereby the entrant must undertake a year of pupillage.

ii) Rules of conduct

- The cab-rank rule is one of the most important rules governing barristers. The rule requires a barrister to accept any brief within his professional competence, regardless of how his client is being funded, the nature of the case or any other factor.
- A barrister must draw the court's attention to all relevant authorities even if they may be harmful to his case.
- A barrister is not permitted to conceal facts from the court, especially if his client has made an admission of guilt to him.

iii) Barrister's liability

- A barrister cannot be sued for negligence in relation to what is said in court and pre-trial work: see *Rondel* v *Worsley* [1969] 1 AC 191.
- A barrister may not sue for his fee even though his relationship with his client is based upon contract, but the instructing solicitor is liable for the barrister's fees.
- A barrister may potentially be sued by his instructing solicitor for negligent advice under the rule in *Hedley Byrne* v *Heller* [1964] AC 465.

c) *Reforms of the legal profession*

The profession has been undergoing considerable change instituted by both governing bodies and recent legislation and reports, eg the Royal Commission on Legal Services (1979) (the Benson Commission) and the Marre Committee Report (1988) and the Courts and Legal Services Act 1990.

i) Barristers

The reforms instituted by the Bar's governing body improve conditions for the practising Bar and in particular for younger barristers. For example:

- a system of funded pupillages;
- lifting restrictions on setting up chambers;
- removal of the need for a barrister's clerk;
- the establishment of a practising library to assist barristers unable to find tenancies;
- lifting restrictions on the advertising of the Bar's specialist skills.

ii) Solicitors

The reforms instituted by the Law Society appear to be less wide ranging:

- firms of solicitors are required to operate a formal system to handle client complaints;

- solicitors are now permitted to publicise specialisation or expertise in particular areas of the law.

iii) The Courts and Legal Services Act 1990

This statute has introduced a wide range of reforms, some of the most important being:

- The institution of a Legal Services Ombudsman to investigate any allegation which relates to the manner in which a complaint to a professional body has been dealt with. The Legal Services Ombudsman has the power to have the complaint reconsidered by the professional body in question or to require that compensation be paid.
- The Advisory Committee set up by the statute has the duty of maintaining and developing standards of education and training of professional bodies. A major criticism of this committee is that its membership is essentially to be dominated by lay persons appointed by the Lord Chancellor.
- The structure for wider rights of audience to be given to solicitors.

iv) The Runcimann Commission has proposed wide-reaching changes to the profession ranging from reviewing fee levels to improved training in areas of scientific evidence for practitioners.

16.3 Recent cases and statutes

Gupta v *Comer* [1991] 1 All ER 289

The Courts and Legal Services Act 1990

16.4 Analysis of questions

The majority of questions on the legal profession concentrate on the arguments about fusion. It is important to consider the dilution of recent reform proposals in the light of the Courts and Legal Services Act 1990.

16.5 Questions

Question 1

'All rules and practices which restrict or limit the way in which a lawyer may choose to practise should be abolished.' Discuss.

University of London LLB Examination
(for External Students) English Legal System June 1987 Q5

General comment

This is a reasonably interesting way of asking a question about that now somewhat hackneyed topic, the fusion of the legal profession. Care should always be taken with questions of this sort so that the candidate does not plunge into a prepared answer without considering whether there are any further implications to the question.

Skeleton solution

- Identify restrictions of practice, eg direct access to client and rights of audience.
- Restrictions on solicitors.
- Participation and role of a governing body.
- Restrictions on barristers.
- Necessity of restrictions.

Suggested solution

This question asks about the restrictions concerning the way that a lawyer may choose to practise. This may refer on one hand to the current structure of the legal profession and the restrictions which emanate from the division into barristers and solicitors, and on the other hand to restrictions on the ways in which lawyers may offer their services generally.

Lord Gifford QC has castigated the legal profession for being a restrictive practice which would be condemned by any other organisation. No doubt, the two most obvious restrictions are the confinement of rights of direct access to the client to solicitors and the corresponding exclusive right of audience in the higher courts to barristers. The Courts and Legal Services Act 1990 has made provision for the extension of rights of audience for solicitors – see s27 and Schedule 4.

After the Benson Report on Legal Services recommended in 1979 that it was in the public interest to have a divided profession as the two branches specialised in different aspects of the work, it seemed that some of the inconsistencies and more old-fashioned practices would remain. If there was not substantial pressure for fusion in 1979 (a book edited by Robert Hazell, *The Bar on Trial*, was critical of the system) the desire for change was increased by the loss of the conveyancing monopoly by solicitors. The loss of this monopoly was initiated by a private MP, Austin Mitchell, but his proposals were taken over by the government. The objectives of ss34–52 of the Courts and Legal Services Act 1990 are to develop legal services by allowing 'authorised practitioners' to undertake conveyancing work formerly restricted to solicitors, barristers, notaries and licensed conveyancers.

The innovation of licensed conveyancers has yet to bite into the rewards of solicitors but already they have been obliged to lower their prices for this simple yet lucrative work. Solicitors are, however, more capable of adapting to change in that they can be approached by their clients directly, indeed, they can themselves initiate the approach. Solicitors are allowed to advertise their services now although there are certain restrictions which curtail the more extreme forms of publicity. In short, individual firms can advertise their specific services in the newspapers and on television and several firms have consulted marketing specialists. For more conservative members of the profession this has seemed to be an abdication of professional detachment but there is no question that it has enabled solicitors to carry the struggle outwards.

Among the major City firms there is much evidence of healthy expansion. There have been considerable recruitment campaigns and a broadening of business into new financial areas. It is likely that mixed partnerships will be permitted in the future so that solicitors can be involved with accountants, chartered surveyors and other professions. There are some who feel that this may endanger the independence of the solicitor – certainly the approach of a lawyer employed by a company will tend to be supportive of company policy rather then detached – but there is no need to fear that solicitors will be contaminated by contact with other professions.

It is generally a mark of professional status that there should be a governing body such as the Law Society which upholds the standards, etiquette and integrity of the profession. It is generally believed that professional men have a dual responsibility: to their clients and to their professional code of conduct. This is seen in the legal profession especially in that there is a duty to the court as well as the client. This does not mean that non-professionals are unscrupulous, simply that the professional must consider his status as an independent person and act so as not to cast disrepute upon his profession. The qualifications which he has obtained are to be protected by preventing others from usurping the function for which he or she has been trained. This is reasonable, but it necessitates a willing subjection to certain forms of discipline, for without this, standards of the profession might deteriorate. The Lord Chancellor's Advisory Committee on Legal Education and Conduct was established to improve and maintain the standard of education and conduct of those offering legal services (see ss19 and 20 CLSA 1990). This appears to 'take over' some of the functions of the Law Society and Bar Council and there is a danger of their role being marginalised.

Professional men sell their advice, not physical goods. It is important to see how that advice can be best offered. Thus barristers are required to work from chambers with a clerk who undertakes the negotiation of fees. Leaving aside the fact that gentlemen do not enjoy haggling about money this has – snobbery apart – a value in that the barrister is able to go about the business for which he has been trained without worrying about the office management. A barrister who acted for clients without this constraint would be subject to disciplinary action. One should, perhaps, ask if the setting up of chambers could be made rather easier as the Inns of Court were, for example, reluctant to allow Lord Gifford to establish a new set outside the already recognised areas of the Inns themselves. This might be thought excessively restricted.

The main question of whether the barristers and solicitors should themselves fuse is more difficult in that there is no thorough and reliable research on the matter. A comparative study would be helpful but this could be inapplicable to the conditions which prevail in this country. We do not therefore know whether the costs of litigation would be lower, or efficiency greater. It is impossible to say whether standards of advocacy would decline and whether justice is better served by the existence of an independent Bar. All is based upon conjecture and assertion.

Certainly there are a number of reforms which would be beneficial. A common form of professional examinations (with specialisations if necessary) would be a good start, already advocated by the Ormrod Committee. It may be unnecessarily restrictive to oblige a newly qualified law graduate to choose a branch of the profession for which he does not know at that time he will be suited or even be successful. There is much good sense in requiring all new lawyers to train as solicitors in the first instance and to decide at a later stage whether they wish to specialise as advocates. It seems restrictive to prevent the solicitor who has undertaken a considerable amount of advocacy from appearing in the higher courts without leaving one professional to sample the uncertainties of another in the middle of his career. As many barristers are not able to practise it seems equally peculiar that they may go and be employed in banks and businesses on the same basis as the solicitors who are often their colleagues, and yet with fewer privileges. There may be much sense in having a split between the generalist and the specialist, between the information gathering of the solicitor and the advocacy of the barrister but it is still possible to ask whether the profession is best structured for its members to find the niche best for them. Unfortunately, the provisions of the CLSA 1990 do not go so far, but are at least a step in the right direction.

Although the Lord Chancellor's initial proposals for reform went much further, the provisions of the CLSA 1990 have gone some way to redressing the problems of the profession. In particular, the restrictions on rights of audience and conveyancing have been to a large effect lifted. The full effects of the legislation will not, however, be apparent for some time.

Question 2

Does a separate Bar serve any useful purpose?

University of London LLB Examination
(for External Students) English Legal System June 1988 Q3

General comment

This is a straightforward (and common) discussion question. It is highly topical at present. The examiner is testing your powers of thought and your ability to see both sides of an argument. Students should read a quality newspaper regularly to keep them up with topical legal developments such as the rights of audience/fusion question. There are often questions of this sort in the English Legal System paper.

Skeleton solution

- Impact of recent government action. The Courts and Legal Services Act 1990.
- Reasons for maintaining the present system:
  - the present system works;
  - better training of barristers;
  - maintenance of specialists.
- Arguments against retention:
  - restrictive practice;

- rights of audience – Courts and Legal Services Act 1990;
- public interest;
- change in training.

Suggested solution

The issue of the future of the two legal professions in Britain has recently received fresh impetus with the publication of the Marre Committee Report and the implementation of the Courts and Legal Services Act 1990. Such impetus is necessary to revive professional and public interest in an issue which is important to all users of legal services. The fact is that both professions are innately conservative, the Bar particularly so, and they will not generally change unless change is thrust upon them. The present Government have shown themselves not averse to radical change in the financial services sector; the change in stockbroking in 1986 and the ending of the solicitors' conveyancing monopoly are examples, and there is a feeling that now is the time for a rethink. What then are the arguments for and against the present system?

One argument against changes, which is of some substance, is that the present division between barrister and solicitor works adequately in practice, and therefore why change it? This is a frequent argument against a lot of changes and may be responded to by pointing out that no system is so good that it cannot be improved upon and our legal professions in particular have faults, some of their own making, others by virtue of the framework in which they exist. There are in addition certain matters which make change the more likely at the present time; the Bar is heavily dependent on state funded legal aid work, the fees for which have not kept pace with fees for other types of work. The Bar has therefore become polarised into those earning relatively low amounts (for professionals) and those who do a high proportion of privately paid work who generally earn reasonable incomes. For the former group and to a lesser extent the latter, they could generally expect to earn a lot more money working for a firm of solicitors, where salaries are paid and where expenses are defrayed against the firm and not against the individual lawyer. The problem is exacerbated by recent substantial rent rises, both in London and the provinces, and these have obviously made the cost of being a barrister much higher. Therefore, while until recently pressure for change came from outside the profession, there is now quite a lot of disgruntledness amongst barristers which invariably must lead some of them to believe they would be better off in a fused profession.

Let us examine the arguments pro and contra more carefully. Firstly it is argued for change that present restrictions are unnecessary and form a restrictive practice. The solicitor must brief a barrister even though he is better qualified to do the case and in particular is far better acquainted with the facts of the case than a barrister who often reads the papers the night before.

The argument that restrictive practices are anti-competitive and are generally there to protect inefficiency is a strong one. The fact is that barristers have a lot to fear from competition and therefore have to hide behind the protection of a restrictive practice in the form of the restrictions on rights of audience of solicitors. This restriction at first sight seems ridiculous; why can solicitors appear in complicated 'chambers' applications, planning inquiries worth millions of pounds and industrial tribunals with matters of great importance to their clients, and yet not be able to make a short application in the Crown Court to, for example, have a hearing date set aside? Similarly, there may be many cases where the person best equipped to deal with a case is the solicitor; he has seen his client, knows the facts thoroughly and is in the best position to appear on his client's behalf. Fundamentally the point is: why should not the solicitor and client decide whether they want a barrister to be employed rather than have the decision made for them? It does not bode well for the idea of a free market.

I believe this view is the correct one and will win the day. The Government appears to have removed rights of audience restrictions with both the High and Crown Court, (the Marre Committee has proposed removing the restriction for the Crown Court only, steering the middle course). However, the converse argument should be put. Put briefly this argument, adopted by the Bar Council, is that barristers are a specialist group who generally have high standards. Many of them go to court every day and therefore rapidly gain maximum experience of advocacy. This is of particular importance in such matters as jury trials where one can only be a good advocate by regular appearances in front of juries. Solicitors would not gain this experience because they would be tied to their offices, and their training and ethos is not advocacy based. The new Legal Practice Course introduced by the Law Society appears to have addressed the problem by including advocacy training. The answer to this argument is simple; it depends on the individual solicitor or barrister, and in practice, as presently happens in the county court, the solicitor is unlikely to appear in court unless he himself feels confident to do so.

We should therefore be cautious about rushing into change too quickly and the strengths of the present system should be weighed against its weaknesses before any decision is taken. I think that rights of audience are likely to change. Fusion is less likely to happen in the short term. In the long term I am not sure an independent Bar will survive if there are wider rights of audience given to solicitors and I am not sure this won't be to the detriment of the consumer. The client will then have a limited choice of advocate, as he does in America, and the cost of legal services will hugely increase. Let us then keep a close eye on what is proposed by way of change.

Question 3

What is the justification for the current division of the legal profession and restrictions on rights of audience? Discuss recent proposals for change and consider whether such changes would be in the public interest.

Adapted from University of London LLB Examination
(for External Students) English Legal System June 1990 Q6

General comment

A very standard question. Difficult to present one's case with some degree of originality. Nevertheless an up-to-date knowledge of the recent legislation is essential and students who present this correctly and succinctly will be awarded high marks.

Skeleton solution

- Description of present divided profession.
- General justification for the two-tier structure:
  - advocacy training and rights of audience;
  - specialists.
- Discussion of Green Paper proposals and subsequent CLSA 1990, with particular attention to:
  - rights of audience;
  - Legal Services Ombudsman;
  - Lord Chancellor's Advisory Committee.

Suggested solution

There are in fact two legal professions and the difference between them has, it seems, hardened into rather unedifying battle lines. The questioning of the traditional divisions of the profession has arisen from the greater competitiveness which is now seen among the professions generally and in particular the blurring of divisions, as there has been encroachment into what have been seen as preserves.

What is the justification for having the legal profession divided into two branches, with solicitors and barristers prepared for their professional examinations in different institutions and apprenticed separately, organised professionally in their distinctive ways and responsible to different bodies, each with its own customs and code of behaviour? More importantly, does such a two tier structure serve the interests of justice? The theoretical justification for a two tier profession is that one branch provides a service that is different from anything offered by the other. The Bar claims that it is a specialist branch – its members are specialists in advocacy or in a particular area of the law. That is the theory, but does this accord with the reality?

There are barristers who, through cumulative day to day experience in the courts, become experts in trial advocacy. However, young barristers now get minimal training in the art of advocacy, though not nearly enough to describe them as specialists in it. By contrast, there are many solicitors who spend most of their time in advocacy in the lower courts and become thoroughly skilled. In addition, the Law Society's new Legal Practice Course makes provision for better training in advocacy. To suggest that barristers are, and solicitors are not, specialists in advocacy is therefore misleading.

A further justification for the present structure is that it provides a pool of specialists to which any solicitor, however small his firm or lowly his clientele, can go for expert advice or advocacy in court. In practice the choice is more limited, and the degree of specialisation is not always high.

Critics of the system advocate the theory that the division and especially the role restricting rights of audience necessarily mean duplication of effort which in turn means duplication of costs and therefore higher fees and often leads to delay and inefficiency. It is true to say that the supposed monopoly of the Bar is illusory. Solicitors already possess rights of audience in 95 per cent of cases civil and criminal. Solicitors may already appear before county court judges, High Court masters, Crown Court judges on appeal from magistrates' court, High Court judges on formal unopposed hearings, and industrial and other statutory tribunals.

Nevertheless, as Zander has put it, there are two or three taxi meters running instead of one. After the solicitor has involved himself in the case, become familiar with all the details and developed a relationship with the client, the case is handed over to another lawyer, the barrister. At all these stages the client is paying for two legal minds when often only one would suffice. As Tony Holland, Law Society Council member, states:

'The old Marshall Hall type advocacy has gone. If one goes into court and hears a civil dispute going on, the advocacy seems of a very dry and dull nature. It's the detailed knowledge of the case that counts. I think a solicitor can put across that detailed knowledge as easily as a barrister, particularly as he had been more in touch with the clients and with the preparation of the case than the barrister has.'

Furthermore, experience in the US and Australasia indicates that a practical division between advocates and administrators exists even in a fused profession. Fusion was rejected by the Benson Report on two principal grounds: standards of advocacy would be reduced and provincial solicitors would lose access to specialist advice. Since Benson the subject of the structure of the legal profession has been constantly on the agenda for discussion by the Law Society and Bar Council.

The Marre Report (1988) concluded that if the two branches of the profession did not initiate change themselves, there was danger that change would be forced upon them. Certainly there is no shortage of critics. The EEC, the Office of Fair Trading, and even the former Prime Minister herself have been making noises about the so-called restrictive practices in the legal profession. The Marre Report provoked Lord MacKay to publish a Green Paper in early 1989 – fusion was not on the agenda, rather other reforms were proposed which would result in the biggest shake up of the structure and work of the legal profession this century. The Green Paper provoked strong opposition from the Bar. The provisions contained therein, somewhat diluted, now form the Courts and Legal Services Act 1990.

Rights of Audience. Since the quality of advocacy is crucial to the administration of justice, advocacy should be restricted to 'advocates' (barristers or solicitors) in possession of a certificate of competence. The CLSA 1990 sets up the Lord Chancellor's Advisory Committee on Legal Education and Conduct. This body will offer certificates for rights of audience on the advice of the Lord Chancellor. The loss of the solicitors' monopoly on conveyancing means, of course, that the Bar will encounter greater difficulty in maintaining arguments for their own security over rights of audience.

As regards education and specialisation, the Lord Chancellor's Advisory Committee on Legal Education and Conduct will review education and accredited specialisms and advise the Lord Chancellor on the appropriate codes of conduct for advice and advocacy work.

The office of Lay Observer has been abolished and replaced with a Legal Services Ombudsman with wide powers to investigate and refer cases and recommend the payment of compensation by the body concerned. This is a move for the better since the Solicitors Complaints Bureau has not yet developed machinery for dealing with complaints which achieves public confidence.

Sections 34–40 of the CLSA 1990 establish a single, regulatory body, the Authorised Conveyancing Practitioners Board, consisting of a chairman and between four to eight members. The Lord Chancellor is responsible for the appointments and is required in doing so to have regard to their experience in, or knowledge of, conveyancing services and associated financial arrangements.

This body has been established to authorise, supervise and discipline the provision of conveyancing services. The objective of this part of the CLSA 1990 is to develop legal services by enabling a wider choice of persons to provide them. The effect of the statute is to allow banks, building societies, and other institutions and individuals to offer conveyancing services to the public. Although this is a wide extension, the statute provides for adequate means of control and supervision.

Section 54 of the CLSA 1990 amends s23 of the Solicitors Act 1974 and allows banks, building societies and insurance companies to undertake non-contentious probate work. They will, however, be subject to regulations to be made by the Lord Chancellor.

Section 61 of the CLSA 1990 abolishes the existing rules that prevent a barrister from entering into a contract for the provision of his services. The statute allows the Bar Council to make rules to restrict such contracts, although none has yet been announced.

The Green Paper was wholly against unregulated contingency fees; the 1990 Act permits instead 'conditional fees'. Section 58 provides that such fees are permissible where the advocate or litigator has a written agreement with the client to receive normal fees or normal fees plus an additional percentage in the event of success, but no fees in the event of failure. The Lord Chancellor will have the power to regulate the percentage of the additional fee. These agreements are not permitted in relation to criminal proceedings and certain other proceedings: see s58(10) CLSA 1990. The main scope of these agreements in practice will be in personal injury and defamation cases.

The changes made represent challenges for the future which, if met with confidence and if enthusiastically tackled, could bring great wealth and increased prospects for the profession as a whole. As the Law Society concludes, the changes 'provide a fair basis for the evolution of a new era in which competence and merit in either branch of the profession can lead to advancement'.

Question 4

'The Government believes that ... rights of audience before particular courts should depend only upon whether advocates can demonstrate that they have the appropriate education, training and qualifications and are bound by appropriate codes of conduct.'

(Civil Justice Review).

Do you agree with this view? What do you consider will be the effect of extending rights of audience as proposed under the Courts and Legal Services Act 1990?

University of London LLB Examination
(for External Students) English Legal System June 1991 Q5

General comment

An inevitable question for this year and many more to come. Tie in the quotation at some point and make your personal response to the final question clear but not by a direct 'I agree/do not agree'. Avoid facile arguments here; the level of general discussion in the press means that a high level of analysis and good supporting evidence will be sought by the examiner. With the question asking directly for a view you can pursue an (almost) one-sided exposition with confidence.

Skeleton solution

- Background to CLSA 1990.
- Basis for analysis. Fairness, efficiency, provision of choice to public.
- Consequences = two sections:
  - a) to legal professions
  - b) to public
- Flaws of CLSA re provision of choice to public.
- Conclusion.

Suggested solution

The arguments leadings to the Courts and Legal Services Act 1990 (as concerns the organisation of the legal profession) have been much rehearsed for over two decades. Until Mrs Thatcher brought in a Scottish Lord Chancellor the status quo had been victorious with only minor nibblings cut from the Bar's monopoly on advocacy. However the 1980s political philosophy abhorred monopolies and as the quote suggests believed that anyone with the ability to conduct legislation should be permitted to do so – solicitors, accountants, architects et al. The necessary element of quality control would be supplied by internal regulation and the Advisory Committee overseeing the training programme and rules of conduct. However the war continues as nine months after the Act the Law Society's proposals for an extension of its rights of advocacy have been met with complete rejection from the Bar.

The argument now centres on what is the correct education, training and qualification for an advocate; however, it seems to be the same defence of staked claims yet again. The Bar went so far as to suggest that the solicitor who prepares a case should not represent it! As Sir William Goodhart QC said this 'seems to be based on the proposition that the more you know about the case, the less suitable you are to present it. If that is not self-evidently wrong, it is very close to it.' Such confused argument merely shows up the truth of the conflict – a fight to maintain comfortable niches and avoid the fierce winds of competition which encourage competence. The Bar in its opposition to the reduction of its advocacy monopoly and the Law Society in opposition to the loss of its conveyancing monopoly have both, in Lord Justice Lawton's words, lost credibility by overstating their objections. The aim of Part II of the Act, to develop legal services by giving a wider choice to the public while 'maintaining the proper and efficient administration of justice', cannot be credibly contested. The damage done to the profession as a whole by this destructive debate is considerable and the school-boy scuffle has obscured the more important issues of the effects of this Act.

The consequences of this part of the legislation fall neatly into two aspects: the effect on the legal profession and the effect on the public. The introduction of greater competition over a reasonable period of time will weed out the advocates who are substandard and enable the rest to adapt to the new state of self-promotion and learn the business orientation required. There will always remain a need for specialist advocates to serve non-advocacy solicitors' firms, whether the advocacy is carried out by the litigation department of an agent firm or an independent practitioner. It may well transpire that the internal rules of the Bar will alter to permit partnerships which can more effectively tender for employment as advocates and compete more successfully with the developing in-house advocacy departments. What will increase is the solicitor's choice of advocate and the number of litigation teams who prepare and present cases at all levels. The junior ranks of the Bar will find it harder to earn a living but they faced this difficulty prior to the inception of the Act. To afford easier entry to a more specialist Bar the traditional rules of practice must change and the Act can only accelerate this process. Specialisation of labour promotes efficiency whereas the restrictive internal practices of the Bar do not. We are likely to see a more unified yet more diversified profession, as a result of this legislation – indeed market pressures may force in fusion through the back door.

Division of labour is also, according to economic theory, a cause of reduced cost to the consumer and the Consumers Association welcomed the Act largely because the wider choice would lead to lower legal fees. This is yet to be proven in practice: it seems likely that solicitor-advocates will value their work by reference to barristers' charges and their own overheads. After the initial round of price-reduction the market for legal services is likely to return to the present situation where quality legal advice costs more than many people can easily afford. The facile argument that only one person need be paid fails in the face of the increased workload of that individual. However the adoption of a prepare and present system should ensure that the advocate knows the case and his client much more thoroughly than in the current 'last-minute-brief' syndrome. There is evidence from criminal cases that the magistrates hear a more accurate picture of the defendant than the Crown Court judge listening to a barrister devilling for the original instructee. The business philosophies of customer satisfaction and payment by returns will have to become the motto of all the legal profession as they have in the commercial world of city solicitors during the 1980s.

However, for an Act which claims to improve access to legal services, several vital areas have been singularly overlooked. The cab-rank rule, honoured in the breach by the Bar, and foisted on to all advocates by the Act, may well disincline firms to offer advocacy. The well respected firm of Bindman and Partners stated in April 1990 that it did not take certain classes of clients and the furore caused obscured the fact that this is common practice for all solicitors' firms. As Professor Zander suggests, forcing advocates to take all cases would be inconsistent with this practice (whether right or wrong) and injurious to the aim of the Act. No attempt has been made to ensure a quality legal service for those cases on legal aid. Even moderately capable advocates can gain better fees elsewhere and, as the Bar does at present, will continue to avoid the cab-rank rule. To be fair the vagaries of the listing system and the propensity for cases to settle or over-run make the double booking of diaries sensible business practice and until a more efficient court system is introduced (perhaps with a judge's clerk actively administering an individual court's list) the problem will be perpetuated. It is hoped that solicitors will continue by the sheer size of the profession to provide for all clients; Professor Zander remarks in the New Law Journal that he has not heard of a client unable to find a solicitor to act for him, and if they are advocates as well, then that client will be assured of representation at court. There is still a strong element in both halves of the profession that believes in providing legal services for the less well off – but this Act does not increase the provision of such services.

The removal of a restrictive monopoly on the provision of advocacy services is welcome but is only a part of the Act. It seems likely that this will increase consumer choice and promote competent, efficient legal services. However, other elements of the Act, in particular the reduction in the conveyancing and probate monopolies, may remove the presence of legal services from the high street and remove the protection given by independent legal advice. Breaking the obsolete barriers within the profession is beneficial to the public but removing the provision of specialist advisers, whose conduct is regulated by a duty to the court and the client not to their paymaster, is contrary to maintaining the 'proper and efficient administration of justice.'

Question 5

Is the Bar's opposition to extended rights of audience in the higher courts anything more than a defence of vested interests? Do you think that the public interest is best served by the changes to rights of audience embodied in the Courts and Legal Services Act 1990?

University of London LLB Examination
(for External Students) English Legal System June 1992 Q4

General comment

Although this is not an unusual topic, the question is quite clear in what it asks the candidate to deal with and therefore requires some very specific knowledge.

Skeleton solution

- What the Bar actually is and what rights of audience are.
- Attitudes to and views on these rights of audience.
- Public interest.
- The changes in the Courts and Legal Services Act 1990.

Suggested solution

The legal profession and its out-dated work methods and attitudes have long been the subject of debate and criticism. The Bar is seen as arrogant and elitist by non-lawyers, and indeed by some solicitors. It is regarded as resistant to change and its approach to the proposed changes in the Courts and Legal Services Act 1990 has done little to alter this view. But it is only when one considers not only the changes in the Act, but also the place of the Bar within the English legal system, that one can really examine its attitudes.

The barristers' role is largely concerned with court work. While a few of the most specialist barristers may act only as expert advisers, more often than not they are required to be advocates. For a great number of the Bar, court appearances are their daily work. It is not surprising, therefore, that they should have a vested interest in the rules on rights of audience. Prior to the Courts and Legal Services Act 1990, the question of who could appear before a court or tribunal was governed more by the individual court procedure than any set of legal rules. Barristers had a virtual monopoly of advocacy before the House of Lords, Court of Appeal and High Court, and for the majority of Crown Court work. (In theory, litigants in person also have the same rights of audience, but these are not often exercised.) Many lawyers choose which part of the profession they wish to enter according to whether or not they wish to appear in court. Just as the solicitors' profession became fiercely protective of its conveyancing monopolies, the Bar jealously guards its rights of audience. Whether one regards this as a defence of vested interests is very much a matter of opinion. If one takes into account the financial uncertainties of the Bar, especially for young barristers at the criminal Bar, one can perhaps find sympathy with their defence of their day to day work. However, if one acknowledges that the legal profession must progress into the 1990s and beyond, then both sides of the profession must be willing to discuss change and compromise.

In the Bar's defence, it should be pointed out that barristers are not the only ones in favour of preserving the status quo. After initial pressure for change from the Law Society in 1984 and furious exchanges between the two sides of the profession, the Marre Committee examined the issue and reported in 1986. The Committee's decision was very much for preserving the status quo. This was not the first investigation into the issue; in 1979 a majority of the Benson Royal Commission on Legal Services had been in favour of retaining the Bar's monopoly on rights of audience on the basis of the 'special skill and expertise' required for advocacy in the higher courts. However, the government became more determined to see change in the profession generally and started to push for that change in the late 1980s.

The government's argument is very much based on what it believes to be in the public interest. This again became a matter of definition. Certainly, it would not be disputed that to receive the best possible service is in the interest of the public and indeed the profession. However, views vary as to what is the best service. It might be said that it is simply the maintenance of the highest standards possible in each discipline, be it advising the client in the solicitor's office or representing his case in court before judge and jury. To achieve these objectives things should be left alone, staying with those who have many years' experience and understanding of their roles and responsibilities; leaving the rights of audience with the advocates and the conveyancing with the solicitors. But this approach is based too much on an unwillingness to respond to change. If one considers that the best service should also be evaluated in money terms, then the Bar certainly looks more like an expensive monopoly than an efficiently run specialist service. Similarly, its resistance to change is seen by sceptics as merely based on financial grounds rather than a desire for the maintenance and furtherance of standards. The Royal Commissions have always taken the former approach – leave it to those who know how. But the loss of the conveyancing monopoly by the solicitors seems to have upset the profession more than the users of that service. Certainly, no cries have been heard about the loss of standards or inefficiency.

The Courts and Legal Services Act 1990 certainly did not reflect the laissez-faire attitude of the Royal Commissions and sought to provide a radical shake-up of the profession. In particular, s27 of the Act deals with rights of audience, attempting to put them on a statutory footing. The government's policy of wishing to stimulate competition in the profession is reflected in the extension of rights of audience in the lower courts to those granted rights by the 'authorised bodies' (including the Law Society, Bar Council and other designated bodies) – these people are not necessarily barristers or solicitors; the basic criteria is that they belong to professional bodies with appropriate rules of conduct and are considered competent. Additional rights of audience can be sought by the Law Society and the professional bodies representing nonlawyers from the Lord Chancellor's Advisory Committee. As soon as the Act received Royal Assent, applications were made by the Law Society to extend the rights of its members and also by bodies representing employed lawyers and the CPS. The Advisory Committee has so far taken a conservative approach. It wholly rejected the proposal that employed lawyers in general, and the CPS in particular, should have extended rights of audience in the higher courts. The applications were rejected on the grounds that employed lawyers lacked the detachment necessary for advocates in the higher courts and that they were unlikely to use such rights of audience often enough to maintain the required level of competence.

It seems, therefore, that while the Act may have purported to be in the public interest by widening the choice available, it has so far been of little effect due to the narrow approach of the Advisory Committee. However, if one regards public interest as being not founded in the principle of free competition, but in the recognition of unique skills for specialist roles, the approach of the Advisory Committee and the Bar to advocacy in the higher courts is the correct one. But as long as change is resisted, by any part of the profession, it will always give ammunition to those who advocate radical change and leave unanswered the wider question of whether we should have a fused profession.

Question 6

See Question 2(b) in Chapter 17.

17 LEGAL AID AND ADVICE

17.1 Introduction

The concept of criminal legal aid is that the costs involved in the conduct of the defence are met by the State as opposed to the individual. The Legal Aid Board administers the scheme and was set up by the Legal Aid Act 1988. Some changes have been made by the Children Act 1989 and the Courts and Legal Services Act 1990. The scheme covers three different aspects, each of which will be dealt with below. Alternative sources of legal advice and assistance will also be considered.

17.2 Key points

a) *Legal advice and assistance*

i) The £5 fixed fee interview provides approximately half an hour's advice to determine qualification for legal aid.

ii) The Green Form scheme:

Contained in Part III of the Legal Aid Act 1988, the Green Form scheme includes aspects as follows:

- the giving of oral or written advice;
- it is advantageous in that many problems can be easily solved with low administrative costs;
- writing letters and preparing cases for tribunals;
- application for the scheme is made by merely filling out the 'green form';
- the legal representative (usually a solicitor) himself calculates eligibility, based on the applicant's resources;
- the solicitor may only allow participation in this part of the scheme if he believes the cost will not exceed two hours of work.

iii) Duty Solicitors

The Duty Solicitor scheme provides free legal advice 24 hours a day to defendants at the police station or on first appearance at the magistrates' court. It is an essential requirement of the Police and Criminal Evidence Act 1984 that the police inform the suspect of the availability of legal advice.

b) *Civil legal aid*

i) Part IV of the Legal Aid Act 1988 allows legal aid to be obtained to pay for all work leading up to and including court proceedings.

ii) Legal aid is available for proceedings in most courts. It is not available in the following cases:

- undefended matrimonial proceedings;
- judicial and administrative tribunals;
- arbitrations;
- proceedings before a coroner's court;
- proceedings involving libel or slander.

iii) In order to be eligible for legal aid, the applicant must be within the financial requirements, ie must have a disposable income of £6,800 per year or less and disposable capital of £6,750 or less. Contributions may be required if the applicant's disposable income is more than £2,294 (lowered in April 1993 from the previous level).

The applicant must have reasonable grounds for taking, defending or being party to the proceedings.

iv) The application for a legal aid certificate must be made on the appropriate forms.

c) *Criminal legal aid*

i) Part V of the Legal Aid Act 1988 applies to criminal proceedings in the magistrates' court, the Crown Court, the Court of Appeal and the House of Lords.

ii) Application in criminal proceedings for legal aid is made to the magistrates' court dealing with the case on which the magistrates will make an immediate decision. The magistrates' clerk is in fact the person who decides if legal aid should be granted.

iii) One factor to be considered in making any decision to award legal aid is the defendant's means. A full assessment of means may take place to determine contributions that the defendant may have to make.

iv) The second factor to be considered is whether it is in the interests of justice that the defendant should have legal representation and financial help to meet the costs: see s21(2) Legal Aid Act 1988. Certain criteria have been set out in s22(2) Legal Aid Act 1988 to assist in making the decisions and to determine if it would be desirable in the interests of justice to grant legal aid. They are:

- where the offence is one which carries a sentence of imprisonment, or would lead to loss of his livelihood or serious damage to reputation;
- the case involves a substantial question of law;
- the accused is unable to understand the proceedings because he is unable to understand English, or has a mental or physical disability;
- the nature of the defence involves the tracing and interviewing of witnesses or cross-examination;
- it is in the interest of someone other than the accused that he be represented.

d) *Costs*

i) In civil legal aid cases, if the assisted person wins, the amount he will have to pay depends on:

- whether the other party is ordered to pay costs and does so, in which case he may receive a part refund of his contributions;
- whether the assisted person is awarded any money or recovers or preserves any property as a result of proceedings, in which case the costs may be deducted from this money or property (this is known as a statutory charge);
- where the assisted person loses the court may require him to pay his opponent's costs. In these cases he will also have to pay the maximum contribution.

ii) In cases where criminal legal aid is granted, the court will decide at the end of the case if contributions are to be paid or cancelled. If the defendant is acquitted all contributions will generally be repaid.

e) *Runciman Commission proposals*

i) Review of Legal Aid fees to ensure their adequacy in attracting sufficient numbers of competent solicitors.

ii) Review of standards of performance by lawyers.

iii) Better provision of funds for defence in criminal matters to allow the use of their own expert research and evidence.

f) *Alternative legal services*

When discussing sources of legal advice it is important to consider those sources outside of the main legal profession.

i) Law Centres – provide a less formal environment for advice, usually based in a town's high street with a 'shop frontage' to make them more approachable.

- They are not centrally administered or funded and so exist on a haphazard and voluntary basis.
- They provide a valuable and informal first source of advice for many people.
- They have been criticised for bias in the way in which they tackle local community issues, sometimes bringing actions against local authorities.

ii) Citizens Advice Bureaux – are centrally organised by the National Association of Citizens Advice Bureaux (NACAB) though not centrally funded.

- Their provision is more uniform with one in almost every town.
- They assist with all kinds of advice, not just legal issues.
- They are well recognised as a valuable agency but are beginning to suffer from lack of funding.

iii) Other advice agencies

- These may take various forms and their existence will be dependent upon localised needs and financing.
- Examples would be Legal Advice Centres, Neighbourhood Advice Centres, Housing Advice Centres and so on.

iv) Free Representation Unit (FRU)

This is run largely on a voluntary basis by trainee barristers and solicitors.

- It receives some funding from the Law Society and Bar Council.
- It provides representation (free) in matters involving unfair dismissal, social security claims, sex or race discrimination and immigration cases.
- It only exists in London.

v) Media, motoring organisations, trade associations, unions and professional bodies all provide valuable sources of legal advice ranging from a 'legal problem page' to specialist advice and representation.

17.3 Analysis of questions

Legal aid has been examined nearly every year by the University of London External examiners. The questions in this area tend to require a description of the present system. The major controversy is the lack of provision of aid to a majority of claimants. In recent examination questions there has been an emphasis on alternative legal services. On occasion, the examiner has examined legal aid as part of a larger problem – see Q1(b) in Chapter 9.

17.4 Questions

Question 1

The government has decided that funding for the legal aid and advice schemes must be reduced in real terms. Prepare a memorandum for the Cabinet outlining the areas in which the limited resources should be applied.

University of London LLB Examination
(for External Students) English Legal System June 1988 Q8

General comment

Government funding for the legal aid system has been the hottest issue facing the legal profession in recent years. This is hardly surprising since nearly all criminal work is paid for in this way and most civil. The question asks you to look constructively at the cuts and say in which areas cuts may be made at the same time as improvements in efficiency. The answer should be in memorandum form as below.

Skeleton solution

- Historical background of present system.
- Discuss the costs involved in criminal legal aid, particularly in the Crown Court with the participation of the jury.
- The Green Form scheme and its disadvantages.
- Availability of legal advice from the Citizens Advice Bureaux.
- Costs of civil legal aid and when it is available.

Suggested solution

Memorandum: Legal Aid expenditure; an outline plan: Introduction and background

The legal aid system, introduced after the Second World War, was placed on its present footing by the Legal Aid Act 1974. Although the system has worked quite satisfactorily the cost of it has increased in real terms from its inception. This increase has been much sharper in the last few years and looks as though it will continue unless something is done about it. There are a number of options which may be broadly grouped into curbing supply and curbing demand. Curbing supply means a ceiling on the amount of money available for legal aid in one year and this restricting the class of people eligible or freezing the level of legal aid in real terms, thus forcing the applicant to find own funding for the additional amount. Curbing demand means curbing the class of applicants eligible for legal aid and placing disincentives on the abuse of the system by way of the court costs system and by way of greater discretion to require contribution from the recipient of aid. Here are some ideas for discussion:

Restricting demand to legal aid before the Crown Court

At present criminal legal aid accounts for a large part of total expenditure and aid before the Crown Court is disproportionately expensive. It is several times more expensive for an accused person to be tried by a judge and jury at the Crown Court with counsel and solicitors in attendance for the defence than for the equivalent trial at the magistrates court, where often only the solicitor for the accused is present. Also Crown Court trials are usually much longer, with a trial for burglary typically taking three or four days in the Crown Court but only one day in the magistrates court: At present there are no disincentives to electing trial by jury, indeed juries are generally thought to acquit more freely than benches of magistrates, and many accused persons prefer to take the risk of a possibly higher sentence in the event of conviction in favour of a much higher chance of acquital. I repeat that there are presently no real disincentives to this course.

This has led to a staggering increase in the Crown Court workload and of course a corresponding increase in cost to the legal aid fund. Much of this time and money is wasted with trivial cases which ought to be tried in the magistrates' court. One suggestion for curbing this demand is to take away the right to legal aid in such trivial cases rather than take away the right to trial by jury altogether. This course would do relatively little political damage because it would be difficult to claim that the Government has taken away a right. Indeed, the right still exists unrestricted, it is the support for the right which will be restricted. Nevertheless such a restriction will probably provoke some opposition particularly from the legal profession.

The Green Form scheme

This scheme constitutes a major part of expenditure. It operates at high street level. Members of the public are entitled to an hour's free advice on supplying only preliminary details of disposable income and capital. Solicitors' practices tend to do as much of this work as possible because often the advice can be given very quickly and even where only ten minutes' worth of advice is given the firm is paid a standard fee for an hour.

This system is wasteful of public money and could be more efficiently administered by Citizens Advice Bureaux. The kind of informal advice given under the scheme does not call for the services of a skilled lawyer and Citizens Advice Bureaux could act as the filter mechanism whereby more serious cases are referred to solicitors under legal aid, if appropriate; more trivial cases are dealt with straight away. There are substantial political barriers to this reform and the Government will need the co-operation of the Citizens Advice Bureaux as well as the Law Society. However, if the reform was successful it would represent a substantial saving.

An overall cut; tightening up eligibility requirements, reducing the level of support, removing some cases from the legal aid scheme:

Legal aid is currently widely available for such things as boundary disputes and relatively trivial consumer disputes which ought to be settled by negotiation but which often get to court. Perhaps consideration could be given to removing such things as boundary disputes from the class of cases for which a litigant is eligible for legal aid. These are often of a very trivial nature and a dispute of this kind does not really touch on the life of the individual in the same way as say, any form of personal injury does.

Another possibility is for a decision to be made on eligibility for legal aid by some kind of independent body. It is presently made by the Legal Aid Board for the area concerned who often rely entirely on the advice of counsel as to whether it is a worthwhile case or not. Counsel can often only make an educated guess as to the outcome of the case and may find it difficult to tell *his client* that the case is a trivial one which ought to be settled in an amicable way. Some kind of independent panel for the area would ensure that a more robust view of borderline cases was taken and that cases with a very small chance of success are brought less frequently.

The other options of freezing legal aid in real terms or restricting the class of applicants further by lowering the threshold above which the applicant is ineligible do not seem attractive at the present time. The Government has gone some way down this road and further restrictions would be politically unacceptable. There is already substantial concern as the fact that people on relatively low incomes are not entitled to any state support as the present system is geared only to those dependent on state benefits.

Question 2

ANSWER ONLY ONE PART OF THIS QUESTION.

EITHER

a) Describe the legal aid system. Are there any ways in which access to legal services for the general public could be improved?

OR

b) 'It is imperative that any consideration of the future shape of the legal profession takes full account of the fact that it is, indeed, a profession. Unbridled competition is for the market place and would be harmful to professional standards.' Discuss.

University of London LLB Examination
(for External Students) English Legal System June 1989 Q7

General comment

A straightforward question requiring a good knowledge of the legal aid system.

Skeleton solution

a)
- Fixed fee interviews.
- Green Form scheme.
- Civil legal aid.
- Criminal legal aid.
- Suggestions for reform, eg contingency fees – to take pressure off the state.

b)
- Mechanisms for supervision of practitioners.
- Dangers of large solicitors' firms 'buying' the skills of the specialist Bar.
- Harm to the consumer.

- Would fusion result in better quality of service at a lower court for the consumer?

Suggested solution

a) A national scheme for the provision of legal aid was established in 1949 and is now governed by the Legal Aid Act 1988. Money provided by the scheme comes from the state-financed Legal Aid Fund. The Legal Aid scheme used to be administered by the Law Society, but is now organised by the Legal Aid Board.

If someone is initially unsure about whether he qualifies for Legal Aid or not, he may ask a solicitor for a 'fixed fee interview' costing £5. This will provide up to half an hour's advice; most solicitors who do Legal Aid work will provide this service.

Under the Green Form scheme, introduced by the Legal Advice and Assistance Act 1972, now contained in Part III of the Legal Aid Act 1988, a person can obtain written or oral advice from a solicitor or barrister on any question of English law and on any steps which it may be appropriate for the applicant to take. This will include the giving of general advice, writing letters, negotiating and preparing a written case if the applicant has to go before a tribunal. If further representation is needed in either civil or criminal proceedings, that must be sought from the Legal Aid scheme proper. The Legal Aid Act 1988 gives the Lord Chancellor the power to extend or restrict advice available and to contract out the giving of the same advice to other agencies.

The name 'Green Form scheme' comes from the method of applying: application is made at a solicitor's office by filling in a green form. This contains questions concerning the applicant's income and capital. The solicitor can calculate whether the applicant qualifies. An applicant receiving Income Support or Family Credit is eligible for free legal advice and assistance unless he has a certain amount of disposable capital. People on low incomes are also eligible for free legal advice; however, there is no longer any requirement for the client to make a contribution as this was abolished in April 1993.

The scope of the scheme is limited by the Legal Aid Act (LAA) 1988 in that advice and assistance may only be given immediately by a solicitor to the extent that the cost of giving it will not exceed two hours. If the advice or assistance will cost more, the solicitor must obtain approval from the legal aid office before giving it.

Part IV of the LAA 1988 covers the provision of legal aid in civil cases. Legal aid may be obtained to pay for all work leading up to and including the court proceedings and representation by a solicitor and if necessary a barrister in any court. Civil legal aid is not available for undefended matrimonial proceedings, judicial and administrative tribunals and arbitrations.

The first requirement for eligibility is that the applicant is within the financial limits as regards both disposable income and disposable capital. If the applicant's disposable income is more than a threshold level a contribution must be paid of approximately one quarter of the applicant's disposable income. If his disposable capital is less than a certain amount no contribution will be payable. There is however an upper limit and if the applicant exceeds this he will not qualify for aid, no matter how expensive the proceedings.

The second requirement for eligibility is that the applicant has reasonable grounds for being a party to the proceedings.

Application for a legal aid certificate is made on the appropriate forms and is considered in two stages, by the assessment officer and the general committee in turn. The process takes approximately six weeks, although an emergency certificate may be issued where delay would cause a risk of miscarriage of justice or an unreasonable miscarriage of justice or an unreasonable degree of hardship. The certificate granted will be marked with any contribution payable and will usually be limited to the taking of certain steps in the proceedings, with a review before legal aid is granted for any further stage in the proceedings. Solicitors and barristers have a duty to advise that cases which do not justify legal aid be discontinued.

If the assisted party loses, he will be liable for his own costs and those of the winning side. As for his own costs he need pay to the Legal Aid Fund only the amount required as a contribution stated on the Legal Aid Certificate. In respect of the winner's costs, the Legal Aid Act 1988 provides that those costs may only be recovered against the fund if the party would suffer severe financial hardship and it would be just and equitable to make an award against the fund.

If the assisted party wins his case, his opponents will be ordered to pay his costs directly into the Legal Aid Fund.

Part V of the LAA 1988 deals with legal aid for those charged with a criminal offence. The defendant applies to the magistrates in the magistrates' court which is dealing initially with the defendant's case. The magistrates' clerk makes an immediate decision on the basis of a 'statement of means' supplied by the defendant. An assessment of the defendant's precise resources may be ordered to take place subsequently to fix an appropriate contribution in the light of his commitments and resources. Apart from financial considerations s21(2) of the LAA 1988 provides that legal aid must be granted where it is desirable in the interests of justice, and this was developed in the notoriously vague Widgery criteria, now in statutory terms in s22(2) of the LAA 1988.

A major criticism of the Legal Aid Scheme is that it provides no help for those of modest income and capital who still do not fall within its low financial limits. The Green Paper on the Future of the Legal Profession suggested the introduction of a contingency fee system as a way of improving access of the general public to legal services. Such a system, under which a litigant pays nothing if he is unsuccessful, already operates in Scotland. It encourages lawyers only to take on cases which have a reasonable prospect of success. But since only one per cent of cases in Scotland are taken on this basis it is unlikely to make much impact. And, in any case, this reform has not been implemented by the CLSA 1990.

The establishment of neighbourhood law centres with their deliberate informality should give ordinary people more incentive to take their problems to a lawyer. But they are precariously underfunded.

b) It is imperative that any consideration of the future shape of the legal profession takes full account of the fact that it is, indeed, a profession. Unbridled competition is for the market place and would be harmful to professional standards.

This part requires more thought and imagination than (a) above.

What is a profession? It can be distinguished by three criteria:

1) the professional applies a body of knowledge in his work;

2) he must always put the interests of his client first;

3) he is answerable to no-one else for how he does his job.

There is absolutely nothing to suggest that the fact that a practitioner needs a corpus of knowledge should put him in any different position from any other person offering his services in the marketplace. A profession is essentially about the sale of skills based on knowledge. Nor is it likely that greater competition will cause lawyers to become more, rather than less, knowledgeable about their specialism.

It is a conventional platitude that the professional must put the interests of his client first, although it is not clear what it means, or whether it is adhered to at the moment. Of course any person who takes on a client will put his interest before that of any opposition; the question is, will he put the client's interests before his own? Given what many would consider to be the excessive fees charged by lawyers, especially solicitors, one may well wonder how at present the solicitor can be said to put his client's interests before his own! The truth is that the selling of legal services is just like the selling of any other good or service: the client will be best served if the service is speedy and efficient, and the price is affordable. That is what the reforms aim to achieve.

The professional is not answerable to anyone for the way in which he does his job. But it is argued that the reforms will make the training and conduct of the Bar subject to Government supervision. One must distinguish the establishment of standards in a profession from the day-to-day supervision of a practitioner. The latter would be quite unacceptable for a professional; the former is not totally at variance with the concept of a profession, but the Government should beware of going too far.

Nevertheless some disquiet has been expressed at the effects of the Government's proposed reforms, by people other than those who might be thought to have a vested interest in keeping the profession uncompetitive. It has been suggested that the big City solicitors' firms will buy up the skills of the hitherto independent Bar, and that the person in need of legal services will be faced with less choice and at higher prices (because barristers at present have lower overheads) than now.

Solicitors argue that allowing banks and building societies to do conveyancing may improve competition, but its adverse consequences will ultimately harm the consumer. There will be no independent advice, a conflict of interest will arise and smaller firms will go out of business reducing the availability of legal sources generally.

It is difficult to tell what will happen. The Government's steamrollering of its plans through, without commissioning a firm of consultants to undertake a study of likely competitive effects of the reforms, and without time for adequate consultation, augurs badly. While improved competition (assuming that there would be no anticompetitive effect) must be good, one might nevertheless lament the passing of the Bar in its present form. But this is a different issue from that of whether professional standards would suffer, and there does not seem to be much evidence for this claim. On one view, the maintenance of professional standards will be crucial in ensuring the competitiveness of the service. One of the things a client expects from a lawyer is a professional service in the three senses outlined above, any lawyer who ceases to offer such a service may find that he is uncompetitive. Quality of service as well as the right price is something a client looks for, and which determines whether an economic agent is competitive or not.

Question 3

'The new Legal Aid Act, together with the Legal Aid Board which it has created to take over the administration of legal aid, will provide a system that is efficient and effective and which will have the flexibility to meet changing demands and circumstances.'

Do you agree that recent changes to the legal aid system will improve efficiency, effectiveness and flexibility? Do you consider that any problems remain?

University of London LLB Examination
(for External Students) English Legal System June 1990 Q5

General comment

A question that requires some knowledge of the Legal Aid System pre the 1988 legislation. In particular, you must be able to identify the changes made by the 1988 Act. Along with a description of the present system, you must critically analyse the efficiency, effectiveness and flexibility of it, with a view to answering the final part of the question. On the whole this is a difficult question to work out in an examination.

Skeleton solution

- Changes made by the 1988 Act, in particular the creation of the Legal Aid Board.
- Operation of the fund on a local basis.
- Description of the system:
  - Green Form scheme;
  - criminal legal aid;
  - civil legal aid.
- Highlight unavailability of aid to middle classes.

Suggested solution

At the beginning of 1986 the legal aid scheme was costing some £320 million a year, treble the amount which it had cost when the Conservatives came into office. It was therefore because he was appalled at the cascading expenditure on the provision of this form of social service that Lord Hailsham LC initiated the Legal Aid Scrutiny which reported in June 1986. In an attempt to respond to deep seated problems the Government introduced its White Paper *Legal Aid in England and Wales: A New Framework*. The White Paper formed the basis of the Legal Aid Act 1988, the first major piece of legislation on the area since the 1974 Legal Aid Act.

The most important reform contained in the new Act is the setting up of a new Legal Aid Board to administer the system.

This Board replaces the Law Society as the administrator and may result in a significant change in the way the system is operated. Firstly, the Government hopes to see a more commercial attitude taken by the Board and membership is not exclusively limited to lawyers but also includes businessmen who it is hoped will bring business acumen to bear on day to day distribution of the large sums of public money that the fund has at its disposal. Section 3 provides for the constitution of the Board and reserves a limited number of places for solicitors and barristers. However, it is exactly this market orientated philosophy which has stimulated widespread criticism of the reforms. Desmond Fennel QC, a former chairman of the Bar Council, has said:

'The inherent defect ... is the application of market forces and competition to the administration of justice.' We shall have to wait and see whether this change in outlook will import improvements to the scheme.

A further change is that the fund is operated on a more local basis. For the purposes of administration England and Wales is divided into 15 areas, each area consisting of an area secretary, a general committee, an area committee (to deal with appeals) and a criminal legal aid committee. This will certainly improve on efficiency and flexibility since the Board will be able to take account of local variations in the availability of lawyers, overheads etc. The Board is further subject to the guidance (but not the supervision) of the Lord Chancellor's Department (s5) although here the Government must not interfere with day to day running as it is essential to the administration of justice that bodies like the Legal Aid Board retain a high degree of autonomy.

As regards the changes in administration, it is estimated that in all £30 million is spent on administering civil and criminal legal aid. This includes a £25 million grant to the Legal Aid Board, £3.5 million spent by the DSS in carrying out means tests, and over £1 million in vetting legal aid bills in the county court. These figures do not include the administration costs borne by the solicitors themselves. Moreover, delays in obtaining legal aid certificates are still prevalent. The Legal Aid Advisory Committee has commented that:

'From the point of view of the ordinary consumer who uses the legal aid system perhaps only once in his lifetime, the delay in obtaining legal aid must seem quite staggering.'

Any system which relies on case by case approval is bound to be costly in administration. Research carried out by the Family Courts Campaign suggests that there might be savings of up to £9 million to the legal aid fund if matrimonial proceedings were to be concentrated in a family court.

The new Act thus marks a shift in attitude away from legal aid benefits as of right to a more market orientated system generally in keeping with the political philosophy of the 1980s and well illustrated in other areas of social policy. The present writer would suggest, however, that the Act represents a palliative and not a cure to the ongoing problems which have not been obviated by the recent reforms.

One of the problems is that legal aid is demand-led rather than being funded from predetermined cash limits. The increase of legal aid costs is not simply an indicator of the greater poverty of the nation or the generosity of the Welfare State. Certainly Lord Hailsham does not see legal aid as analogous to the NHS in that he has said that whilst the state should provide for the sick, few people have to have recourse to the courts – the Government has no interest in multiplying legal actions.

Legal aid has three aspects. The Green Form scheme permits written or oral advice on any question of English law; this includes general advice, drafting letters, negotiating and pre-action steps, and is limited to two hours' worth of advice. This scheme was criticised by the Legal Aid Scrutiny which suggested that initial advice should be given by advice centres and in particular by the Citizens Advice Bureau. The Law Society has attacked this proposal as it claims that the client would often need to be referred to a solicitor and that this is thus an unnecessary duplication. A major survey recently undertaken by Drs Baldwin and Hill concluded that the scheme:

'far from being a wasteful or misdirected use of scarce resources, represents a crucial element in publicly funded legal aid services in this country.'

Civil Legal Aid – as for eligibility, two conditions apply:

i) that the applicant's income and capital fall within the financial limits, and

ii) that the applicant has reasonable grounds for being party to/defending the proceedings.

Criminal Legal Aid – application to magistrates' court which makes an immediate decision based on a statement of means and by the notoriously vague Widgery criteria, given statutory form in s22 of the 1988 Act. Indeed, disparities in interpretation of the criteria have been attacked in the House of Lords as inequitable yet the meaner clerks are simply trying to adhere to the Lord Chancellor's guidelines; in fact the liberality of the present criminal legal aid criteria has been highlighted by recent cases of the very wealthy being represented under the scheme. Thus Maria Aitken was able to obtain aid even though she has a large amount of capital and more recently Ernest Saunders, former chairman of Guinness, was able to obtain aid even though his assets exceeded £1 million.

Conversely, the capital limits for civil legal aid have failed to keep pace with other social security means tested benefits. Considerable concern has been expressed that the capital limits operate unfairly towards people on low incomes with savings, particularly the elderly (*Opren* case). The Royal Commission on Legal Services in Scotland recommended that capital should be wholly disregarded, while the Benson Commission thought it should be assessed on more generous terms. More recent reforms had made more generous allowances for pensioners' capital savings.

The operation of the statutory charge presents problems, especially in matrimonial cases. Legal aid is more akin to a loan rather than an outright grant. As far as possible, the legal aid fund seek to recoup the legal costs paid out on behalf of all applicants, firstly from costs paid by the other side, secondly from contributions paid by the applicant and thirdly by the applicant property 'recovered or preserved' in the proceedings. This last rule is the statutory charge.

Berlins outlines cases of petitioners who can barely cover the cost of the proceedings from monies recovered from respondents due to the effect of the statutory charge.

The 'middle income trap' should finally be considered. There has been a polarisation of the scheme whereby those on income support are automatically granted aid while those just above the limit are refused it. Zander points out that most empirical studies have shown that it is precisely this middle income band of people who tend to use lawyers most frequently yet possession of modest means denies such people necessary financial help for pursuing worthwhile claims.

Whilst it is certain that the previous format could not have survived without modifications, the 1988 Act has not eliminated many of the criticisms concerning the adequacy of legal aid. With the growing demand for assistance, the increasing size of the legal aid budget and the recent cut-backs in funding by the Government, the issues remain as controversial and insoluble as ever.

Question 4

See Question 1(b) in Chapter 9 as mentioned in 17.3 above.

18 TRIBUNALS AND ALTERNATIVE DISPUTE RESOLUTION

18.1 Introduction

Tribunals developed in the late 1940s and are now an established and useful part of the English legal system dealing with more cases than the county courts. Alternative Dispute Resolution is a newer but growing area.

A TRIBUNALS

18.2 Key points

a) *Organisation and role*

i) This is governed by the Council on Tribunals under the Tribunals and Inquiries Act 1992.

ii) Tribunals specialise in dealing with specific subject matter such as the Industrial Tribunals or Social Security Appeal Tribunals.

iii) The internal organisation varies from tribunal to tribunal. Some general points are common:

- They are not part of the main court hierarchy.
- However, if a case is within the tribunal's jurisdiction it must be commenced there.
- Tribunals often use the Court of Appeal as a higher appellate body.
- To hear cases they will use a chairman with legal knowledge assisted by two lay-wingmen (not lawyers) from the relevant specialist background.

b) *Characteristics*

They were essentially introduced to provide cheap, quick and informal processes for decision making. The Franks Report in 1957 identified three key features: 'openness, fairness and impartiality'.

i) To encourage informality, procedures are not governed by strict rules.

ii) The chairman may choose whatever approach best suits that aim of informality.

iii) Litigants in person are encouraged.

iv) Legal aid funding is, therefore, not available, in order to discourage the use of legal representatives. This has led to discussion and criticism.

v) In recent years, tribunals have been criticised for becoming inflexible in their approach and procedures and for excessive 'legalism'.

B ALTERNATIVE DISPUTE RESOLUTION

18.3 Key points

The phrase 'Alternative Dispute Resolution' (ADR) encompasses several possibilities, all designed to find ways of resolving disputes without using the court system. The aim is to reduce time and costs and sometimes acrimony so as to allow for an ongoing relationship between the parties.

a) *Settlement*

This is the most commonly known form of ADR, and is used in many civil cases. Whilst it is quicker and cheaper than a full trial, questions have arisen as to the equality of bargaining power between the parties and undue pressure on the plaintiff.

b) *Ombudsmen*

A recent trend, often found in the financial services sector. The Courts and Legal Services Act 1990 created the office of the Legal Ombudsman to deal with allegations of misconduct or negligent services in the legal profession.

c) *Arbitration*

An informal system of trial operates for small claims in the county court and often by agreement between the parties in commercial matters. The parties will often agree in advance of a dispute to use an arbitrator and be bound by his decision. The system has the advantages of speed, privacy and in some cases specialist knowledge.

d) *Conciliation*

Sometimes called mediation. In conciliation, a third party assists the disputing parties to negotiate a compromise solution.

The system is considered to be advantageous due to speed, low cost and a considerable reduction of hostility. The use of conciliation in the United Kingdom is still limited, but it is growing, especially in family and commercial matters. it is commonly used in the United States where it is considered extremely valuable by its users.

18.4 Analysis of questions

Questions in this area may focus solely on the tribunals and their relationship with the main court system. However, as alternative dispute resolution becomes more popular in practice, examiners may choose to focus upon it.

18.5 Question

Consider the alternative means available to resolve a legal dispute other than by way of a court hearing. Your answer should specify any advantages that such means may have over a court hearing.

University of Wolverhampton LLB (Hons) by Distance Learning
English Legal System Examination September 1993 Q3

General comment

This is a straightforward question provided the candidate has a thorough knowledge of all the alternatives and puts some thought into their suitability.

Skeleton solution

Introduction:

- adversarial process;
- expense;
- delay;
- complexity;
- need for alternatives.

Tribunals:

- origins;
- features;
- success.

Alternative dispute resolution:

- settlement;
- arbitration;
- Ombudsmen;
- conciliation;
- mini-trials;
- the features and success of ADR.

Conclusion.

Suggested solution

The English legal system is said by many to be the envy of the world. However, it is not without criticism especially when it comes to the finer points of procedure and processes. Based on an adversarial system, the court hearing is intended to elicit the facts through a 'contest' between the two sides with the judge acting as umpire. This process can be daunting for the uninitiated. Furthermore, the complex rules that surround it mean that expensive legal representation is required and the litigant is often left bemused, out of pocket and far from feeling that he has had a fair hearing. This expense and complexity, along with the delay caused by an increasingly overburdened civil system have led to the growth of alternatives, often intended to provide a more efficient and less hostile solution to the dispute. It should be noted that these alternatives are only appropriate to civil proceedings. Broadly speaking, they can be divided into the headings of tribunals and alternative dispute resolution (ADR).

The origins of the tribunal system can be found in the late 1940s and early 1950s. Despite their legal 'youth' tribunals are now an established part of the legal system, dealing with more cases each year than the County Courts, and regulated by legislation (Tribunal and Inquiries Act 1992). They operate alongside the main court hierarchy, with compulsory jurisdiction over their subject matter and often an ultimate right of appeal to the Court of Appeal. They were introduced to provide a quick, cheap and informal forum for decision making. The Franks Report of 1957 was the first thorough examination of their use and identified three valuable characteristics of 'openness, fairness and impartiality'.

These characteristics are advantages of the system and to a large extent still exist today. The internal organisation of tribunals is generally intended to be quite unlike that of the traditional adversarial court hearing. Specific tribunals now deal with specific areas of law eg Industrial Tribunals, Employment Appeal Tribunals, Social Security Appeal Tribunals. Cases are heard by a legally qualified chairman assisted by two specialist lay advisers from the appropriate field of expertise, which allows for a more balanced final decision. The litigant in person is encouraged and no strict rules of evidence and procedure apply, in order to try and foster the feeling of informality and accessibility. The lack of legal representation should ensure costs are minimal and opponents 'equal'.

Whilst they are acknowledged to have avoided many of the problems of the main court system, there are criticisms to be made of tribunals. Legal aid funding is not available (in order to discourage legal representation) but this does not prevent the wealthy party (eg an employer) from using his lawyer to represent him, nor does it allow for the expertise of a government social security administrator who may appear before a tribunal on a regular basis. Increasingly, tribunals are criticised for becoming inflexible in the approach with excessive legalisation of their procedures. This is especially true where lawyers are often used or where decisions are reported, as in the case of Industrial Tribunals, creating a system of precedent. The Social Security Appeal Tribunals have been criticised for arbitrary decisions and procedures, particularly with the growth of more complex rules of administration and narrower rights of appeal. They are also often not without delay and confusion!

Despite these criticisms tribunals still remain a valuable and indeed essential part of the legal process which is much more accessible to the individual than the courts.

Alternative dispute resolution, or ADR as it is known, is a growth area in the modern legal system. Its popularity is due to the general features of speed, economy and, in particular, privacy and comparative lack of hostility. The phrase covers several different approaches which are usually used at the choice of the parties, unlike tribunals with their compulsory jurisdiction.

Perhaps the commonest form of ADR is the traditional concept of 'settlement', ie where two parties have commenced proceedings but through negotiation reach an out of court settlement, bringing an end to the matter. This is undoubtedly quicker than going to full trial (although it often takes place 'at the doors of the court') and removes the uncertainties of judicial decision-making. However, there have been criticisms regarding undue pressure on the plaintiff, especially against an experienced and powerful defendant, to settle at an unreasonably low level of damages. But it is a part of the civil process which is now essential: without many cases being settled, the civil system would be subject to even more delay and possibly even collapse.

Arbitration is another well known form of ADR, now partially regulated by legislation and an everyday part of commercial life. This involves the parties agreeing (sometimes at contract stage) to use a specialist arbitrator to decide any dispute. This is not a process of negotiation as the arbitrator will make a decision which is legally binding (though the jurisdiction of the courts cannot be ousted). It is favoured because of its speed, the specialist knowledge of the arbitrator, privacy and, in commercial matters, the ability to maintain an on going business relationship. It is sometimes regarded as a cheaper means of dispute resolution, although this is not always the case. One example of arbitration is the Small Claims procedure in the county court where all claims for less than £1000 are automatically referred to the District Judge who will hold an informal, sometimes inquisitorial hearing to decide the issues. Survey statistics suggest that even the losing party feels the Small Claims system is fair.

A newer development is that of the Ombudsman, often seen in the financial services sector but now a part of the general legal system since the 1990 Courts and Legal Services Act. Such a person is intended to investigate and whenever possible resolve allegations of misconduct without the need for any form of hearing. Whilst this clearly removes the anxiety and expense of normal legal proceedings, some Ombudsmen have been criticised for lacking any real disciplinary powers.

The newest form of ADR is that of conciliation, not to be confused with reconciliation or arbitration. This involves negotiation under the guidance of a specialist third party whose expertise lies not in the legal issues but in the skills of mediation. The conciliator assists the parties in finding a compromise, without imposing a decision. This process is very popular in the United States where many major corporations regard it as an essential part of any potential proceedings, saving them billions of dollars. In the United Kingdom it is in its infancy, although it has great potential in family and commercial matters due to the privacy, speed, low costs and amicable nature of the process. Pilot schemes have been greeted with praise but the system has not yet received government backing, although a voluntary scheme – the Centre for Alternative Dispute Resolution – is achieving growing success.

There has also been minor use in the UK of 'mini-trials' where both parties agree to conduct a trial before a chosen expert (eg a QC) who will give a legally based decision. An obvious advantage here is again speed, but the parties also feel that they have had a chance to properly present and argue their case before a legal authority. To date, the American west coast concept of 'Rent a Judge' where retired judges can be hired to hear legal arguments has not spread to the English legal system!

In conclusion, there are nowadays many alternatives to the traditional adversarial process. Whilst these enjoy varying degrees of success, it is submitted that anything that helps to reduce the problems of a constantly criticised civil system is worthwhile.

19 LAW REFORM

19.1 Introduction

The concept of law reform involves the consideration of how changes in the law are brought about and the adequacy of our system. It requires discussion of both legislative reform and the role of the judiciary. Students should, however, check whether law reform is on their syllabus as this varies from one examining board to another.

19.2 Key points

a) *Ideas for reform*

These can come from many sources:

i) Pressure groups such as JUSTICE, Liberty, Shelter and Legal Action often call attention to 'gaps' in the law.

ii) The legal profession – the Bar Council, the Law Society or the judiciary – may call for change.

iii) Events and the media may highlight problems especially where an apparent failing in the law has failed to adequately deal with a tragic disaster, eg the Zeebrugge Ferry or juvenile crime.

iv) Politicians and public opinion may provide a call for change in miscarriage of justice cases.

v) Government often gives the impetus for reform.

b) *Official reform bodies*

i) Law Commission

- The Law Commission (for England and Wales) and the Scottish Law Commission are the only permanent bodies dedicated to law reform in the United Kingdom. They consider changes in the law and codification of existing laws. The Law Commission began in 1965.

- Issues are referred to it by the Lord Chancellor. The Commission then thoroughly researches the issue and consults with interested parties before issuing a final report and draft Bill to place before Parliament.
- It is regarded as a very capable body but has not enjoyed huge success in getting its proposals introduced due to lack of political impetus and parliamentary time.

ii) Law Reform Committee

Part of the Lord Chancellor's Department, this committee is made up of academics, lawyers and members of the judiciary. It is not a permanent body and has been little used in recent years.

iii) Criminal Law Revision Committee

This has previously been a very useful body made up of leading academic and professional lawyers. It was responsible for the Theft Acts of 1968 and 1978 but has not been called together since 1985.

iv) Ad hoc committees

- Royal commissions are formed to investigate and suggest reform in a particular area of the law. The most recent was the Runciman Commission on Criminal Justice which reported in July 1993. Royal commissions are made up of both practitioners and academics and produce comprehensive reports and proposals into their area of inquiry.
- Internal government procedures such as departmental committees and the civil service have been used increasingly in recent years. They are a much quicker and cheaper way of investigating proposals but are not regarded as the most comprehensive method of review.

c) *Criticisms of the present system*

The temporary nature of all but the Law Commission.

i) The failure of Parliament to discuss valuable Law Commission proposals due to lack of time or political interest.

ii) The lack of a body dedicated to a systematic review of the law.

d) *Role of the judiciary*

Whilst the judiciary claim to merely apply and not create the law, they do have a role in law reform.

i) The use of the doctrine of precedent allows the judges to create binding law for future decisions.

ii) The 1966 *Practice Statement* gives the House of Lords greater scope.

iii) The role of the higher courts as an appellate body allows the law to be amended.

iv) There are many examples of where the courts have been responsible for major developments in the law, eg *Hedley Byrne* v *Heller* [1964] AC 465; *Central London Property Trust Ltd* v *High Trees House Ltd* [1947] KB 130, and more recently, *R* v *R (a husband)* [1991] 4 All ER 481 which revised the law on marital rape.

Nevertheless, the judges claim to be reluctant to act as a creative body and will often steer away from it. They have also been known to make many errors.

c) *Alternatives*

i) Ministry of Justice

This is often discussed in the context of providing a body responsible for review and reform of the law, which would be directly accountable to Parliament.

ii) Codification of the law

Whilst this might 'simplify' the law and provide certainty, it would of course, be at the expense of flexibility. Many areas of English law have proved too complex to be codified.

iii) A 'fast route' through Parliament for uncontroversial or 'technical' reform. This would overcome the problem of pressure upon parliamentary time.

iv) A commitment by Government to put before Parliament a certain number of Law Commission proposals per year. This suggestion arises out of the fact that the Government approves of many Law Commission drafts but they are never placed before Parliament as Government Bills.

19.3 Analysis of questions

This is a topic that many students fail to consider in detail. However, if it forms part of their syllabus students should give it careful thought as it can provide a detailed but straightforward source of examination questions.

19.4 Question

'The official law reform agencies have failed to meet the need to reform the law'.

Discuss the effectiveness of these agencies and whether they are the only source of legal change.

University of Wolverhampton LLB (Hons) by Distance Learning
English Legal System Examination June 1993 Q6

General comment

This question requires special care because students must consider some alternative sources, as well as the need for reform.

Skeleton solution

- Sources of ideas and 'need'.
- Official bodies; their existence and success.
- Alternatives; judiciary.
- Conclusions.

Suggested solution

The issue of reform of the law does not generally attract media attention, nor is it considered controversial. Nevertheless, law reform is an essential part of the English legal system. Generally, one thinks of change coming through Acts of Parliament, but the process begins long before and may not reach fruition in a statute.

When one examines the origins of the process of reform that the real need can be clearly seen. As society evolves and new situations arise socially, morally and technically the law must change to keep pace with those changes, eg the need to protect against criminal damage and theft of computer programmes or to change the law on marital rape. The pressure for change may come from various sources. Pressure groups such as JUSTICE, Liberty, Legal Action, Shelter and environmental lobbies often draw attention to gaps in the law. Media people and Members of Parliament may provide a vociferous source of pressure, especially where a controversial issue or tragic event needs to be dealt with. The legal profession, the judiciary and academics have been known to highlight changes required. These are just examples which show that the pressure and need for reform undoubtedly exists.

Having identified this need, one must consider how far it is being met: it is in examining this area that the inadequacies of the system can be clearly identified.

The official reform bodies are various. The most important, and only permanent, body is the Law Commission for England and Wales which was founded in 1965 in response to calls for a Ministry of Justice. Issues are referred to the Commission by the Lord Chancellor's department. The permanent, specialist staff then investigate the law and consult interested bodies before submitting a fully-informed report and draft Bill to the Government. The next stage of the process should be presentation to Parliament for debate. However, despite receiving government approval, many reports are simply shelved due to the pressures on parliamentary time. This is especially true of technical or legalistic reforms (eg patent legislation or land law) which do not attract the political interest for the government or MPs, although they may be vital.

The quality of the Commission's reports and Bills is widely agreed to be excellent and where a proposal does eventually get put into practice it is usually well drafted and workable. But unless some way can be found to get these draft Bills through Parliament they will fail to meet the need for change no matter how carefully considered and created they are. One proposal has been a special 'fast path' through Parliament, making greater use of the House of Lords, for non-controversial legislation. However, this idea has not received government backing and would itself require parliamentary discussion which it is unlikely to receive in a Parliamentary timetable already considerably behind schedule due to the Maastricht debates.

Over the years, there have been various other types of non-permanent reform agencies. The Law Reform Committee, made up of academics, lawyers and judges, has not been used in recent years. The Criminal Law Revision Committee of leading academics and practitioners has been very successful in the past, having been instrumental in producing the Theft Acts. However, it has not been called together since 1985. Various ad hoc committees may be used, the most well known of which are probably the Royal Commissions, the most recent being the Runciman Commission on Criminal Justice (Cm 2263) which reported in July 1993. There have been several Royal Commissions over the past decades which have dealt with matters such as changes in the law of tort and reform of the legal profession. Their composition usually provides wide representation of interests with members from the legal profession, academics, judges and experts in the relevant subject matter. Their failing lies not in the quality of their investigation and proposals, but in their lack of power to persuade government to adopt their ideas.

In the past decade or so increasing use has been made of government department reviews to propose reform. These are favoured because they are quicker and less expensive than the other bodies. However, they have been criticised for a lack of clarity in their proposals, especially where a Bill is rushed through Parliament against a backdrop of political and media attention eg the Dangerous Dogs Act.

Frequently attempts at reform are made through the use of Private Member's Bills, which may be introduced by any Member of Parliament in the limited parliamentary time allocated. These rarely achieve first reading and often lack clarity or completeness because the Members of Parliament have no immediate access to parliamentary draftsmen. Their best chance of success is if they are adopted as a government Bill, as happened in the case of the abolition of the solicitors' monopoly on conveyancing, originally proposed by a Labour back bencher.

There are, then, many official ways to introduce change. Many of them fail to receive the necessary backing to become law, though they may have dealt very thoroughly and efficiently with the original need at draft stage. One route for reform that is not subject to the uncertainties of political life is via the judiciary's use of precedent.

Although not an 'official body' the judiciary are an active agency for change. Whilst judges generally claim to be declaring the law, not creating it, in practice they are responsible for many changes and developments. This is especially true of the common law with the use of the doctrine of precedent allowing the higher courts to bind future decision makers. The 1966 *Practice Statement* gave the House of Lords considerable scope and over the years they have been responsible for many changes in all areas of law. Even persuasive authorities have provided a valuable source of change eg *Hedley Byrne* v *Heller* (1964) establishing a new area of negligence and *High Trees* (*Central London Property Trust Ltd* v *High Trees House Ltd* (1974)) establishing a new principle of contract law. Arguably, they have sometimes been responding to a social need, such as reforming the law on marital rape in *R* v *R (a husband)* (1991), even though their response might be said to be rather slow! Often, however, they have simply been amending a mistake, for example in criminal law with the case of *R* v *Shivpuri* (1986), and often their decisions have attracted a great deal of criticism from academics for the lack of specific expertise.

How far the judges meet the need for reform is therefore debatable, and they certainly would not regard themselves as a reform agency. They do, however, provide a sometimes useful alternative to the official bodies.

The lack of a consistent review of the law and the inability of the Law Commission to force its proposals through show that the system often fails to respond to the demand for change. Proposals to reform this aspect of the law have ranged from relatively minor changes in parliamentary procedure through to the introduction of a Ministry of Justice. None, however, has yet been adopted and so the problem remains and the need is unmet.

20 UNIVERSITY OF LONDON LLB (EXTERNAL) 1993 QUESTIONS AND SUGGESTED SOLUTIONS

UNIVERSITY OF LONDON
LLB EXAMINATIONS 1993
for External Students
INTERMEDIATE EXAMINATION (Scheme A) and
FIRST AND SECOND YEAR EXAMINATIONS (Scheme B)

ENGLISH LEGAL SYSTEM

Friday, 18 June: 10.00am to 1.00pm

Answer FOUR of the following EIGHT questions

1 'There is no such thing as the intention of Parliament. The concept is a convenient fiction necessary to make sense of statutes.'

Discuss.

2 'Depicting judges as the crucial decision makers in the legal system is a falsehood. All the important decisions in the legal process have been made much earlier in the process.'

Is this an accurate statement?

3 'The present selection, exclusion, exemption and challenge procedures ensure that juries will never be representative of the public conscience.'

Discuss.

4 'The great challenge to the legal system is to ensure that legal services are available to all who need them at a cost they can afford.'

To what extent do you believe that the English legal system achieves this objective?

5 'The widening of the group eligible for higher judicial office under the Courts and Legal Services Act 1990 will break down some of the traditions which make it difficult to rebut the charge that judges inhabit a judicial ivory tower remote from the problems of the ordinary citizen.'

Explain and discuss this statement.

6 What features of the civil justice process lead litigants to settle their claims out of court? Are there any dangers for litigants in this practice?

7 'There is a pressing need for further development of the appellate process in criminal cases, not only to produce a more coherent system, but also to ensure that the objectives of justice, due process and consistency of decision making are better achieved.'

Do you agree with this statement, and what changes do you think should be made to the criminal appeal system?

8 David, a youth of 15, is alone driving his older brother's (Paul aged 18) car when he is stopped by PC Black and PC Tripper because he did not indicate while making a sudden turn. The police search the car, find Paul's driving licence (which indicates his age) and find a large quantity of cannabis in the glove compartment. PC Black exclaims: 'This is a serious matter, Paul. You had better come with us to the police station, and you had better be careful of what you say because we can use it.' On the way to the station David states 'that stuff is not mine. I know nothing about it.'

At the station David is cautioned and he asks to make a telephone call, but is told 'You can make one later.' A tape recorder is running while he is interviewed, but he keeps silent for one hour. After being told 'this could take a long time, you had better come clean', he admits that the car is his older brother's and that his brother 'makes a bit of money on the side selling drugs to his friends'. David is charged with driving without a valid licence and without proper insurance, while the police apply for a search warrant to search the house where Paul lives.

Discuss the police actions and consider whether David's statement could be used as evidence against his brother.

Question 1

'There is no such thing as the intention of Parliament. The concept is a convenient fiction necessary to make sense of statutes.'

Discuss.

University of London LLB Examination
(for External Students) English Legal System June 1993 Q1

General comment

It is important to appreciate the particular theme which the examiner wishes to be used in this answer on statutory construction. The assertion in the question invites comparison of the literal and purposive approaches to construction. The literal approach concentrates on the precise words used in a statute; the purposive approach tries to discover the 'real' intention of Parliament by looking beyond the literal words and taking account of matters extraneous to the statutory text. Whilst the literal approach is based on a fiction that Parliament always intends what it says in a statute, the purposive approach rejects the fiction in an attempt to find the 'real' intention.

A mere catalogue of the canons of construction is not enough. The canons should be cited only by way of illustrating the above theme.

Skeleton solution

- Constitutional roles of Parliament and judiciary in relation to enacted law.
- Definition and scope of the Literal Rule.
- Exceptions to the Literal Rule.
- Illustrations of the Golden and Mischief Rules.
- Use of presumptions and of grammatical canons.
- The rule relating to use of Hansard as an aid to construction and the effect of the decision in *Pepper* v *Hart.*
- Has there been a switch from a literal to a purposive approach?
- Discussion of the implications.

Suggested solution

Under the British constitution it is Parliament which makes law and it is the judiciary which must interpret and apply such law. Therefore, if it is a fiction to talk of the 'intention of Parliament', it is a fiction made of constitutional necessity as much as judicial convenience; judges need 'rules of recognition' to tell them what is law (the sovereignty of Parliament is one of the most fundamental of such rules) and what particular laws mean (the canons of statutory construction serve this purpose). The concept of the 'intention of Parliament' as the underlying theme for purposes of statutory construction provides at least a constitutional basis and some kind of limit to what would otherwise be very wide, if not absolute, judicial discretion in the application of statute law.

Judicial respect for parliamentary sovereignty has traditionally persuaded the majority of judges to follow a literal approach to statutory construction. Encouragement of a literal interpretation has been given by parliamentary draftsmen who have used very detailed and precise language to demonstrate 'the intention of Parliament'. The literal approach permits a departure from a literal interpretation only in very limited circumstances.

For example, if statutory language is ambiguous and would result in 'manifest absurdity' if a particular meaning were chosen, then the judge has discretion to avoid that meaning and to construct an alternative so as to achieve consistency with the rest of the statute and a sensible result: *Becke* v *Smith* (1836), applied *R* v *Allen* (1872). Such departure is permitted under the 'Golden Rule' of statutory construction. Departure from a literal interpretation in cases of ambiguity may also be encouraged under the 'Mischief Rule', which allows the judge to search for 'the intention of Parliament' by looking at the history of the Act in question, including reports of law reform bodies which contributed to the making of that Act: *Black-Clawson International Ltd* v *Papierwerke Waldhof-Aschaffenburg AG* (1975).

Apart from the Golden and Mischief Rules, the literal approach permitted a degree of judicial latitude through use of certain presumptions of parliamentary intention (eg against retrospectivity unless express words of retrospectivity were used) and certain grammatical rules, such as the ejusdem generis rule, to cut down the meanings of phrases which would otherwise have an extremely wide literal meaning which no sensible legislature would have intended.

Until recently judges refused to use a source of material which, prima facie, appeared to contain the best evidence of parliamentary intention, namely, Hansard, the official reports of parliamentary proceedings. The refusal was based on two main objections; first, the risk of being misled by speeches of government intentions which might not, after going through full parliamentary passage, be translated into the words of the Act (see per Lord Reid in *Re Black-Clawson* (above)); and, second, the practical difficulty lawyers would have in gaining access to Hansard and the consequent increase in the costs of litigation for private parties and for the Legal Aid Fund: see further *Davis* v *Johnson* (1979), *Hadmor Productions* v *Hamilton* (1983) and *Beswick* v *Beswick* (1968), all House of Lords decisions.

Recently the House of Lords made use of the 1966 *Practice Statement* in order to depart from the above precedents so as to lift the ban on Hansard: in *Pepper* v *Hart* (1992) it was held (majority of 6 to 1, Lord Mackay LC dissenting) that a judge may consult Hansard if he believes that ambiguity in a statute may be resolved by reference to the intentions expressed during parliamentary debates. Hence 'the intention of Parliament' is no longer a constitutional fiction used to buttress the artificial and mechanical literal approach. It has become something capable of proof to justify a purposive approach to construction:

'The courts now adopt a purposive approach which seeks to give effect to the true purpose of legislation and are prepared to look at much extraneous material that bears on the background against which the legislation was enacted': per Lord Griffiths in *Pepper* v *Hart*.

The implications of the decision are profound. First, it could lead to a flood of references to Hansard adding greatly to the costs of litigation (the basis of Lord Mackay's dissenting judgment in favour of keeping the ban on Hansard). Second, it affects the constitutional role of the courts because, as Dawn Oliver has pointed out ([1993] PL 5 at 12–13 especially), judges will no longer need to use presumptions of parliamentary intentions if they can ascertain them by direct reference through Hansard. The presumptions have been used to uphold the rule of law and principles of good administration, but reference to Hansard might well disclose that an executive-dominated Parliament did not intend such principles to operate! The substitution of the actual intention of Parliament for the fictitious presumed intention might well undermine the power of the courts to operate as checks against a powerful executive.

Question 2

'Depicting judges as the crucial decision makers in the legal system is a falsehood. All the important decisions in the legal process have been made much earlier in the process.'

Is this an accurate statement?

University of London LLB Examination
(for External Students) English Legal System June 1993 Q2

General comment

This is not a typical question and examinees would need to think very carefully about the object of the exercise, particularly as the question comes in an unusual form. Although it concerns judge-made law, it is clear that the emphasis is not on the operation of the doctrine of precedent (which examinees may have been hoping for) but rather on the pre-trial influences and decisions that affect the conduct of the trial and hence the way the judge formulates his ultimate decision. The review would need to cover both criminal and civil forensic processes.

Skeleton solution

- Character of judicial decision-making.
- The process of inductive reasoning.
- The influence of precedents.
- The criminal forensic process.
- Roles of police, Crown Prosecution Service and law officers of the Crown.
- The contrast with inquisitorial systems and the French institution of 'juge d'instruction'.

- Recommendations of Runciman Commission on Criminal Justice.
- The civil forensic process and role of the judge under the adversary system.
- The role of law reporters.

Suggested solution

In the English legal system judges make decisions on a case-by-case basis of inductive reasoning, making general rules from a particular set of facts. Their legal reasoning will form precedents for other judges, often of a binding character, so the influence of common law on the development of the rules and principles by which society is governed cannot be overstated. Nevertheless, common law by its nature depends on the accidents of litigation and the forensic process by which cases are brought to court. The law of evidence will decide what the judge may or may not hear. As the assertion in the question suggests, many people take crucial decisions in this forensic process.

In the criminal process it is the police who make the initial decision of whether to charge someone with an offence and increasingly there is a tendency to caution petty offenders as an expedient way of avoiding the time and cost of the trial. The Crown Prosecution Service, established in 1985, decides whether to continue or discontinue a prosecution, and some kinds of prosecution may require the consent of the DPP or Attorney-General. The CPS takes all important decisions concerning the preparation of the prosecution, including the evidence to be called. English judges have no part to play at this stage.

This is in contrast to Continental inquisitorial systems under which members of the judiciary are actively involved from the start in the collection of evidence. In France the 'juge d'instruction' is called to the scene of every serious crime and participates in the collection of evidence, including the questioning of witnesses. The juge d'instruction will also supervise the conduct of forensic laboratory tests. At the trial a different judge takes a proactive role in ensuring that all relevant evidence is heard, including if necessary calling a witness which neither side has called.

In view of recent notorious miscarriages of justice in the English system, some of which were due to police malpractice and faulty presentation of incomplete evidence, there has been a growing demand for judges to become more actively involved in the pre-trial stages of a criminal case. The Royal Commission on Criminal Justice (July 1993) recommended pre-trial case monitoring by judges, albeit with the aim of speeding up procedures rather than descending to the collection and supervision of evidence. In complex cases of certain length the Commission recommended a preparatory hearing before the empanelment of the jury so that the judge could define and clarify the issues. Even these modest reforms, if implemented, would be a significant inroad into the traditional attitudes of judicial aloofness from anything to do with the pre-trial collection and preparation of evidence.

In civil procedure the trial judge is again largely a passive, reactive figure in an adversary system under which each side plays a tactical game in deciding what evidence to disclose in court. There remains a heavy reliance on oral testimony and a reluctance on the part of the judge to get involved in reading written evidence in advance of the trial for fear that it might 'cloud his vision' when he comes to adjudicate on the actual dispute when it is waged in his courtroom. Historically he is like the umpire at a game of cricket, there only to answer the shout, 'How's that?' (ie who has won according to the rules). If, as is common, the parties choose to settle out of court, or choose alternative dispute resolution procedures, he may not even be asked that question!

Hence the ability of a judge to formulate the substantive principles of civil and criminal law depends heavily on the way others take decisions at much earlier stages. Even the citation of a precedent as a binding source of law may now depend on whether a law reporter has chosen to publish it, because the House of Lords has discouraged counsel from citing unreported precedents: *Roberts Petroleum Ltd* v *Kenny Ltd* (1983). Gone are the days when one could say that English law is what it is because a judge has so decided, rather than because a reporter has so reported!

Question 3

'The present selection, exclusion, exemption and challenge procedures ensure that juries will never be representative of the public conscience.'

Discuss.

University of London LLB Examination
(for External Students) English Legal System June 1993 Q3

General comment

A straightforward question on the jury, which emphasises the aspects of composition, particularly method of selection and the rules on eligibility for jury service. It will be important to set out the statutory lists of exemptions and excusals and to consider whether they are justifiable and serve a useful purpose; also the rules on challenges for cause and the related topic of multi-racial juries (*R* v *Ford* (1989)) should be addressed. The basic theme behind the entire discussion should be whether the rules on composition produce juries representative of society generally and of the public conscience (discuss Devlin's concept of the jury as enforcers of public morality).

Skeleton solution

- Constitutional significance of the jury.
- Problems of research into jury behaviour.
- General eligibility rules.
- Critical account of lists of exemptions, disqualifications and excusals.
- Critical account of methods used to produce random selection.
- Multi-racial juries.
- Reform proposals.

Suggested solution

Trial by jury is generally accepted today as a constitutional fundamental; it ought to provide a trial by one's equals, who should be unbiased and a microcosm of society. However, practical reality may not reflect this high-sounding principle for a number of reasons and there has long been concern over whether the rules regulating the composition of juries produce representative and responsible groups of jurors. Unfortunately, modern empirical research into the jury system is inhibited by the Contempt of Court Act 1981, s8, which the Royal Commission on Criminal Justice (July 1993) recommends for repeal. Unless and until such repeal occurs, analysis of juries may have to depend largely on anecdotal evidence.

In regard to selection the qualification is very liberal: anyone on the electoral register aged 18 to 70 inclusive and who has been ordinarily resident within the UK for any period of at least five years since the age of 13 is eligible, unless exempted or disqualified by statute. Those exempted involve mainly people who are concerned with the administration of justice, such as judges, magistrates, police officers and lawyers. Such exclusion would seem justifiable on the ground that members of such groups might tend to become 'case-hardened' by their profession and lack what Sir Sebag Shaw described as 'the great merit and advantage of being anonymous and amorphous'. Presumably no-one quarrels too much with the exemption of the mentally ill by the relevant statutes. But the exemption of members of the clergy is, perhaps, more surprising and contentious, because they would be particularly valuable in reminding a jury of public conscience and of the need to enforce public morality. Such duties were described by Lord Devlin as essential to the proper performance of a jury's functions ([1991] LQR at 398–404 especially). The Royal Commission on Criminal Justice (July 1993) has recommended the lifting of the exemption affecting members of the clergy.

Disqualified from jury service are those who have received serious custodial sentences (eg of five years or more), presumably on the ground that they will have a deep anti-police, anti-establishment bias which will prevent them from hearing a case fairly (they may also be incapable of reflecting public conscience). Less easy to justify is the disqualification of those sentenced to imprisonment or custody of any duration during the last 10 years (even if not actually served, eg because suspended), or any order for community service during the last 10 years, or who have been placed on probation during the last five years.

Certain eligible groups may be excused as of right because of more pressing employment duties of public need, eg doctors, nurses, MPs and members of the armed forces. Service is also voluntary for jurors aged 65 to 70 inclusive.

Subject to the above list of exemptions, disqualifications and excusals, selection of jurors is random, with names picked by computer from the electoral register. However, people may not register for the vote for all sorts of reasons and the Society of Black Lawyers has argued for wider eligibility rules based on random selection of driving licences and social security numbers. Research suggests that in many cases a black defendant is faced with an all-white jury even in areas where there is a sizeable ethnic minority population. At common law the trial judge has no power to ensure the empanelment of a racially-balanced jury: *R* v *Ford* (1989). The Royal Commission on Criminal Justice (July 1993) recommends that in exceptional cases either side should be able to apply to the trial judge to ensure the selection of a jury containing up to three people from ethnic minority communities. One or more of this group of three should come from the same ethnic minority as the defendant or the victim if either side should so request and if the trial judge deems it appropriate.

Such reform might help address the difficulty caused by the abolition of peremptory challenges in 1988, because the remaining right to challenge for specific cause is useless unless the system adapts American-style procedures of examining individual jurors in an effort to detect bias or general unsuitability.

In his book *What Next in the Law?* (1982), pp70–78 especially, Lord Denning argued that random, untested selection can produce 'irresponsible jurors' and that the system should be reformed to ensure that the suitability of jurors is assessed through interviews and character references. Some have even gone as far as to argue for the reintroduction of the property qualification, under which jurors had to be home owners, which had been abolished by statute in 1972. Whatever reforms are eventually chosen, the above arguments have served to alert one to the drop in public confidence in the jury system as part of the general unease about the administration of justice in recent times.

Question 4

'The great challenge to the legal system is to ensure that legal services are available to all who need them at a cost they can afford.'

To what extent do you believe that the English legal system achieves this objective?

University of London LLB Examination
(for External Students) English Legal System June 1993 Q4

General comment

Although the main theme of the answer should involve a critical analysis of the operation of the legal aid scheme, it is important not to overlook the broad approach taken by the assertion in question. Therefore the provision of legal services outside the legal aid scheme should also be discussed from the viewpoint of the consumer and taxpayer, eg law centres, legal expenses insurance, alternative dispute resolution procedures, etc. Reform proposals should also be discussed, eg the case for a Contingency Legal Aid Fund.

Skeleton solution

- Constitutional importance of access to justice and legal aid.
- Costs of legal aid and recent cutbacks.
- Scope of civil legal aid.
- Law centres.

- ADR.
- Legal expenses insurance.
- Reform proposals.

Suggested solution

Access to justice is generally accepted today as a constitutional fundamental, and some would go as far as to put it on a level with access to medical aid. If so, the lessons of the National Health Service are a useful reminder of how difficult it is to provide a subsidised state service in an economy of limited resources and burgeoning national debt (the current account deficit is approximately £50 billion for the financial year 1993–4). The total cost of the legal aid scheme at present is just over £1 billion per annum, having risen more sharply in recent years than any other field of public spending. Lord Mackay LC has repeatedly warned that such a rate of growth cannot be sustained and severe cuts, particularly in the area of financial eligibility criteria for civil and criminal legal aid, have been implemented from 12 April 1993. Is this the right way forward?

In regard to criminal cases the Royal Commission on Legal Services (1979) recommended that legal aid should be granted as of right (at present it is automatic only for charges of murder) because it is wrong in principle for the accused to pay one penny towards proving his innocence. He should pay costs only if convicted and only according to his ability to pay. However, in practice the discretion to grant criminal legal aid (albeit subject to discrepancies between areas) appears to be exercised on a reasonably generous basis since 98 per cent of Crown Court cases are funded by legal aid and 90 per cent of magistrates' courts cases are funded under the ABWOR part of the Green Form scheme. What is causing concern is the apparent pressure being applied by the Lord Chancellor's Department (now fully responsible for magistrates' courts since April 1992) for less generous exercise of discretion, and there is a proposal being mooted for the Legal Aid Board to take over the administration of criminal legal aid from magistrates' clerks, partly to achieve greater consistency in awards, but also to ensure 'value for money' for the taxpayer. But can access to justice be measured on an accountant's computer in this way? Should it? One fears that the presumption of innocence could be insidiously undermined if an accused were forced to find the means to finance a defence, particularly when faced with the awesome powers of the state-financed Crown Prosecution Service.

Civil legal aid has already suffered cuts as a result of more stringent monitoring since responsibility for its control was assumed by the Legal Aid Board in 1988. In fact the process of cutback had begun in the years prior to 1988 as a result of failure by LCD to raise eligibility criteria in line with wage and price inflation: in the period 1979–1992 nearly 14 million people became ineligible for legal aid according to research conducted by the London School of Economics (albeit disputed by LCD). It is estimated that a further seven million will become ineligible as a result of the April 1993 cuts and the subsequent freezing of eligibility levels for future years. Even Lord Taylor, Lord Chief Justice, a pillar of the establishment, has savagely denounced the effect of such cutbacks ((1993) The Times 4 February). The introduction of comparatively low fixed fees for work in the Crown Courts and a proposed introduction (for summer of 1993) of a similar system for work in the magistrates' courts has led to predictions from the Law Society to the effect that many firms will find it uneconomic to undertake legal aid work, thereby causing problems of access to justice in some areas.

Not surprisingly there have been accusations that the legal aid scheme is 'in crisis' and that nothing less than a Royal Commission on Legal Aid is needed to examine the problems: view, Tony Holland ([1993] NLJ 101). Some solutions can, perhaps, already be found in the system, although they may need nurturing and, dare one say it, better funding from the state, eg law centres to assist and represent parties in court, and out-of-court mediation, conciliation and arbitration services coming under the umbrella of 'Alternative Dispute Resolution'. The Government is trying to encourage the growth of legal expenses insurance, which is very low in the UK compared to, for example, Germany and Sweden.

Other solutions could be imported from foreign systems, eg the setting up of a Contingency Legal Aid Fund to assist those who fall outside the legal aid scheme to finance litigation if they are genuinely unable to meet the full costs (ie those caught by the so-called 'middle income trap'). Such a fund is made up of contributions from successful plaintiffs in all civil cases (in Hong Kong it is financed out of the state lottery and since a lottery is to be introduced in the UK this might be worth studying for its feasibility).

However, it may well be that the way to tackle the problem is to find ways of reducing the costs of criminal trials and civil litigation (eg by allowing lawyers to charge USA-style contingency fees; or by introducing simplified do-it-yourself procedures for simple debt, housing disputes etc). The nature of the problem is so huge and the possible solutions so diverse and difficult to weigh that one is tempted to conclude that Tony Holland's call for a Royal Commission on this subject makes great sense.

Question 5

'The widening of the group eligible for higher judicial office under the Courts and Legal Services Act 1990 will break down some of the traditions which make it difficult to rebut the charge that judges inhabit a judicial ivory tower remote from the problems of the ordinary citizen.'

Explain and discuss this statement.

University of London LLB Examination
(for External Students) English Legal System June 1993 Q5

General comment

A straightforward question on the composition, selection and outlook of the judiciary. Note that the question requires first an explanation (ie a narrative) of the changes made by the Courts and Legal Services Act 1990, and second a discussion (ie involving critical analysis) of the impact of those changes. Try to give each part of the question equal emphasis.

Skeleton solution

- Position prior to CLSA 1990.
- Effect of CLSA 1990 on solicitor circuit judges and on rights of advocacy generally.
- Likelihood of more solicitor judges and impact in terms of women and ethnic minority judges.
- Likely change in judicial outlook as a result.
- Critical account of extent of changes made by CLSA.
- Other reform proposals, eg setting up of Judicial Appointments Board and Judges' College.

Suggested solution

Until the passage of the Courts and Legal Services Act 1990 (CLSA) appointments to the High Court bench and above were restricted to barristers (usually QCs) of at least 10 years' experience of advocacy or barristers who had become circuit judges with at least two years' experience of judging cases in the Crown Courts or county courts. The immediate effect of the Act was to allow circuit judges who had originally qualified as solicitors to become eligible for appointment, though it was not until June 1993 that the Lord Chancellor made the first such appointment (that of Sachs J). Approximately one-tenth of the 500 or so circuit judges are solicitors, so more such appointments can be confidently expected in the near future.

CLSA 1990 also made possible the eventual extension of rights of advocacy to those lawyers who obtain the approval of their professional bodies and a panel of senior judges. In the short term this should mean rights of advocacy for solicitors in all proceedings in the High Court and above; this in turn should ensure the eligibility of solicitors who exercise such rights on a regular basis for appointment to the High Court bench, since CLSA repeals the statutory rule which restricted such appointments to barristers. In the very long term the effect of CLSA 1990 may be to extend rights of advocacy (and hence create eligibility for judicial appointments) to 'para-legals', ie those without formal legal qualifications but who have gained legal experience by working regularly in the field of citizens' advice agencies.

So what is the likely impact of these changes? Is it really likely that, by itself, CLSA 1990 will change the traditional assumptions on which judges are chosen and the traditional attitudes which judges display? The existing English judiciary is predominantly public-school and Oxbridge-educated, white, male, aged 50 or over, and generally regarded as being out of touch with society. The reason? Because that is also the make-up and character of the narrow pool from which such judges were chosen: the Bar. If the CLSA does lead, as anticipated, to an increase in the number of solicitor-judges, this in turn should imply an increase in the number of female and ethnic minority judges in the High Court because of the larger numbers of women and ethnic minority solicitors in private practice compared to those in private practice at the Bar, so the reforms should lead at least to a broader based, more representative judiciary.

Further, circuit judges such as Sachs J, and solicitors in private practice, probably have much greater familiarity with and understanding of the practical everyday problems of those who come into contact with the law than a barrister who may have spent all his formative years in the cloistered atmospheres of (in order) prep school, boarding school, Oxbridge, Council of Legal Education and the Inns of Court. Even if that is not the case, it appears to be the public perception, and it is the restoration of public confidence in the quality of the judiciary which should surely be uppermost in the minds of those contemplating reforms to the way judges are chosen.

But does CLSA 1990 go far enough? Invitation to become a High Court judge remains by invitation only of the Lord Chancellor, although advertisements for vacancies on the circuit bench, along with 'job descriptions', are to be introduced during 1993. Although one accepts the integrity of the Lord Chancellor and his assertion that the best qualified candidate is selected regardless of sex, race, religion or politics, there remains general unease over a selection process (which is mirrored in the selection of QCs) which is shrouded in secrecy and which takes account of such subjective criteria as a person's 'standing' and 'temperament'. Reliance on character references provided by those already integrated in establishment positions (judges, heads of chambers, etc) fuels fears of an 'old boy network' in which only those who fit the traditional mould and who hold the 'right' attitudes will progress up the judicial ladder.

Consequently, some have argued for the establishment of a Judicial Appointments Board to act as an independent advisory body to the Lord Chancellor. Such a Board would have a broad-based composition, operate as openly as possible (though interviews with candidates might be in private so as to avoid the excesses of the American system), give reasons for all recommendations and seek to control the political influences that affect judicial appointments. Although the present Lord Chancellor has rejected such reform, he has accepted the need for 'suitable lay people' to become formally involved in selection procedures, and Lord Taylor LCJ, in his Dimbleby TV Lecture (1992) conceded the case for a 'lay observer' to advise the Lord Chancellor on judicial appointments.

Finally, it is suggested that changes to the appointments system may not in themselves solve all the problems associated with a remote, aloof judiciary. Such changes should go hand-in-hand with better and more intensive training, including compulsory continuous training/refresher courses during tenure. The Royal Commission on Criminal Justice (July 1993) recommends more resources for the Judicial Studies Board and proper monitoring of judges' performances. This could eventually pave the way for a Judges' College to provide a fuller and more structured course than the present system of training.

Question 6

What features of the civil justice process lead litigants to settle their claims out of court? Are there any dangers for litigants in this practice?

University of London LLB Examination
(for External Students) English Legal System June 1993 Q6

General comment

The problem with this question is that it does not invite a straightforward narrative of the pre-trial and trial stages in a civil action (for which the examinee was probably well prepared) but rather a selection of those aspects of the procedures that have a deterrent effect, particularly on plaintiffs, in conducting litigation. Hence careful selectivity of issues is crucial, plus ability to discuss in a lively and relevant way matters which many might find dry and uninspiring. An examinee who rises to the challenge and responds well is likely to be rewarded with high marks.

Skeleton solution

- Historic legacy of delay in civil litigation.
- General character of the adversary system and the role of the court.
- The procedural and financial burdens facing a plaintiff (bring in the clawback rule operated in legal aid cases).
- Attempts at reform following recommendations of Civil Justice Review.
- Exchange of witness statements.
- More positive case management by the court.
- The importance of the Summons for Directions stage.
- The tactic of payment into court and the general effect of rules on costs.

Suggested solution

The major problems facing a litigant are ones of cost, delay and complexity. Ever since Charles Dickens wrote about the horrors of the Chancery Division in *Bleak House* ordinary people probably have visions of fat, greedy lawyers making rich pickings out of civil pleading. Dickens' fictional *Jarndyce* v *Jarndyce* dragged on for 20 years or so; modern litigation may not equal that feat but it is not unknown for personal injury actions (usually defended by rich insurance companies) to take up to a dozen years to settle from the issue of the writ.

The main root of the problem is the adversary system which treats the two opposing sides as equal and puts the burden on the asserter to prove the assertion he is making. Generally the court (especially if it is the High Court) takes a passive, reactive role, responding only to formal requests from one or both sides rather than behaving in an active, even proactive fashion, by, for example, taking charge of service and exchange of documents and supervising and enforcing strict timetables. Even the most conscientious plaintiff will quickly tire of having to take the initiative in all procedural manoeuvres, and if his physical and mental character does not tire, his financial pocket will quickly become exhausted. Whilst legal aid provides a safety-net, the 'clawback' rule may well deprive an ultimately successful plaintiff of some, if not all, of the fruits of his victory: the sorry fate of Mrs Hanlon must have persuaded many divorcing wives of the attractions of trying to settle their dispute out of court: *Hanlon* v *Law Society* (1981).

The Civil Justice Review 1988 served to highlight some of the awesome problems facing a modern litigant and subsequent reforms may have helped to alleviate them. Probably the most significant of the pre-trial procedural reforms is the compulsory exchange of witness statements, including statements of medical evidence in personal injury cases: Courts and Legal Services Act 1990 s5. This reform has minimised the risk of 'surprise witnesses' at the trial since pleadings do not generally require the pleading of evidence. The importance of the reform was commented on by Lord Donaldson MR in *Mercer* v *Chief Constable of Lancashire* (1991) in which he observed a 'sea change' in judicial attitudes to the conduct of litigation.

This change has taken the form of increased positive case management by judges and the adoption of procedures designed firstly to identify the real issues in dispute and secondly to enable the parties to assess their relative strengths at the earliest possible moment: what Donaldson called the 'cards on the table' philosophy. This new approach tended to make for shorter trials and savings of cost, as well as encouraging reasonable and sensible out of court settlements (as distinct from the unreasonable ones frequently forced on exhausted litigants under the old 'cards to the chest' tactical waiting game).

Lord Donaldson also indicated his expectation that High Court Masters (probably at the Summons for Directions stage) should take the case 'by the scruff of the neck' and sort out the real issues between the parties, ensuring that neither side is taken by surprise (ambush) at the trial. Instead of the old type of stocktaking to prepare for the battlefield of the trial, the Summons for Directions stage should be used, for example, to receive written testimony of witnesses so as to reduce the need for oral testimony at trial, with consequent savings of cost and time.

The Civil Justice Review had recommended even more radical reform: that the Summons for Directions should be held at an earlier stage and that the Master should have power to lay down a strict timetable for every preliminary. Parties should be required to report back to the court at regular intervals on the progress of the case, with penalties being imposed for unjustified delays. Whilst Lord Mackay LC has accepted this principle of case monitoring, he has stated that its implementation must await full computerisation of the courts ([1991] MLR 173–4).

On average it takes approximately three years for a case to reach trial after the issue of a writ. On any view that is surely too long. Computerisation and case monitoring are urgent reforms if litigants are to have confidence in settling their claims in reasonable time and at reasonable cost.

Finally, a word on payment into court: this is a tactic frequently employed by the defence to tempt the plaintiff into (sometimes) an unreasonable, unfair settlement out of court. It takes a brave plaintiff to reject such an offer, even if it appears palpably unfair, because, in his mind, there is knowledge of the risk (even if it is a low one) that the trial judge (who has no knowledge of the actual amount paid in) might award the same amount or even a lesser sum, causing the plaintiff to become liable for all the costs incurred from the date of payment in. The costs might well outstrip his compensation, and he ends up a winner but out of pocket: this happened recently to the actor Bill Roache ('Ken Barlow' for over 30 years in TV's 'Coronation Street'): *Roache* v *News Group Newspapers* (1992). The publicity surrounding such cases would surely act as a further deterrent to plaintiffs in pursuing legitimate claims if faced with the tactic of payment into court and perhaps the time has come to review the whole issue of costs and how they should be borne.

Question 7

'There is a pressing need for further development of the appellate process in criminal cases, not only to produce a more coherent system, but also to ensure that the objectives of justice, due process and consistency of decision making are better achieved.'

Do you agree with this statement, and what changes do you think should be made to the criminal appeal system?

University of London LLB Examination
(for External Students) English Legal System June 1993 Q7

General comment

A predictable kind of question on the criminal appeal system, one of the most topical subjects within the English legal system. It is important to note the emphasis on the objectives of justice, due process and consistency, and to relate existing rules and proposed reforms to the particular objective(s) which appear(s) most relevant. A lively critical discussion would be expected because of the passion generated by notorious recent miscarriages of justice which the appeal system took so long to put right.

Skeleton solution

- Recent cases of miscarriage of justice.
- Anomalies affecting appeals from magistrates' courts and from Crown Courts.
- Rehearings, burden of proof and grounds for appeal.
- Court of Appeal's approach to fresh evidence and role of Home Office in referring cases to CA.
- Recommendations of Runciman Commission on Criminal Justice and the proposed Criminal Cases Review Authority.
- Critical conclusions.

Suggested solution

In recent years there have been celebrated cases of miscarriage of justice in which the Court of Appeal (Criminal Division) had dismissed appeals (sometimes in robustly dismissive language) and then found grounds for allowing them, usually after a lengthy interval in which there had been sustained public campaigns. The roll-call of such cases has become infamous: the Birmingham Six, the Guildford Four, the Maguire Seven, the Tottenham Three, Judith Ward ... Many of these and other cases involved specific problems of police malpractice but they also raised concerns about the manner in which the Court of Appeal heard the appeals. So it is not difficult to agree with the statement in question that a more coherent appellate process needs to be introduced. How could this be done?

First, a simple anomaly needs to be corrected to produce consistency in the appeal system. Appeals from magistrates' courts to the Crown Courts against convictions take the form of complete rehearings but appeals from Crown Courts to the Court of Appeal do not, taking place instead 'on paper' based on the court transcripts and legal submissions (oral) thereon:

'It seems perverse, to say the least, that a person appealing from a magistrates' court against a conviction for speeding has the right to a full retrial in the Crown Court while a person convicted of murder in the Crown Court has no such right to a full retrial in the Court of Appeal': view, Tregilgas-Davey ([1991] NLJ 668).

This anomaly probably contributes to the comparatively lower success rate for appeals to the Court of Appeal than to the Crown Court.

The objectives of justice and due process are probably not served by other anomalies in the criminal appeal system. For example, the switch in the burden of proof onto the appellant when appealing to the Court of Appeal (this does not happen in appeals to the Crown Court). Probably the most decisive difference is that the Crown Court may allow appeals on the broad ground that the conviction was against the weight of the evidence, whilst the Court of Appeal is confined by the straitjacket of criteria set out in the Criminal Appeal Act 1968, s2 ('unsafe and unsatisfactory'; 'errors of law'; 'material irregularities') and the effect of s2's proviso that an appeal should nevertheless be dismissed if the Court of Appeal is satisfied that no miscarriage of justice has actually occurred. In order to be so satisfied the Court of Appeal must perform the fact-finding functions of a jury without the advantage of seeing and hearing the testimony of witnesses under examination of counsel (the bare transcript cannot convey the true atmosphere of the trial or the manner in which witnesses gave evidence).

A similar restrictive approach has been taken by the Court of Appeal to the receipt of fresh evidence. There seems to be a heavy suspicion of such evidence: why was it not given at trial? (Negligence of counsel is not an excuse unless so flagrant as to amount to material irregularity at trial: *R* v *Clinton* (1993)); is it credible (again the Court of Appeal must usurp the jury's function to assess credibility). Retrials are possible before new juries but may not be practicable because of lapse of time since the original trial, so the Court of Appeal may be forced to accept the task of assessing credibility (and may well prefer to give the benefit of the doubt to protecting the public rather than to the appellant).

Finally, one must not overlook the historic role of the Home Office and a unit called C3 (under-resourced and with few lawyers) in referring dubious convictions to the Court of Appeal. There has been a long campaign for an independent advisory body, better resourced and able to act of its own motion and on an inquisitorial basis, to take over the Home Office's role in this area, and the recent Royal Commission on Criminal Justice (July 1993) has endorsed this idea with its recommendation of a Criminal Cases Review Authority (CCRA).

The Royal Commission also recommends other reforms to deal with the problems outlined earlier: the redrafting of the Criminal Appeal Act 1968, s2 to provide for a single broad ground of appeal based only on the safeness of the conviction. Material irregularities would be covered by this broad ground and should include negligence of defence counsel in tactical handling of the case – simple, not flagrant, negligence would suffice. If appeals are allowed on such grounds and retrials before new juries are not practicable, the conviction should be quashed rather than upheld (thus restoring the presumption of innocence at the appeal stage). The Commission recommends that a broad approach should be taken to the issue of fresh evidence, with the possibility for the Court of Appeal to refer it for investigation to the new Criminal Cases Review Authority if not already investigated by that body.

The Government and most civil liberties groups have welcomed these recommendations which are expected to be included in a Criminal Justice Bill for the 1993–4 session of Parliament. Such reform may well help restore public confidence in the handling of criminal cases, although not all the response has been uncritical, eg retired judge Sir Frederick Lawton and the distinguished QC Sir Louis Blom-Cooper have expressed reservations about any new independent appeals tribunal which might not operate on normal judicial principles and pose a threat to the rule of law. They would prefer to see a remodelled Court of Appeal to include an internal investigation unit for cases of alleged miscarriage of justice, a concept found for example in the French system and known as 'police judicaire'.

Question 8

David, a youth of 15, is alone driving his older brother's (Paul aged 18) car when he is stopped by PC Black and PC Tripper because he did not indicate while making a sudden turn. The police search the car, find Paul's driving licence (which indicates his age) and find a large quantity of cannabis in the glove compartment. PC Black exclaims: 'This is a serious matter, Paul. You had better come with us to the police station, and you had better be careful of what you say because we can use it.' On the way to the station David states 'that stuff is not mine. I know nothing about it.'

At the station David is cautioned and he asks to make a telephone call, but is told 'You can make one later.' A tape recorder is running while he is interviewed, but he keeps silent for one hour. After being told 'this could take a long time, you had better come clean', he admits that the car is his older brother's and that his brother 'makes a bit of money on the side selling drugs to his friends'. David is charged with driving without a valid licence and without proper insurance, while the police apply for a search warrant to search the house where Paul lives.

Discuss the police actions and consider whether David's statement could be used as evidence against his brother.

University of London LLB Examination
(for External Students) English Legal System June 1993 Q8

General comment

As with all 'problem-type' questions it is important to address the precise issues raised by the facts and not to be distracted into discussion of irrelevant matters, even though one may be anxious to display wide-ranging knowledge. Avoid a bare narrative of the provisions of relevant statutes or a mere citation of case law authority. Each statutory or common law rule must be explained in clear connection with the particular fact(s) in the problem which make it relevant. A critical account of such rules is unnecessary.

Skeleton solution

- Legality of the search of the car; legality of the seizure and retention of the cannabis; the rule on written records.
- The caution on the right of silence.
- Whether there had been a lawful arrest.
- The propriety of the interview at the police station; the rules protecting juveniles.
- Rights to have someone informed of the arrest and to legal advice.
- Admissibility of confessions obtained by oppression, improper inducements or as a result of other illegal or improper police actions.
- Remedies against the police (discussed here during the course of the answer rather than as a concluding summary).

Suggested solution

a) *The police actions*

The police were entitled under the road traffic legislation to stop David on the ground that he had committed a summary offence (failing to indicate). They should then have taken his name and address from the driving licence with a view to serving a summons on him later (it appears they had no suspicion at the time that David was under 18 or that the car belonged to someone else). They were not entitled to search the car, unless they had reasonable grounds for suspecting that they would find drugs (or stolen or prohibited articles). There appeared to be no concrete basis for such suspicion from the facts given, so it is advised that the search of the car was illegal and that Paul would have a right of action for trespass to his property which can be brought against the local Chief Constable under the Police Act 1964.

It follows that the seizure of the drugs was also unlawful because following an unlawful search, and the normal right of retention of such evidence is not available to the police: *R* v *Chief Constable of Lancashire, ex parte Parker* (1993). (It might have been different if the evidence of crime had been discovered during a search of premises, ie buildings, under the Police and Criminal Evidence Act 1984 (PACE) s19).

The police also failed to make a written record of the search of the car, as required by PACE.

Since the discovery of the cannabis was sufficient to raise suspicion of criminal activity against David, he should have been properly cautioned in accordance with Code C, para 10 of the Code of Practice on Questioning issued under PACE, which applies even where the suspect has not yet been arrested. It is enough that he might be questioned about offences on a basis where he is not on equal terms with the police and hence in need of the protection of the right of silence: dicta in *R* v *Christou* (1992). The recommended words of caution are: 'You do not have to say anything unless you wish to do so, but what you say may be given in evidence'. Minor deviations from this formula will not constitute a breach of para 10 provided that the sense of the caution is preserved. It is arguable whether PC Black's advice was a minor deviation for this purpose; the failure to emphasise that David had a right to say nothing at all might be regarded as a major deviation. If so, it would affect the admissibility of the statement David made in the car on the way to the station.

It is also not clear from PC Black's language to David whether he had arrested him or merely invited him to go voluntarily to the police station to answer questions under PACE s29. If it was clear to David and the officer that David had been given no free choice by PC Black's words, then he was being arrested and should have been informed of the reasons: PACE s28. Failure to communicate clearly the fact of arrest or the reasons for it will render the detention unlawful and give David the right to sue the local Chief Constable for the tort of false imprisonment: *Lewis* v *Chief Constable of South Wales* (1991).

At the station it appears, prima facie, that David was cautioned and his interview tape-recorded as required by Code C of the Codes of Practice. However, Code C provides a number of other safeguards for a suspect during interview which do not appear to have been observed in David's case. As soon as David's age as a juvenile became apparent to the questioning officers, they should have ensured that another adult (not a police officer) was present to protect David's interests. The police also had the duty to inform David's parents of his detention as soon as practicable and to request their presence at the station.

Although David had no right to insist on making a telephone call (a popular myth in this country), he did have the right under PACE s56 to have someone informed of his arrest, and his request for a phone call should have been interpreted as a request under s56. The police should make contact on behalf of David as soon as practicable, so their delay was probably a breach of s56 unless they can show that the delay was necessary for the proper administration of justice.

Under PACE s58 and Code C David should also have been informed of his right to legal advice.

The above breaches of PACE and Code C probably do not give rise to causes of action in tort, but they could form the basis of a complaint to the Police Complaints Authority, and may be relevant also to the issue of admissibility of evidence (below).

b) *The incriminating statement against Paul*

This came as part of a confession, since David was at the same time admitting to the offences with which he was subsequently charged. The confession was the result of being told that he might be held for 'a long time', impliedly incommunicado: quite severe pressure on a young lad. Implicit in such advice is the promise of early release if a statement is made, so David's confession is probably the result either of 'oppression' or an 'improper inducement' rendering it unreliable. Whichever applies, the result is to render the confession automatically inadmissible under PACE s76.

Even if the confession had been voluntary the trial judge might still exercise a discretion under PACE s78 to exclude the incriminating statement against Paul from Paul's trial if, as a matter of justice, it would be unfair to receive it and prejudice that trial, particularly in view of the catalogue of illegal and improper actions by the police that led up to its making.